D1759304

RORSCHACH TEST

RORSCHACH TEST

Theory and Practice

Rajendra K. Misra
Meena K. Kharkwal
Maurita A. Kilroy
Komilla Thapa

With an Introduction by Paul M. Lerner

Sage Publications
New Delhi/Thousand Oaks/London

First published in 1996 by

Sage Publications India Pvt Ltd
M-32 Greater Kailash Market-I
New Delhi 110 048

Sage Publications Inc
2455 Teller Road
Thousand Oaks, California 91320

Sage Publications Ltd
6 Bonhill Street
London EC2A 4PU

Published by Tejeshwar Singh for Sage Publications India Pvt Ltd, phototypeset by Pagewell Photosetters, Pondicherry and printed at Chaman Enterprises, Delhi.

Library of Congress Cataloging-in-Publication Data

Rorschach test: theory and practice / Rajendra K. Misra . . . [et al.].
    p.   cm.
    Includes bibliographical references.
    1. Rorschach Test—Interpretation—Handbooks, manuals, etc.
I. Misra, Rajendra K., 1936–
RC473.R6R67   155.2'842—dc20   1996   96–28316

ISBN: 0–8039–9328–5 (US-hb)   81–7036–563–5 (India-hb)

Sage Production Editor: Sumitra Srinivasan

CONTENTS

PREFACE

Raghupati Sahai 'Firaaq' Gorakhpuri (1896–1989). Professor of English at Allahabad University. A literary legend. In one of his poems titled *Aadhee Raat Koe* ('In the middle of the night'), 'Firaaq' portrays dark trees *looking like* their own shadows; like towers, bridging earth with sky; a feeling of infinite, quiet, stillness. He describes the village like a live exotic dream of romantic scenes, reflected in the mirror of moonlight. Dimming earthen lamps (*chiraagh*) are falling asleep. Up in the sky, stars are beginning to yawn.

It's almost as if Mother Nature showed 'Firaaq' a giant inkblot 'Midnight', like a Rorschach card, and asked, *'What might this be?'*. And he responded with a beautiful, 10 stanza, 91 line, poignant poem *Aadhee Raat Koe*. The first 10 lines of the poem are:

Aadhee raat koe

Siyaah payier hain ab aap apnee parchhaiaan,
Zameen say taa maho-anjum suqoot kay meenaar,
Jidhar nigaah karain ik athaah gumshudgee,
Ek, ek ker kay fursudaa chiraghoen kee palkaien
Jhapak gayeen hain—joe khulee hain, jhapakane walee hain
Jhalak rahaa hai 'pura' chaandeen kay darpan main
Raseelay qaif bharay manzaroen kaa jaagta khwaab
Falak pay taarone koe pahlee jamhaayeaan aayeen.
(Dark trees have turned into their own shadows,
Like the towers of quiet silence,
Bridging earth with the moon and stars.
All around exists a sense of infinite stillness.
Dimming earthen lamps are gradually falling asleep,
Those still half-awake, may soon close their eyes.
Reflected in the moonlight-mirror is the village:

A live, exotic dream of romantic scenes.
And, way up, high in the sky,
Stars are beginning to yawn.)

—'Firaaq' (Pandit, 1987, p. 21)

As children, most of us have looked at clouds, mountains and trees and 'imagined' them to be animals, persons and other objects around us. That's what the Rorschach test does. A set of vague-looking inkblots are shown to the person whose personality we are trying to understand. He/she is then requested to tell us what these blots look like: 'What might this be?'

Based on what is seen (e.g., humans, animals and household objects) and what factors have influenced whatever is seen (e.g., shape of the blot, its color and shading), inferences are made about his/her personality, e.g., (*a*) cognitive resources, (*b*) emotions, and (*c*) relation between cognition and emotions. Since whatever is 'seen' and/or 'experienced' on the blots is based on how that person has conceptualized his/her world, the percepts have a symbolic, representational significance. The objects seen signify something. They represent a part of the world outside his/her internal world.

Percepts may contain a simile (a figure of speech in which one thing is seen *like* or *as* another dissimilar thing: 'stupid *as* a donkey', 'boring *like* a politician's speech', etc.), or a metaphor (a figure of speech in which there is an implied comparison between a word of phrase usually used for one object as applied to another object): 'storm in a tea-cup', '*prem nagar*' or '*shahray mohabbat*' ('city of love'), etc.

Similes and metaphors play an important role in this 'making-sense-out-of-ambiguities' process. Whenever we see something unfamiliar, we tend to compare it to something we are familiar with based on our past experiences. Comparing an object to other objects appears to be an effective way of making them meaningful. For example:

Fire: A red flame may remind us of a ritual in which fire 'looked like' the one we are seeing now.
Life: '*Zindgee khwaab hai; khwaab men phir bhalaa such hai kyaa, or bhalaa jooth hai kya! Sub sach hai*' (Life is a dream; how could a dream be true or false? It's all real!).

—A song in Raj Kapoor's film *Jaagtey Rahoe* ('Beware'), released in the fifties.

Femininity
'Fraility, thy name is woman'.

—Shakespeare.

Naari! tayray roop anaik (Woman! you have multiple forms).

—Jaishankar Prasad.

Dost naheen koi tum saa, tum saa naheen koi mister,
Kabhi tum darling, kabhi mahboobaa, kabhi tum bholi-bhalee
sister
(There's no friend like you, none like you, mister!
sometimes you're a pretty woman, then, look like a beloved,
and, then, you appear to be an innocent sister).

—A song in film *Khamoshi* ('Silence'), released in the sixties.

In *Metamorphosis* (first published in 1915), Franz Kafka (1883–1924) transforms its main character, Gregor Samsa, into a beetle: 'Gregor slowly lugged himself toward the door . . . threw himself against the door, held himself upright against it—the pads on the bottom of his little legs exuded a little sticky substance . . .' (Kafka, 1988, p. 14).

R.K. Narayan (1909–), in *Swami and Friends* (first published in 1935), sees the world through the eyes of the ten-year-old Swami, '. . . the closeness of the tree-trunks and their branches intertwining at the top gave the road the appearance of a black cavern with an evil spirit brooding over it' (Narayan, 1992, p. 157).

In his incisive monograph on prostitutes, *Yey Kothey-waaliaan* ('These dancing girls'; first published in 1960), Amritlal Nagar (1984), another literary giant who lived and worked in Lucknow, India, describes them as 'fairies-for-sale' ('market-fairies'). '*Kaheen apnay naseeb kay kaaton per aur kaheen gulaab-sage bichhayae, baazaar kee pariaan sukh-dukh kee neend soe raheen theen*' (The fairies-for-sale, were asleep: some on the beds of cruel thorns of their fate; others, on beds of roses) (Nagar, 1984, p. 69).

Authors, artists, poets and playwrights make ambiguities meaningful. So do we. We all carry a little of Kafka, Narayan and Nagar within us. We interpret things, events and people around us. Phrases like, 'what do you mean', 'it doesn't make sense' and 'in other words' reflect our efforts to make things meaningful. Writers and artists interpret objects creatively. They connect them often with unusual similes and metaphors, with myths, folklores and fairy tales. Sometimes, these links are apparent; sometimes not.

A person who takes the Rorschach test links inkblots with the objects he/she is acquainted with. Whatever is seen (*content*) is a sample of his/her psychological world; the world inside him/her. The *process* by which inkblots are connected with the outside world reflects his/her personalized, unique way of seeing the world around him/her.

Hermann Rorschach was more interested in *how* the blots were seen. His *Psychodiagnostics* (first published in 1921) (Rorschach, 1975) focuses on the *process of perception* rather than on the *content of perception*. However, in his posthumously published paper containing 'blind' analysis of the Oberholzer's patient (ibid.) he does talk about *content* and its clinical significance in personality assessment.

In the present work, although we do not intend to minimize the role of the *process* of seeing the blots, we primarily want to stress the critical role of the *product*: the *content*. Along with many others, e.g., Rapaport, Gill and Schafer (1945, 1946), Schafer (1954), Schachtel (1966), Mayman (1967), McCully (1971), and Lerner (1991), we feel it is as important to look at the content— the product—as it is to look at the process underlying a response in a protocol.

The *experiential* aspect of the Rorschach process is personal to the testee as well as meaningful and phenomenologically real. Underlying and associated with the content is the vast wealth of the testee's inner world: personally and emotionally charged experiences involving culture, myths, archetypes, folklores and fairy tales. Trying to understand the testee's personality without focusing on the cultural–experiential aspects would be ignoring more than half the story of a personality as projected by the Rorschach test.

ORGANIZATION OF THIS BOOK

We have written this book for a beginner, for someone who is curious to find out what the Rorschach test is all about. There are two goals:

1. to place the test in a context consisting of the clinical—cultural— experiential aspects of the world around us, and

2. to describe ways (systems, methods) of looking at the Rorschach protocols for understanding human personality.

For the first goal we have tried to:

1. describe the life and times of Hermann Rorschach (the *zeitgeist*) (Chapter 1),
2. stress the close relationship between the test and literature and the arts (Chapter 2), and
3. look at the test in the Indian context (Chapter 3).

Before addressing the second goal (namely, different systems), we thought it would be helpful to outline the basic Rorschach procedure (seating arrangements, instructions, recording and tabulating responses, etc.). This is done in Chapter 4.

The next four chapters address the second goal. We describe four different systems or ways of looking at the protocols. These are:

1. John Exner's *Comprehensive System* (Chapter 5),
2. Robert McCully's *(Jungian) Archetypal Approach* (Chapter 6),
3. Roy Schafer's *Psychoanalytic Ego Psychology Approach* (Chapter 7), and
4. Paul Lerner's *Psychoanalytic Object Relations Approach* (Chapter 8).

A brief overview of each of these four systems is given here.
Exner's Comprehensive System: In Exner's recent version of the Comprehensive System (Exner, 1991, 1993), a detailed and comprehensive scoring and tabulation of the various Rorschach responses is organized into a structural summary. Then, empirically based, step-by-step interpretive statements (hypotheses) are developed in terms of 11 key variables and seven clusters. The 11 key variables are (in order of priority):

    (*i*) schizophrenia index (SCZI),
   (*ii*) depression index (DEPI),
  (*iii*) D>Adj D,
  (*iv*) coping deficit index (CDI),
   (*v*) Adj D is minus,
  (*vi*) Lambda (L),
 (*vii*) reflection responses,
(*viii*) experience balance: introversive,
  (*ix*) experience balance: extratensive,

(*x*) passive movement response, and
(*xi*) hypervigilance index (HVI).

The seven clusters (alphabetically) are:

(*i*) affect,
(*ii*) controls,
(*iii*) ideation,
(*iv*) interpersonal perception,
(*v*) mediation,
(*vi*) processing, and
(*vii*) self-perception.

Exner (1991, 1993) helps readers 'walk through' a protocol step-by-step and formulate interpretive propositions (hypotheses) about the testee's personality as shown on the Rorschach test.

Robert McCully's (Jungian) Archetypal Approach: McCully (1971) provides an extremely rich and experientially meaningful framework for understanding the human personality through a Rorschach protocol within a Jungian archetypal system. There are five main concepts in McCully's system:

(*i*) pragmatic schema,
(*ii*) Rorschach experience,
(*iii*) laws governing the Rorschach process,
(*iv*) archetypal influences in Rorschach plates, and
(*v*) placement of the responses on the Rorschach process quadrants.

Let us take a quick look at each of these five elements in McCully's system.

(*i*) *Pragmatic Schema*: In the pragmatic schema, McCully compares the concept of karma in Hindu philosophy with the Rorschach concept of experience type (erlebinstypus); looks at archetypes as the *great connectors*; describes the specific archetypes of, (*a*) knowing, (*b*) opposites, (*c*) anima–animus (Yin–Yang), (*d*) self–persona, and (*e*) creativity; and finally, discusses the relationship between the unconscious and symbols.

(*ii*) *The Rorschach Experience*: Rorschach experience involves looking at the test situation as (*a*) an intrapsychic confrontation, and (*b*) looking at the Rorschach response as the end-product of a creative process.

(*iii*) *Laws Governing the Rorschach Process*: There are two sets of laws affecting the Rorschach process: (*a*) the laws of altered perceptions, and (*b*) the laws of symbols. Under the former are included the law of excluded awareness and the law of altered visual perception. Among the laws of symbols are the law of incomplete understanding, the law of psychic correspondence and the law of mutual projection.

(*iv*) *Archetypal Influences in Rorschach Plates*: Rorschach cards have the potential to arouse certain archetypes. The responses need to be examined for archetypal material. McCully suggests the archetypal potential of the various cards:

- Card I: Archetypes of matriarchal power, feminine functioning.
- Card II: Archetype of opposites.
- Card III: Archetypes of persona, shadow.
- Card IV: Archetype of patriarchal world, fatherhood.
- Card V: Archetype of good and evil.
- Card VI: Archetype of masculine power.
- Card VII: Archetype of femininity; archetype of temptation.
- Card VIII: Archetype of male–female, interpersonal bonds, non-specific energy.
- Card IX: Archetype of goals and growth within the context of karma and experience type.
- Card X: Archetype of source of life, *sansara* (the 'Hindu notion of [the] vast wheel of life on which all things turn') (McCully, 1971, p. 163).

(*v*) *Rorschach Process Quadrants*: There is the A–B horizontal axis of withdrawal (A), on the left end of the axis, and expansion (B) on the right side. Cutting across at mid-point of this horizontal A–B axis is the vertical axis C–D. The top of this axis (C at the top), represents the conscious level, while the lower end (D) represents the unconscious level of psychic functioning. A particular Rorschach response could be placed in any of these quadrants based on the extent it reflects the withdrawal–expansion and the conscious–unconscious dimensions.

McCully suggests using his system as a supplement to a formal, structural method of analyzing and interpreting a protocol. His culturally rich way of looking at a Rorschach protocol does, however, appear internally consistent. We feel it may also be used independently of other systems.

Roy Schafer's Psychoanalytic Ego Psychology Approach: Schafer (1954) conceptualizes Rorschach responses from a psychoanalytic ego psychology perspective. His system presupposes a good knowledge of psychoanalysis and clinical psychology. The most important feature of Schafer's approach is its integration of the quantitative and qualitative aspects within a psychoanalytic framework.

For the quantitative aspect he uses the scoring system developed and used by David Rapaport (Rapaport, Gill and Schafer, 1945, 1946; Gill, 1968). For the qualitative part, he suggests looking at the Rorschach responses in terms of the:

(*i*) situational dynamics of the test situation,

(*ii*) location of the responses on a dimension of psychic functioning (primary process at one end of the continuum and secondary process at the other),

(*iii*) shifts and fluctuations in the levels of psychic functioning,

(*iv*) interaction between (*a*) impulses, (*b*) defenses, and (*c*) adaptations, and

(*v*) examining the contents of the responses with special reference to (*a*) response process, (*b*) thematic analysis, and (*c*) coping mechanisms.

One of the most important features in Schafer's system is his suggestion to ensure that the interpretive process meets six specific criteria, namely,

(*i*) criterion of sufficiency,

(*ii*) criterion of depth,

(*iii*) criterion of manifest form,

(*iv*) criterion of intensity,

(*v*) criterion of hierarchic level, and

(*vi*) criterion of adpative/pathological coping strategies.

Schafer's system is comprehensive, rich, as well as clinically meaningful. It still retains the freshness it had when it was first published in 1954.

Paul Lerner's Psychoanalytic Object Relations Approach: Lerner (1991) has creatively synthesized the quantitative components of the Rorschach responses with the most recent advances in the psychoanalytic system, e.g., self psychology and the object relations approach. His system looks at the protocols most comprehensively from a clinically rich and meaningful perspective without compromising scientific rigor.

Lerner (1991) recommends what may be called a *level-based core character* framework for conceptualizing a personality emerging out of a Rorschach protocol. The main features of Lerner's system include:

(*i*) relatively less emphasis on quantitative scores,

(*ii*) identifying responses for (*a*) form level, (*b*) kinesthesias, (the number of responses in which the subject saw/experienced movement), and (*c*) responses with human content,

(*iii*) detailed response-by-response analysis for evidence of character features (of personality and levels of personality organization), thought organization, affect organization and core dynamics,

(*iv*) examining the sequence,

(*v*) examining the content, and

(*vi*) developing an integrated personality picture of the subject.

His system may be described in terms of:

(*i*) psychoanalytic diagnostic scheme,

(*ii*) levels of personality organization, and

(*iii*) inference process.

(*i*) *Psychoanalytic Diagnostic Scheme*: Lerner suggests eight representative core characteristics for a diagnostic scheme:

- hysterical,
- obsessive–compulsive,
- depressive,
- masochistic,
- infantile,
- narcissistic,
- schizoid, and
- paranoid.

(*ii*) *Levels of Personality Organization*: There are six levels of personality organization:

- level of instinctual development,

- level of ego weakness,
- level of defensive organization,
- level of internalized object relations,
- level of superego development, and
- level of ego identity.

(*iii*) *Inference Process*: Inferences about the personality of the testee in Lerner's system are drawn at two-tiers: (*a*) first order inferences, and (*b*) transformation process.
   The first order inferences are drawn at three levels:

- level of form,
- kinesthesias, and
- human responses.

The transformation process involves 'translating' data into narrative statements. Based on the clinical, qualitative significance of the responses, the formal scores and the examiner–testee interactions, the tester attempts to develop an internally consistent and theoretically sound profile of the testee in terms of four areas:

- character structure,
- thought organization,
- affect organization, and
- dynamics.

The chapters on each of these four systems include illustrative protocols.

SUMMARY ·

In summary, this book is addressed to students, clinicians and academicians interested in the Rorschach test. The focus is clinical—cultural—experiential. The cultural canvas covers India. The four systems presented are those of Exner, McCully, Schafer and Lerner. Students, clinicians and researchers using the Rorschach test may decide to use any one of these four systems. However, in view of the synthesis of formal features with the psychoanalytic theory and its recent advances as systematized in Paul Lerner's psychoanalytic object relations approach, we would recommend his approach.

A word of caution. *Please, do not mix the systems!* Each one of these four systems is rooted in a specific context of concepts. Each approach is also internally consistent. Mixing them up would be confusing in the least, if not chaotic. The personality profile emerging out of a *mixed approach* may look like a bunch of bananas hanging off a guava tree! Or, like what they call *gondoe-goal* in West Bengal or *ghapach* in Bihar!

ACKNOWLEDGEMENT

We want to thank Paul M. Lerner, Ed. D., A.B.P.P., for taking time out of his busy schedule to read the manuscript of this book and write its introduction. A Rorschacher of international repute, Dr. Lerner is a graduate of the Toronto Psychoanalytic Institute. He completed his post-doctoral training in clinical psychology at the Menninger Foundation, Topeka, Kansas. Dr. Lerner is a past president of the Society for Personality Assessment and a member of The International Society of Rorschach and Other Projective Methods. He maintains a private practice of psychoanalysis, psychotherapy and psychological testing, and is a member of the Department of Psychology at the University of Tennessee. He has authored and coedited four books and more than 45 articles and book chapters on the Rorschach. His recent book, *Psychoanalytic Theory and the Rorschach* (Lerner, 1991), received the 1991 Menninger Alumni Scientific Writing Award.

We would like to thank the publishers of the Rorschach plates, Hans Huber Publishers, Berne, Switzerland, for granting permission to reproduce the Rorschach cards to help locate the various responses in the illustrative protocols.

Hari Shankar Asthana, Ph.D., now retired professor and chairman of the psychology department and also former vice-chancellor of Sagar University, Sagar, India, read an earlier draft of this book and offered many helpful suggestions. We thank him. It may be mentioned here that Dr. Asthana was trained in the Rorschach by Samuel Beck, and in turn trained the senior author of this work, R.K. Misra. Also, he has the credit of publishing the first paper on the Rorschach test in India (Prasad and Asthana, 1947).

Mr. Tejeshwar Singh, Managing Director, Sage Publications, New Delhi, India and an anonymous reviewer provided many valuable suggestions for improving this book. We appreciate their comments.

This book is an outcome of the enthusiasm and interest shown by the participants in the Rorschach workshops conducted by the senior author in India. The first (ever) workshop was held in February 1990 at the Department of Psychology, Lucknow University, Lucknow, India. Dr. Prabha Gupta, currently professor and head of the Department of Psychology deserves the credit for hosting this workshop. We wish to thank her.

Later, an intensive four-day workshop (February 1992) and another two-day workshop (February 1993) were held at the Department of Psychology, Allahabad University, Allahabad, India. Dr. Rama Charan Tripathi, currently professor and head of the Department of Psychology, Allahabad University, hosted these two workshops. We are grateful to him.

Evidence of the interest in these workshops and the fact that to date there is no textbook on the Rorschach in India in spite of people using this test for a number of years (as shown in two review articles by Prabhu, 1984; Raychaudhuri, 1988), prompted us to put together in one place the basics as well as the recent advances in the Rorschach test. This book is an attempt in that direction.

A comment about the style. Some readers may notice a somewhat 'radical' style of this work, involving poets, authors, films and mythology, mixing Hindi, Urdu and Hindustani with English. They might even feel it is 'non-academic'. We, however, did this with the intent of re-constructing the close link between the academia and the common worlds of common people.

Disciplines are separated to facilitate detailed studies of specific phenomena, not to fragment them. Often, specializations end up in isolation, continue the asymptotic process of separation, and in turn feed the illusion of isolated (and, therefore, implicitly superior) existence. Maybe that's the way to do it. Maybe not. We don't know.

What we do know is that to study psychology we need to venture outside the castle of campuses and departments. There is as much psychology outside as there is within the walls of academic settings. Thus, we decided to converse with our readers about what the Rorschach test is all about and how it interfaces with our everyday life.

The test constructed itself into a context. Over the years, it had become increasingly alienated from the mainstream. Obsessed with one version of science, some of us have been forcing the test to 'fit' the 'respected' canons of physics. Years ago, we remember Kendall, the British mathematical statistician, saying that copying (aping?) non-applicable models often ends up in *scientification of non-knowledge (SONKING)*. We wanted to *de-SONK* the Rorschach test; re-construct it. That's why we have selected a 'radical' style.

Creative writings, culture and films—all are part of our psyche, specially the Indian psyche. Enjoying the luxury of accessing two feature-length films each day, 365 days a year (India produces about 900 films a year), with 70 per cent of the 800 million Indian population living in villages, with exposure to Western affluence (e.g., through satellite TV), breathing and living a philosophy of doing more with less, enchantingly flooded with festivals and rituals, the Indian psyche reflects a unique blend of paradoxes and contradictions. The Rorschach test samples this psyche; hence, the adoption of a style linking (re-constructing) it with 'Firaaq', Kafka, Nagar and Narayan, Devdas and Lady Macbeth, and movies like *Teesri Kasam* and *Gaman*.

We hope students, teachers, clinicians, and researchers will find this work helpful and consider using this fascinatingly complex tool in academic, clinical and research settings.

Lyndhurst, Ohio   *Rajendra K. Misra*
November 1995   *Meena K. Kharkwal*
                                             Maurita A. Kilroy
                                              Komilla Thapa

INTRODUCTION

Now, virtually 75 years after Rorschach published his classic text *Psychodiagnostics*, Misra and his colleagues have prepared this volume designed to acquaint students and clinicians alike with recent advances in the use of the Rorschach. This book is timely. In India, in the United States, across Europe and in most areas of the world, the past two decades have witnessed a significant resurgence of the Rorschach for the understanding and study of people— a virtual revival of the 1940s and 1950s.

Prompting this renewal of interest in the Rorschach has been the empirical work of Exner (1991, 1993) together with major shifts in psychoanalytic theory. With respect to the latter, the relatively recent integration of modern object relations theory, a broadened psychodynamic developmental theory and a systematic psychology of the self into the mainstream of traditional psychoanalytic theory is now providing the conceptual basis for a more comprehensive and systematic Rorschach theory.

This book is intended to be informative and useful, and both purposes are reflected in its organization. Chapters on Hermann Rorschach, his life and his times, on literature and the Rorschach, and its place in India are followed by instructions in administering the Rorschach and then an outline of four different approaches to Rorschach interpretation. Underlying the text is the authors' commitment to a clinical—cultural—experiential orientation.

In keeping with the intent, organization and underlying value structure of the book, in this introduction I will address the following three areas: a comparison of an empirical approach with a conceptual approach to the Rorschach, the meanings of an experiential Rorschach psychology and the role of empathy in an experiential approach.

EMPIRICAL APPROACH VERSUS CONCEPTUAL APPROACH

Two overarching approaches for using and evaluating the Rorschach pervade the contemporary scene—an empirical psychometric approach as represented in the work of Exner and a conceptual approach as exemplified in the writings of McCully, Schafer and Lerner. Although not mutually exclusive, the two approaches differ significantly in several important ways including basic sources of information, the role accorded to the person and the examiner, and the place of a personality theory that is independent of and lying outside of the test itself.

Empirical Approach

The empirical approach began with Hermann Rorschach (1921/1942) himself when he compared previously selected diagnostic groups and found that certain 'signs' or scores occurred more frequently in some groups than others. While this approach has spanned the Rorschach's history and has cut across theoretical orientations through a number of major books and publications, Exner and his colleagues (Exner, 1991, 1993) have become the most thorough, instrumental and contemporary representatives of the empirical approach.

Exner's Comprehensive System represents an attempt to systematically bring together into one overall system the empirically defensible elements of five earlier approaches to the Rorschach. Underlying the System is an insistence upon standard administration, accurate scoring and empirically supported interpretations.

With regard to test-based sources of information, the Comprehensive System admits three—the structural summary, the sequence of scores and the patient's verbalizations including, but to a limited degree, the content of responses. Exner's distrust of Rorschach content served as a corrective counter-reaction to years in which content was misused. Although Exner is beginning to address content as a springboard for interpretation, there are other approaches which are systematic and provide more information than is available through the Comprehensive System.

The structural summary is the heart and soul of the Comprehensive System, and other sources of information serve to refine and extend inferences derived from the summary. Included in the structural summary are the quantitative or structural features of a test record—the scores and their relationships. The way in which Exner organizes the scores, and based upon empirical findings the meanings he attributes to them, constitutes a lasting contribution to the Rorschach literature.

In his pursuit of standardized administration, Exner accords the person of the examiner, in terms of his or her experiences and skills, little value. Indeed, the examiner is seen as a source of error or bias, and his or her role is reduced if not eliminated altogether.

In the tradition of Hermann Rorschach, Exner does not tie the method to any specific theory of personality. This atheoretical stance restricts the Comprehensive System's clinical usefulness. For example, inferences derived from the System are descriptive, pragmatic, jargon-free, useful and sturdy. However, they also lack overall integration. Thus, while the final descriptive picture that emerges is helpful, it does not have the coherence, clinical sweep, or depth which an independent theory of personality would afford.

Viglione and Exner (1983) note that studies based on the Comprehensive System are united by understanding the Rorschach primarily as a 'problem-solving' task that activates consistent styles of coping behavior. Accordingly, 'The data gleaned from the subject's responses or solutions, provide a glimpse of how the individual works with the world, how he responds to ambiguity and challenge' (ibid., p. 14). This problem-solving orientation to the Rorschach, with its emphasis on habits and decision operations, stands in marked contrast to the method seen in terms of a 'projective process' and tied to a theory of personality independent of the test.

Beginning in 1970, Exner has set out to develop a Rorschach system that allows a standard method of using the instrument, that can be easily taught, has high interscorer reliability and can provide interpretive hypotheses that can withstand validation demands. Having accomplished each of these, he has brought a rigor and objectivity to the Rorschach which has served to re-establish the method's scientific credibility and respectability.

Conceptual Approach

In contrast with Exner's Comprehensive System and other empirical approaches to the Rorschach, the works of the other theorists in this volume—McCully, Schafer and Lerner—represent a conceptual approach. The roots of this approach are found in the writings of Rapaport (Gill, 1967) and his attempts to tie the Rorschach to psychoanalytic theory.

Rorschach did not wed his procedure to a particular theory; Rapaport did. He envisioned the relationship between method and theory as a two-way street. In one direction he saw theory offering the clinical tester a bedrock of clinical conceptualizations, with the possibility for greatly broadening and enriching test-derived inferences. In the other direction, he saw how the test itself provided a means for operationalizing concepts that were elusive and abstract, and how this process could facilitate the testing of key psychoanalytic formulations and thus, in time, could add to the evolving scope of psychoanalytic theory.

Unlike empirical approaches with their emphasis on formal scores and their interrelationships, examiners who assess from a conceptual perspective admit other sources of information, including the thematic content of the response, the patient's more spontaneous and evaluative comments, the sequence of responses and the multilayered vicissitudes of the patient–examiner relationship. The psychologist's task, as Schlesinger (1973) has noted, is to be attuned to all of these sources of information and to integrate the data of one with that of another. Each source must be given its due and must be seen as having its own consistency and relationship with the other levels of observation. The art of psychological testing then consists of sensitively shifting attention from one to another of these sources, while drawing and checking inferences throughout the course of testing.

Examiners who test from a conceptual position, in contrast to those who employ an empirical approach, place major emphasis on the patient–examiner relationship and its role in assessment. Each recognizes that an intricate interpersonal relationship with realistic and unrealistic aspects is intrinsic to testing, and that this relationship has a significant impact on the patient's test productions and can also provide a wealth of information in its own right. Several concepts including transference/counter-transference, self object transference and projective identification have been evoked and used to conceptualize the relationship.

In marked contrast to the empirical approach, a conceptual approach assumes an intimate relationship between the test and a theory of personality independent of the test. Several authors subsequent to Rapaport have outlined the specific functions offered by theory for Rorschach testing, especially but not exclusively, psychoanalytic theory.

Sugarman (1991), for example, has identified four such functions: (*a*) organization, (*b*) integration, (*c*) clarification, and (*d*) prediction. For Sugarman, an implicit theory of personality aids the Rorschach examiner in comprehending and organizing data that are complex, often exceedingly rich and at times inconsistent. As such, a comprehensive theory of personality allows the examiner not only to organize the mass of material, but also to integrate pieces of data that at first glance seem unrelated. The third function, clarification, means that personality theory can assist the clinician or researcher in filling the data gaps in an informed manner. Finally, regarding prediction, Sugarman reminded us that it can be successful only insofar 'as the behaviour being questioned is mediated by the personality variables tapped by the testing' (ibid., p. 134).

Beyond the functions served by theory, it is important that the examiner who assesses from a conceptual perspective be aware of the impact his or her theory has upon Rorschach interpretation. One's theory tends to determine the framework within which the interpretation is cast, the level at which the interpretation is pitched, the role accorded to the examiner, how the patient–examiner relationship is conceptualized, and the mode of observation and data gathering. For example, suppose on Card I a patient saw 'damaged bat with holes in its wings that was unable to fly'. An examiner from a self psychology perspective might well focus on the 'damaged bat' aspect of the response and infer an early narcissistic injury as experienced in a 'sense of being damaged or flawed'. An examiner from a developmental perspective might instead emphasize the 'unable to fly' part of the response and infer 'difficulties in separating and individuating'. Even though the two inferences are compatible, they reflect differing points of emphasis and different ways of conceptualizing core dynamics. As suggested previously, the empirical and conceptual approaches are not mutually exclusive. Increasingly, stimulated largely by the needs of front line clinical workers, efforts are being made to explore the ways in which the two approaches may be integrated. Those who approach the Rorschach from a conceptual vantage point are recognizing that more can be gleaned from the formal scores than they allowed, and that issues of reliability and validity need to be taken seriously. At the same time, those with an empirical bent are beginning to reconsider Rorschach content as a valuable source of information and are also thinking about the issues of self and interpersonal relations in a broader and more substantive manner.

Toward an experiential Rorschach psychology, Misra and his colleagues explicitly point out that their orientation is clinical—cultural—experiential. The term experiential has particular meaning when applied to the Rorschach; therefore, I will attempt here to provide a context for a better understanding of what is meant and implied by an experiential approach to the Rorschach.

The roots of a more experiential approach to the Rorschach are to be found in the shifts in emphasis in psychoanalytic theory and the contributions of the early Rorschach theorists, especially Schachtel (1966) and Mayman (1967). Within psychoanalytic theory there has been a gradual movement away from an experience-distant metapsychology couched in a mechanistic natural science framework of impersonal structures, forces and energies to a more experience-near clinical theory concerned primarily with experiences and subjective meanings.

Schachtel (1966) not only provided a rationale for the test as a whole and for each of the major determinants, but also articulated a clear description of what is meant by an experimental approach. He puts it this way:

I call the main approach I use . . . 'experiential' because it consists mostly in the attempt to reconstruct, to understand, and to make more explicit the experiences that the testee underwent in taking the test and his reactions to these experiences, specifically his way of approaching or avoiding and of handling the experiences of the inkblots in the context of the test task (ibid., p. 4).

Mayman's (1967) contributions included outlining a systematic approach to Rorschach content, clarifying the multileveled language of psychoanalysis, bringing to the Rorschach a set of concepts and a level of language that are relatively experience-near, and steadfastly arguing for a clinical–intuitive approach to the interpretation of the Rorschach data.

An experiential approach to the Rorschach involves a particular attitude toward the testing process and the nature of the Rorschach data, a set of test rationales that apply to the test as a whole and to each of the scores, a systematic method for evaluating content and a particular view of the interpretive process.

As Schachtel suggests, in Rorschach testing the examiner attempts to understand and re-construct as much of the totality of the testee's experience of the test as possible. To do so, the examiner must first appreciate that the testing experience takes place within the context of a specific 'test task' and a particular 'test situation'.

By 'task' is meant the specific directions; for example, 'Tell me what you see' or 'What might this be?' In paying close attention to the test directions, the examiner recognizes that Rorschach responses reflect and are influenced by the subjective meanings the patient ascribes to such directions. That is, Rorschach performance involves what the testee believes must be done to deal with the task.

The 'test situation' and the subjective meanings it has for the patient also influence Rorschach performance. Of the various aspects of the 'test situation', the consideration that testing takes place in the context of an interpersonal relationship is of prime importance. At some level, the testee recognizes the ultimate necessity to communicate a response to another person. Therefore, from this perspective, it is assumed that Rorschach protocol cannot be fully understood without an awareness of its interpersonal aspects.

An experiential perspective provides various sources of information about the patient that can serve as a springboard for developing clinical inferences. These include: (*a*) the formal aspects of the test responses, including test scores and their interrelationships, (*b*) the content of the patient's specific response, including the attitude toward the response, (*c*) the patient's behavior in the testing situation and how the patient interacts with the examiner, and (*d*) the exact sequence of responses.

Examiners who test from an experiential perspective insist upon test rationales, that is, explanatory concepts and formulations that connect behavior with its psychodynamic underpinnings on the one hand, and with test performance and test responses on the other. As Schachtel (1966, p. 2) noted, 'No amount of validation or Rorschach-test-score meaning can substitute for the understanding of what goes on in the test'. When an examiner feels comfortable and secure relying on a fixed meaning for a particular score based on authority or research, it becomes far more difficult to always experience anew whether such meaning really applies to the actual concrete response, or whether other, even more important meanings may apply.

For example, it has long been held (and supported by research) that the white response indicates negativity and oppositionality. Using a rationale developed by Schachtel (1966), I (Lerner, 1991) found that in a select group of narcissistic patients, the space response (in Schachtel's terms, the attunement to hollow areas) reflected subjective feelings of emptiness and hollowness, not just negativism.

An experiential approach views Rorschach content as an immensely rich and valuable source of information. It further holds that the analysis of content can be approached in an informed and systematic way. Mayman (1977) laid the conceptual groundwork for such an approach in his careful and astute analysis of the human movement response. He identified five determinants of the human movement response and then demonstrated how each could be related to core aspects of self and object relational experiences. I (Lerner, 1991) have shown how three of these components— fantasy, kinesthesia and object representation—could be applied to the content of non-movement responses as well.

To briefly recap, the Rorschach has been used to infer from the patient's test performance the more basic and enduring structures in his/her personality. The experiential approach holds that the patient's phenomenological experience is also a vital aspect of assessment.

EMPATHY AND INTERPRETATION WITHIN AN EXPERIENTIAL APPROACH

Based upon Rorschach's belief that his test could elicit conclusions about an individual's characteristic way of experiencing, but not about the content of such experiences, Rorschach theorists and clinicians have tended to focus on the more formal and structural features of a test protocol as the basis of interpretation. As one reviews this practice, it becomes apparent that interpretations drawn from the structural features of a Rorschach tend themselves to have a primarily structural emphasis.

With utmost regard for this time-honored approach and full appreciation of the contributions that have issued from it, I would point out that it is not without limitations. There is more to a Rorschach protocol than the determinants and there is more to a person than that which can be explained from a structural perspective.

As indicated in the previous section, there is also the experiential aspects of a protocol and of the testee. This aspect of the test record and of the person does not lend itself to the more objective and formal analyses we bring to structural features. Instead, it calls for a different approach—a complementary one. It begs for an approach with a more phenomenological orientation—an essentially subjective frame of reference.

At the center of such an orientation, I would suggest, is empathy. Empathy as an information gathering activity, as a way of coming to know another if you will, has been insistently espoused by Kohut (1978). In his paper, 'Introspection, Empathy, and Psychoanalysis', he argued that access to psychological depths could be obtained only through specific modes of observation: introspection into one's own subjective state, vicarious introspection and empathy into that of another.

Empathy is applied to Rorschach interpretation in the following way. The examiner uses the individual's entire production—the response and the accompanying verbalizations—as a jumping-off point for tuning into the testee's underlying subjective state. Herein, the examiner asks, 'To have arrived at this response and said these things, what might the patient have been experiencing at that moment?' The following examples illustrate this process.

In Card I the patient responded, 'It looks like something menacing, coming toward me, the hands are up'. On inquiry he added, 'Legs, body, arms, hands protruding out. The bulk of the image is large. There is a white dot which could be a mouth'. The examiner attuned to the content of this response, especially the rich affective elaboration, would empathetically understand the patient as indicating that he, the patient, felt frightened by a powerful, malevolent and engulfing force. Because it was the patient's first response, the examiner considered its possible transferential meanings. That is, the examiner wondered if the patient might also be conveying his fear that the test would overwhelm and envelop him.

A second patient offered three responses to Card I, of which two required extensive inquiry. As testing progressed the examiner found himself having to inquire less and less as the patient herself volunteered the necessary information as part of her initial response. For example, on Card IX she responded, 'I see a flower, an iris. The entire card. This area are the petals; the color and the tones within the color make 'it appear velvety'.

On the basis of the patient's heightened attunement to what he the examiner needed, her unasked for willingness to provide it and his own diminishing role, the examiner empathetically noted the patient's hypersensitivity to the needs and expectations of others, her ease in accommodating to these expectations and her subtle movement towards self-sufficiency.

These examples illustrate how a more phenomenological orientation built around the examiner's empathy is applicable to a wide range of features in a Rorschach record. It can be applied to obscure aspects of a protocol such as where the patient positions himself or herself vis-à-vis the response (that is, 'looking down on dark clouds'), peculiar ways of expressing a response (that is, 'this looks batty to me'), or a patient's tendency to self-inquire.

The place of empathy in the interpretive process, as conceptualized here, occupies a middle ground between what has been termed 'wild interpretation' on the one hand, and exclusive empiricism on the other. Unlike the former, there is comparatively little reliance on symbolism, the examiner does not offer his or her own associations to the individual's response, and one attempts to stay close to the data. Empathy, not association, is the basis of knowing. In contrast with strict empiricism, this interpretive approach admits sources of data that would be otherwise excluded. Here, the clinician's role is maximized. His or her skills, judgement and sensitivities are valued and made use of.

SUMMARY

Rorschach Test: Theory and Practice is designed to update students and clinicians with the latest advances in the use of the Rorschach. The book accomplishes this and more. The Rorschach is placed in both a historical and cultural context, and four different approaches to Rorschach data are presented. Because each approach is presented in a clear and straightforward way, the reader will find the book especially practical and useful.

In keeping with the authors' commitment to a clinical—cultural—experiential orientation, my intent here has been to supplement their work. I have compared two contemporary and overarching approaches to the Rorschach, and have explicated what is involved in a more experiential Rorschach psychology. I have also suggested that a more formal, structural interpretive approach to Rorschach data should be complemented with a more phenomenological orientation based upon empathy.

Paul M. Lerner

1   THE *ZEITGEIST*

Events occur in contexts. They are surrounded by backgrounds. Placed against their backgrounds, events acquire significance. In this chapter, we will try and place the Rorschach test in a context. We will first outline the climate in which Rorschach lived and worked. Then, we will briefly describe some events and activities in Rorschach's life and work. Both the events around him and the ones in his life and professional work when looked at against each other provide a rich phenomenological framework for appreciating his test.

The first section describes the context—the spirit of the times in which Rorschach worked. This is followed by the section on Rorschach's life and work.

SECTION I: THE SPIRIT OF THE TIMES

There are six features characterizing Hermann Rorschach's times:

1. psychoanalysis,
2. schizophrenia,
3. Gestalt school of psychology,
4. phenomenology,
5. movements in art, e.g., Cubism, Dadaism, Expressionism, Fauvism and Futurism, and
6. Existentialism.

We will take a brief look at each of these.

Psychoanalysis
While working on hysteria with Joseph Breuer in the 1880s, Freud discovered the role repressed memories played in developing

pathological behavior. He formulated the concept of the unconscious. Experiencing difficulties in using hypnosis to bring these memories out at the conscious level, he developed the method of free association. It involved asking patients to tell any/everything that came to their minds. In the years to come, Freud's writings provided insights into abnormal behavior. His work on dreams (Freud, 1900) focused on representation. Objects and experiences in dreams *represent* otherwise painful repressed wishes in acceptable and comfortable form. These are metaphorical expressions of unconscious material.

In many ways, the person taking the Rorschach test undergoes the same dream-like, surrealistic experience. The test instruction, 'What might this be?', tends to place the testee in a frame of mind where he/she feels that the inkblots on the cards could be many different things, and that the tester wants him/her to figure out what they might be. The Rorschach test in this sense seems to be an operational version of the free association method.

Schizophrenia

Bergholzli Mental Hospital, Zurich, Switzerland. Rorschach was working there with Eugen Bleuler (1857–1939) researching mental disorders. It indeed was a pleasant coincidence that Carl Gustav Jung (1875–1961) was also there at the same time working on schizophrenia. Jung completed his doctoral dissertation titled, 'On the Psychology and Pathology of the so-called Occult Phenomena'. And the title of Hermann Rorschach's dissertation was 'On Reflex Hallucinations and Kindred Manifestations'. Both Jung and Rorschach worked under Bleuler. Historical accident? Maybe.

McCully (1971) carefully examines the link between Jungian philosophy and Rorschach's test experience in terms of inkblots arousing archetypes. Jung's word association method involves testees giving the first word that comes to their mind after hearing the stimulus words. In the Rorschach method, the subject is asked to tell what the inkblot might be. The underlying process is the same in both, namely, making connections between something you come across and the things that come to mind. The Jungian word association subject selects one from the many words that may come to his/her mind. The Rorschach subject selects one percept from the many that may be aroused by the blot.

In schizophrenia, pathology in thinking is more obvious than in other mental disorders. We are not trying to 'connect' schizophrenia with Jung and/or Rorschach. We are, however, trying to 'contextualize' the Rorschach test. Both Freud, through his works on the unconscious and the free association method, and Jung, through his studies of schizophrenia and the word association method, provided a meaningful, experiential, phenomenological context to Hermann Rorschach's work on using the form interpretation method as a diagnostic tool for understanding psychopathology.

The Gestalt School of Psychology

Max Wertheimer (1880–1943), Kurt Koffka (1886–1941) and Wolfgang Kohler (1887–1967) founded the Gestalt school around 1912 by focusing on perceptual processes and discovering laws of perception, e.g., open form seeks completion by closure, something we often notice in Card III of the Rorschach test when the gaps in the leg-like areas are 'filled-in' by some testees and a whole human form is seen; other testees may not 'want to' fill in the gap. They see it as say a fish. Gestaltists pointed out that perceptual fields are organized as *figures* and *grounds*. In Card II, the middle white space (the background) may sometimes be seen as a figure (spaceship going up surrounded by fire and smoke), or on Card VII, the inside white space is seen as an island surrounded by water. The law of good figure (*Pragnanz*) stresses that the need to see a 'good' figure often ignores non-fitting details and tends to 'modify' it to make it look good. The quality of symmetry in all the Rorschach figures recognizes this tendency; yet, at the same time, minor seemingly incongruent details are added to 'assess' the testee's ability/need to see 'good' figures. Associated with form and shape in this good figure law is yet another tendency on the part of the perceiver, namely, to inject an additional dimension in seeing things, that is, movement. Some Rorschach cards have a greater potential to arouse a sense of movement (e.g., Card II, Card III) than others (e.g., Card IV, Card VI).

Phenomenology

Edmund Husserl's (1859–1938) inaugural lecture, 'Pure Phenomenology: Its Methods and its Investigations', was delivered at the University of Freiburg in Breisau, Germany, on 3 May 1917 (Van

Breda, 1989). We may consider this date as the formal beginning of the movement of phenomenology, that is, appearance is reality.

The Rorschach cards *arouse* certain feelings/emotions in the testee. They may also *suppress* some other feelings and emotions. A testee may get upset by looking at certain cards or excited by looking at others, e.g., 'Please take that away' (Card IV), 'I don't want to look at it'; or, 'Wow! that's pretty, I'd like to hang it on my wall' may be the response on seeing Card VIII. From the point of view of the tester, these *experiential* expressions are real and meaningful.

Phenomenology is a science of the apriori (Husserl, 1973). Experience occurs before knowledge. Husserl points out that, '. . .progressive phenomenology constructs apriori (yet, with a strictly *intuited* necessity and universality), on the one hand, the *forms* of conceivable worlds and, on the other hand, conceivable worlds themselves, within the limits set by all conceivable forms of being and by their system of levels' (ibid., p. 154, emphasis in the original).

A woman saw two men chasing a woman in a car on Card I; another person saw Lord Shiva (*Shivling*) on Card IX; a third saw a man being attacked by two pythons on Card X. Each of them constructed an apriori *form* on the basis of the limits set by the shape, color and shade of the selected blot area. It was an intuited necessity, guided by the conceivable world in his/her mind. The inkblots *limited* the range of experiences, but the experience per se was phenomenological.

Art Movements

The fifth element in the *zeitgeist* of the Rorschach test is movements in the field of art: Cubism, Dadaism, Expressionism, Fauvism and Futurism.

Cubism focuses on looking at objects simultaneously from different perspectives. That is usually what a testee does in the Rorschach test situation when he/she turns the cards around, brings them closer to or away from the eyes, looks at them from a flat perspective ('edging'), etc. Pablo Ruiz Picasso (1881–1973), the Spanish sculptor and painter who worked in France, and George Braque (1882–1963) are considered to be the main founders, promoters and launchers of the Cubism movement.

Dadaism (literally, the *da-da* sounds of a hobby-horse), was founded in Zurich, Switzerland, in 1915. It was an intense, emotionally violent, anti-establishment movement. Artists in this movement opposed just about everything that was conventional and traditional. Why should things be seen in a traditional sense? they asked. Why are only certain objects considered to be artistic over others? 'Beauty is in the eyes of the beholder'. *Dil lagaa gadhee say toe paree bhee kya cheez hai?* ('Who cares for a fairy when you are in love with an ass!') goes a Hindi saying.

Dadaism was led by Jean Hans Arp (1887–1986), a Franco-German artist. He made objects demonstrate 'the absurdity of this world' to the rich. Then, there was the famous American artist Marcel Duchamp (1887–1968), who did indeed pick up a urinal, title it *Fountain*, sign his name as R. Mutt, and submit it as an entry for an art exhibition in 1917! The sponsors of the exhibition, however, did not consider it suitable for the exhibition. It was rejected. It was, however, a strong statement about absurdism: art is not confined to objective criteria.

In the Rorschach situation, it is not uncommon to come across unusual perceptions. Card I may look like a bat to some, but to someone else it may be two alien monsters kidnapping a headless woman to the limits of the outer world. Two persons sitting at a table enjoying a cup of tea could be the image on Card III for one, and two men-like women (or women-like men) carrying a bleeding human head, for another. Why should things look traditional to us? asked Dadaists. Something similar happens in the Rorschach: in spite of similarities, inkblots look different to different people. Dadaists believed that:

a society which could produce something so horrible as the First World War was an evil society whose philosophy and culture should be totally destroyed because it was socially and morally bankrupt . . . established that art meant nothing anymore . . . chance had as much meaning and made much more sense than the art of a rotten society (Lambert, 1991, p. 39).

A little *da-da* lives inside each one of us and often comes out in the open during the Rorschach experience.

Expressionism, epitomized in Vincent van Gogh (1853–1890), the Dutch painter, literally dipped, drenched and wallowed in emotions. Objects were great and fine. But what one needed to experience them, believed Expressionists, was having a mental state in which those objects were embedded.

A Rorschacher often finds it easy, but many a time has to struggle, to figure out the psychic, cultural and mental context of the percepts seen by his/her patients. A subject *expresses* himself/herself with no inhibition on the one hand, or by withholding everything on the other. Either extreme, or the points in between, express features of his/her personality.

Fauvism stressed bright, sharp colors. It was a reaction to the dull and the academic. It was full of passions. The Fauvists, literally wild beasts, e.g., Henri Emile Matisse (1869–1954), loved to distort reality by (*a*) challenging conventional forms, and (*b*) enriching objects with bright, often frightening, colors.

Sometimes, don't our testees scare us by distorting Rorschach card images and adding frightening colors? 'Fire in hell' (Card I). 'Green scum' (Card IV). 'Colorful butterfly' (Card V).

And then there was Futurism, founded in Italy around 1909–1916. Giacommo Balla (1871–1958) was one of its main leaders. Futurists, were literally futurists. They ignored the past. Why worry about what has happened? Focus on the future. *Beetee taahi bisaar kay, aagay kee sudhi laye* ('Let bygones be bygones; let us look forward, to the future').

That's exactly what Futurists were all about. Let us burn and destroy the museums, they said, because these are grim reminders of the past. 'The real contribution of the Futurists now', says Lambert (1991, p. 22), 'seems to be their "simultaneity", a way of putting together things that happen together in time: sound, light and movement'.

Existentialism

The sixth and final trend characterizing the spirit of the times when Rorschach worked on his test was the literary movement of Existentialism. While existential philosophy was articulated by Soren Kierkegaard (1813–1855): *experience precedes essence*, it could really be traced back to Dostoevsky's (1821–1881) *Notes from the Underground*, first published in 1854 (Dostoevsky, 1992).

Much later, in 1915, the theme of existential despair was presented with great intensity in Franz Kafka's (1883–1924) *Metamorphosis*. Greg Samsa is transformed into a giant beetle and *experiences* his world: his domineering father (who in anger tries hitting him by throwing apples at him, he misses quite a few times, but then one of them does end up hitting him and getting lodged in his 'shell'), his ambivalent mother, a caring sister, the 'cold' maid, an uncaring boss, the picture on the wall, along with other series of intense experiences.

On the Rorschach test, we see testees exhibiting their world— the world as they see and experience it. Empathy plays a critical role in helping the examiner see their world from their eyes.

In summary then, psychoanalysis, schizophrenia, Gestalt, phenomenology, Cubism, Dadaism, Expressionism, Fauvism, Futurism and Existentialism constituted the main elements of the times in which Hermann Rorschach lived and worked. As we mentioned in the beginning of this chapter, we are trying to contextualize the Rorschach test by looking at the *zeitgeist* on the one hand, and at Rorschach's life and work on the other. We have presented a glimpse of the *zeitgeist*. Let us now look at the other piece: the life and work of Hermann Rorschach.

SECTION II: HERMANN RORSCHACH'S LIFE AND WORK

Ellenberger (1954) provides an extremely rich clinical–experiential perspective appreciating Rorschach's life and contributions centering around the form interpretation test. A brief summary:

1. 4 November 1884: Zurich, Switzerland, Rorschach is born.
2. 11 July 1897: Rorschach's mother passes away. Later, his father re-marries his wife's sister.
3. 7 March 1902: Rorschach loses his father.
4. In school, Rorschach is given a nickname *Klex* (inkblot!) by his friends; he was destined to work on the inkblots later. *Karm siddhaant* ('Law of *karm*') at work.
5. 1906: Rorschach visits Russia and falls in love with the country and its people.
6. Around 1914: While in medical school, Rorschach observes an autopsy; later, he dreams about it. 'I had a dream in which I felt my own brain cut off from the mass of the hemispheres and fell forward exactly as it had happened in the autopsy'

(see, Ellenberger, 1954, p. 178). Split between the self and non-self!

7. 21 April 1910: He marries Olga Stempeliu, a Russian girl.
8. 1912: Rorschach graduates from medical school, receiving an M.D. (Psychiatry) under the supervision of Eugen Bleuler (who, incidentally, also supervised Carl Gustav Jung's work and also coined the term schizophrenia). The title of Rorschach's doctoral dissertation was 'On Reflex Hallucinations and Kindred Manifestations'.
9. 1912: He publishes a paper based on his doctoral dissertation: 'Reflex Hallucinations and Symbolism within a Psychoanalytic Framework'. He also published many other important papers on clinical issues between 1912 and 1914, e.g.,

   (i) *Clock and Time*: He observed that among certain neurotics, their interest in clocks could be traced back to an unconscious desire for their mother's breast.
   (ii) *Choice of a Friend by a Neurotic*: Parental images tend to influence the choice of friends made by neurotics.
   (iii) *Analytical Remarks on the Painting of a Schizophrenic*: Rorschach had one of his patients copy a painting, 'The Last Supper' (a 6th century mosaic showing Christ eating with his 12 disciples the night before his death). The patient, noted Rorschach, drew long-hair on all disciples except Judas (who betrayed Christ and helped the Romans identify him by kissing him, leading to Christ's crucifixion the next day).

10. 1914–1922: In addition to doing clinical work Rorschach undertook studies of religious sects in the context of culture and mythology, e.g.,

    (i) The sect, *Forest-Brotherhood*, led by Bingelli who, among many other things, demanded that the sect members worship his penis because it was holy. Bingelli also called his urine 'heavenly drops' and offered it as a medicine to his disciples. He would profess that the treatment for his disciples from demonic possession was to have sex with young girls.
    (ii) *Unternahrer's Sect*: The followers of this sect believed that incestual relations were *holy*. Rorschach points out that Unternahrer believed that the thought content of the

neurotics reflected what he called *low mythology* and that archetypes indicated *high mythology*.

(*iii*) During this period, Rorschach also studied personality differences as reflected on his test among the Bernese and Appenzeil communities. 'A Bernese who becomes schizophrenic is more apt to fall into a profound catatonic state than is Appenzeller' (Rorschach, 1975, p. 97). Bernese are serious; Appenzellers maliciously humorous. Appenzellers maintain their extratensive style even when they show schizophrenic symptoms; they also almost exclusively manifest auditory hallucinations. On the other hand, the Bernese suffering from schizophrenia most commonly indicate kinesthetic hallucinations.

(*iv*) Rorschach's interest in culture and mythology was further illustrated in his papers which appeared in the *Swiss Journal of Folklore*, including the one on the superstition associated murder case.

11. *The Munsterlingen Monkey*: Rorschach may be credited with starting 'pet therapy' long before it became a helpful adjunct to psychotherapy. He would bring in his pet monkey to the mental hospital not only to have his patients entertained by its tricks, but also to observe his patients' reactions while they were being entertained. The monkey was a *live* Rorschach card to which his patients responded.

12. While working at the Munsterlingen Hospital, Rorschach also organized plays and fancy dress shows for his patients. Not only did he organize them but would also often dress up in disguise and appear in these shows. Jungian *persona* at work!

13. June 1921: Rorschach's classic work introducing his test is published, *Psychodiagnostics: A Diagnostic Test based on Perception*.

14. 2 April 1922: Rorschach died of complications while suffering from appendicitis. Age 37!

Here, we have given an overly brief summary of this great man—a psychiatrist and a researcher. We would recommend that readers consult Ellenberger (1954) for an exciting and informative picture of Rorschach's life.

SUMMARY

In this chapter, we have attempted to look at the *zeitgeist* of the Rorschach test. Section I described some of the features characterizing the spirit of the times around the end of the last century and the beginning of the present century. Section II provided a brief overview of Rorschach's biographical details. Treating and researching mental patients, Rorschach's work reflects the influence of things happening around him: psychoanalysis, schizophrenia, Gestalt school of psychology, phenomenology, Cubism, Dadaism, Expressionism, Fauvism, Futurism and Existentialism. The Rorschach test is a figure against the background of the intellectual—cultural—experiential climate of the times.

Rorschach responses reflect our world, the world as we experience it. So do the creative writings of authors, novelists, poets and playwrights. The rich relationship between the Rorschach test and literature is the content of the next chapter.

2 LITERATURE AND THE RORSCHACH TEST

He was on the faculty of the English department in Lucknow University, India, back in the fifties. Professor A.T. Bhattacharya. Very well read. Very popular. Once, in one of his lectures, he said, 'The function of literature is to make life beautiful'. You see a panhandler, a rickshaw-wallah or a vendor on the streets in Hazratganj or Aminabad. Chances are, you may ignore them. However, said Prof. Bhattacharya, if you read a story about them in a newspaper or a magazine, the same pandhandler or rickshaw-wallah or vendor starts looking different. They become meaningful. You tend to see them, or think about them differently. Like a city or a building becomes famous when it is used as a location for shooting a film.

After reading Amritlal Nagar's (1984) *Yey Kothey-waaliaan*, the ladies of the evening are seen differently, perhaps with sympathy and concern rather than hate or anger. Something similar happens after seeing the movies *Teesri Kasam* or *Umrao Jaan* or *Pretty Woman*.

Kafka's (1988) *Metamorphosis* is most likely to change your way of looking at bugs and beetles. The percepts of the office clerk, domineering father, caring sister and helpless mother acquire unique intensity in hitting your psyche whenever you think of, or come across, them. Kafka reinterprets these concepts and many others (e.g., existential despair and the anxiety of non-achievement).

Narayan's (1992) *Swami and Friends* re-frames the image of a ten year old in our mind. We begin empathizing with his world. The school building, classroom, desks, ink-pots, friends and bullies all begin to arouse benign, nostalgic emotions. The next time you watch kids going to school, you start wondering which one among them could be Swami.

All these three authors—Nagar, Kafka and Narayan—start with a gentle nudge and then, step-by-step, almost subliminally, pull us away from our mundane reality and guide us into a surrealistic world of objects, episodes and fantasy. That's what Professor Bhattacharya's comment was all about. *Literature beautifies life.*

A process similar to creative writing occurs in the Rorschach experience. The testee usually starts very matter-of-factly with Card I, and moves through Cards II, III, IV, V and so on. By the time he/she reaches Card X, you have a good sample of the objects and object relations he/she has incorporated from the world outside.

In this chapter, we interface literature with the Rorschach. We will look at three authors, Nagar, Kafka and Narayan, and their works: Nagar's *Yey Kothey-waaliaan*, Kafka's *Metamorphosis* and Narayan's *Swami and Friends*. We will also look at three protocols: Shakher, Ibrahim and Mary. The intent is to illustrate parallels between the literary process and the Rorschach process.

The discussion is divided into three sections. Section I is a brief overview of the three literary works. Section II contains the protocols. And, finally, Section III, makes some comparative observations.

SECTION I: PROSTITUTES, VERMIN AND THE BOY

Yey Kothey-waaliaan

Nagar's narrative about prostitutes alternates between sensitively done case studies on the one hand, and his reflections on the lifestyles of prostitutes and suggestions for bringing them into the mainstream of society on the other. Somewhat sensitive to the fact (stigma?) of writing about them, Nagar defensively (although, honestly and sincerely) clarifies that he did this work somewhat hesitatingly and under pressure.

The year was 1950. The first president of the Republic of India, Babu Rajendra Prasad wished that someone would do a study on prostitutes and bring their plight to the attention of policy makers. In fact, he himself wanted to put something together about this issue but obviously could not find the time for it. Pandit Rudra Narain Shukla, a well-known and highly respected journalist, thought that this job should preferably be done by an author who writes in the Hindi language. So, without even consulting about the project with Nagar (in good faith, though), he issued a press statement that Nagar was going to do this. Nagar, naturally, felt uncomfortable about it.

The topic (news!) was discussed at a literary club, a club comprising literary giants including Bhagwati Charan Verma, Gyan Chand Jain and Rudra Narain Shukla. And following a lively debate, the project was '(re)assigned' to Nagar. He had to write about the ladies of the evening because (*a*) the president of the country wanted to address this problem and Nagar was *the* most suitable person to do this, and (*b*) therefore, the Lucknow literary circle 'requested' (in fact, ordered) Nagar to undertake this project. That was it!

The result? *Yey Kothey-waaliaan*, first published in 1960. Perhaps, this is the first ever book-length work in Hindi (maybe, in any Indian language) in India. It is a poignant picture of the hurt and helplessness of prostitutes. It is *experiential*. Phenomenological. A classic piece synthesizing a literary–scientific approach to a social problem.

Maybe it was a coincidence and possibly did factor into the decision of the Lucknow literary group. All his life Nagar lived in his ancestral, family home located in the *Chowk* in Lucknow—an old, historical, royal neighborhood where prostitutes also lived and 'worked'.

Based on interviews and case studies, the book *looks like* a collection of *Rorschachs* of women who, starting their career as students of music and dance, were later pressured by a combination of economic hardships and a need for stability, and (if they were lucky) ended up as the mistresses of the rich. Many (the unlucky ones) however, just withered away in pain and humiliation.

In *Lulu kee Maa* ('Lulu's mother'), for example, Nagar profiles a married woman with a child and an unemployed husband who is literally forced by her husband and a pimp to prostitute, and thus avoid death by starvation. In 1940, Nagar and his friend Mahesh Kaul (later the famous film director) together shared one room in a two bedroom apartment. The woman, her child and husband lived in the other room! People 'visiting' the lady had to pass through the room shared by Nagar and Kaul! They (Nagar and

Kaul) often ended up babysitting for Lulu during his mother's 'business hours'. Finally, feeling uncomfortable with this delicate yet embarrassing situation, they decided to move.

'*Abee, Lulu kaa kyaa hoye gaa?*' ('What about Lulu now? Who would watch him?') asks Lulu's anxious mother when Nagar and Kaul say goodbye to her. As readers of this poignant narrative, we also often wonder what indeed did happen to Lulu after Nagar and Kaul moved out of the apartment.

Then, there is the sad story of Badray Muneer, a lady, who following a tiring, humiliating 'career', grows old and (adding salt to injury) suffers from veneral disease. She is dumped by her 'boyfriend' (pimp?). She has no money to buy food or medicines for treatment. A compassionate friend offers a place to live in a makeshift 'room'. Existentially, she is dead. She is, however, waiting for physical death.

Quite sometime ago, Nagar and some of his friends had visited her a couple of times to hear her sing and had known her as a respectable artist/musician. Wishing for some help, bedridden Badray Muneer sends a message to Nagar wondering if he would visit her. He does, and also gives her some money for treatment. On his way out, Nagar overhears her ecstatic voice: '*Main kahti thee, Khuda nahin hai! Khuda hai! Khuda hai!*' ('I used to say, there was no God. There *is* God; there *is* God').

Interspersed with sensitive narratives (reading like Freud's case studies), Nagar in this book reviews problems of (*a*) prostitution in the villages in India, (*b*) traditional dancing girls who pride themselves as students of classical music on the one hand, and the so-called 'cheap' ones who would trade sex for money on the other, (*c*) the concept of 'the other woman', and (*d*) the issues and concerns around rehabilitating these ladies into the social mainstream.

Yey Kothey-waaliaan presents intense portraits of prostitutes—Nagar's perceptions of these ladies; his Rorschachs; what they *look like* to him. Literature is somewhat like an embellished, fabulized Rorschach of the world of objects as it exists in the mind of the author, poet or playwright. So are the Rorschach responses. Let us look at another creative Rorschach: the world from the eyes of a vermin.

Metamorphosis

'When Gregor Samsa woke up one morning from unsettling dreams, he found himself changed in his bed into a monstrous vermin' (Kafka, 1988, p. 3). Thus begins Kafka's *Metamorphosis*.

Gregor, a traveling salesman, takes the five o'clock train to go to work when he is not on the road visiting customers. Although he is transformed into a *gobraila* (dung-beetle), he still realizes that he has to catch the train. Can *gobrailas* think? Kafka's does. He also feels. Gregor, the vermin, feels helpless and has to struggle to get out of the bed. He just can't seem to do it. After undergoing numerous, existentially agonizing experiences, he hopes his family (an ex-army officer and pathologically assertive and domineering father; a homely, fragile mother; and a caring sister) would perhaps realize his predicament and help him out. The authoritarian father fluctuates between anger and disgust. His mother alternates between fear and pity. It is only his sister, Grete, who still cares for him and tries to make his life as less painful as possible. Gregor's existence is discomforting. Painful. He thinks. What comes to mind is Descartes' 'I think, therefore, I am' (*Cogito ergo sum*).

In addition, he also *feels* the world around him. He was *ashamed* because trying to sleep under a couch was quite uncomfortable: his back almost got crushed under it; he could not raise his head up either. Staying like that the whole night was no fun, but he realized its inevitability, '. . . for the time being he would have to lie low, and by being patient and showing his family every possible consideration, help them bear the inconvenience which he simply had to cause them in his present condition' (Kafka, 1988, p. 23).

And then, one day, he dies. A 'somebody' ends up as a 'nobody'. His dead body is referred to as *the stuff*. The housemaid disposes of it. And (proudly) announces to the family, '*Well, look, you don't have to worry about getting rid of the stuff next door. It's already taken care of*' (Kafka, 1988, p. 57, emphasis added).

Metamorphosis is a three-part story. The first part depicts Gregor's transformation and the reactions of the people around him (family, office manager, cleaning woman).

The second part intensifies the reactions of others as well as Gregor's world-view (*weltanschaung*). He is hurt. Physically too, painfully crawling around with an apple lodged in his back!

The third and final part of the story begins with a reiteration of this wound. '*Gregor's serious wound, from which he suffered for a month, the apple remained imbedded in his flesh, . . . seemed to have reminded even his father that Gregor was a member of the family'* (Kafka, 1988, p. 40, emphasis added). In the end, after Gregor is dead and the 'stuff' has been disposed of, the three (father, mother and sister) take a trolley-ride into the country. Visible in them is a sense of relief. Among many other things, they would now be able to move into a smaller, less expensive apartment.

Metamorphosis is a trans-existential experience—a Rorschach experience. It is, at one level, what the beetle's world *looks like* percept, and describes how a family of four faces (experiences) its world when one of them, the wage-earner (who is also helping to repay the money borrowed by the family), one morning is suddenly transformed from an effective, powerful member, into a helpless dung-beetle. And, at the second level, there is Gregor's—the *gobraila's*—world of object relations, comprising of him and the other three.

In *Metamorphosis*, Kafka, the narrator, creates multilayered Rorschach protocols and weaves a *see-through* screen between them. They are separated, although in an integrated way. You see one, then the other, and then, yet another, in relation to each other. And that's how the individual responses in a Rorschach protocol appear. They look separate. Yet, when you see them in relation to each other, they begin to evolve into a bigger, separated (yet integrated) picture of the total personality.

After Nagar's prostitutes and Kafka's vermin, we now move on to Narayan's hero, Swaminathan, and his world.

Swami and Friends

This is a story of a ten-year-old boy Swaminathan (Swami), who is in the first form, section A, at the Albert Mission School, and four of his friends—Pea (the shortie), Mani (the bully), Rajam (the son of the police superintendent) and Sankar (the nerd)—in the small town of Malgudi (an imaginary town near Madras, India, and the setting for Narayan's stories and novels).

In Swami's world, just outside the inner circle of his four friends, are his father, mother, grandmother and his small newborn brother. On the periphery are a few others: the 'fire-eyed' Vedanayagam, his classroom teacher; the history teacher, D. Pillai; the scripture teacher, Mr. Ebenezar; the district forest officer, Mr. M.P.S.

Nair; Ranga, the cartman, etc. Narayan narrates what the world *looks like* to Swami (like the Rorschach experience prefaced with 'this looks like . . .').

'After the delicious freedom of Saturday and Sunday, it was difficult to get into the Monday mood of work and discipline. He shuddered at the very thought of school: *that dismal yellow building; and fire-eyed Vedanayagam, his class-teacher, and the Head Master with his thin long cane* . . .' (Narayan, 1992, p. 3, emphasis added).

This is the nucleus of Swami's world of objects. 'Yellow building' looks *dismal*; Vedanayagam is *fire-eyed*; the *thin, long cane* becomes an extension of the head master. There are objects. There are object relations; the inner world representing (symbolizing) the outer world.

The outer world is usually mundane. Cut and dry. It becomes meaningful when it is *incorporated* into the inner world. This is because (*a*) we often (if not always) incorporate whatever out there *looks* important to us (and things become important when they get invested with our feelings and emotions), and (*b*) incorporated objects ('charged' as they are with emotions) influence how we feel and act in relation to the world outside. The Rorschach responses sample the objects in our inner world as well as the relations between these objects. Here is an example of the object world and emotional metaphors.

In one of the many interesting episodes involving the issue of turf-control between Mani, the bully, and Rajam, the son of Malgudi's superintendent of police (the intelligent, affluent, newly arrived student in Swami's class), Mani and Rajam talk with each other through Swami. 'Mani faced Swaminathan steadily and asked, "*Are you a man?*" Swaminathan turned to Rajam and repeated, "*Are you a man?*" Rajam flared up and shouted, "*Which dog doubts it?*" Swaminathan turned to Mani and said ferociously, "*Which dirty dog doubts it?*"' (Narayan, 1992, p. 17, emphasis added). The plain word 'dog', when re-communicated, was turned into 'dirty dog'. That's what emotions do: embellish objects.

Challenges to our ego are often handled by embellishing objects. Rajam's status is challenged by Mani sarcastically. Sarcasm is intensified by downgrading (representing) *manhood* to *doghood*! And, it is degraded additionally by making it a *dirty dog*. We don't care what something *actually is*. The important thing is *what does it look like* to us. It is appearance, not reality. *Appearance is reality*.

We distort reality. Distortion is emotionally gratifying. It gives us licence to do, say, or think about it (i.e., reality) in a personally satisfying way. We all do it. Levels of impairment in reality testing are reflected in *shifts* and *spreads* in *psychic functioning* (Schafer, 1954). At one end is the fantasies of poets, authors and psychotics (with a difference however, insofar as poets come back to reality after wandering in the world of surrealistic imagery but psychotics feel little or no pressure to 'wake up' and thus, rarely come back to reality), and on the other hand is the 'reality-bound' objects of 'scientists'. Between these two ends are folks like us. The average people. We fluctuate within a relatively short range. Rorschach responses reflect this fluctuation and help us make some meaning-ful observations about the world as it *appears* or *looks like* to our testee.

When Swami runs away to escape the wrath (the dreaded cane) of the head master and then gets lost in the forest, his (free-floating) anxiety takes control. 'He would not mind even if it were twelve o'clock when he reached the Trunk Road', enters Narayan into Swami's psyche, adding, 'There was something reassuring in its spaciousness and in the sparseness of vegetation. But here the closeness of the tree-trunks and their branches intertwining at the top gave the road the *appearance of a black bleak cavern with an evil spirit brooding over it*' (Narayan, 1992, p. 157, emphasis added).

We might recall here that the trees in the middle of the night *look like* 'tall towers' to 'Firaaq'; here, in a dark forest at night, trees and their branches *look like* 'an evil spirit' to Swami. In one case, trees are 'bridging earth with heaven'; in another, they represent an 'evil spirit brooding over it [the road]'.

Rorschach's Card IV often brings out responses like 'big foot' or a 'big dark tree' or 'a river flowing down a valley' or 'a giant coming towards me', etc. To Swami, the intertwined branches of the trees and the closeness of tree-trunks *looked like* a 'black bleak cavern with an evil spirit brooding over it'. He finds the sparseness of the Trunk Road *reassuring*; he does not feel 'closed-in' by the fluid, infiniteness of the forest and the brooding evil spirit. His anxiety is structured. Bounded.

Having looked at the percepts of prostitutes (Nagar), a beetle (Kafka) and a boy (Narayan) as *Rorschached* in creative writings, we may want to place these percepts against three Rorschach protocols to illustrate that the way an author looks at the world around him/her and picks up certain objects and views the world from these vantage points is the same as the way a testee in the Rorschach situation looks at his/her world from the vantage points provided by the Rorschach cards. The process is similar.

The difference is in the perspective. An author selects his/her own perspective (Nagar chose the ladies of the evening, Kafka the beetle, and Narayan the ten-year-old Swami). On the other hand, a subject gets assistance in selecting the perspective by being given the Rorschach cards.

The next section contains the protocols of three persons: (a) Shakher, a twenty-seven year old Indian male, (b) a thirty year old male from the Middle East, Ibrahim, and (c) Mary, a twenty-eight year old American female.

SECTION II: SHAKHER, IBRAHIM AND MARY

Shakher's Responses

Card I: Well, there are a couple of faces; child in the middle; well, I see a parent and a child; colors are very dark; looks like, the parents don't like each other; they are trying to go away from each other; and the child is, kind of, mad; child has split personality? I don't know; that's all I see right now.

Card II: Some kind of crime; just a crime; bloodshed; that's all I see.

Card III: Well, two women, female sex, whatever; and something; crime; some kind of killing; killing each other; looks like, they are fighting over one man; each one is saying, they want him; that's all.

Card IV: This is real tough; this is longest of all; all these pictures have, have similarity in some way; two girls; looks like, females; two women; that's all.

Card V: I know this animal; I don't know the name in English; flying; just flying; looks like, they are hungry for food; that's all.

Card VI: Jesus, Christ; and looks like, he is hanged or something; lot of bloodshed; looks like somebody is trying to preach; carpet; just for some decorations; looks like, two human beings together; I don't know if that makes any sense; looks like, that guy who is preaching, he has a lot of followers; he has lot of people helping him.

Card VII: Two children; and two pigs; and looks like, two children are fighting; looks like, I don't know if I should say this; looks like a woman's vagina; that's all.

Card VIII: Mountain; big, tall mountains; high mountains; and some bears, trying to reach there; grizzly bears; beautiful mountains; beautiful flowers; different colors, pink, light orange, colored flowers.

Card IX: Two pregnant women? Sunset or sunrise, whichever you may say; some kind of ocean in between; and far away sunshine; it is sunrise; beautiful lovely colors; and then a garden; and some flowers in there; fire somewhere; and twins; looks like, they are twins.

Card X: I don't know what's the name in English; some kind of animals of a different nation, you know; two animals fighting over some kind of bone; a parachute trying to go in the sky; and pink flowers and some kind of musical words; they use some kind of musical language; green flowers; green things in the garden; looks like, all these paintings are for kids; like a five-year old kid made these paintings; and that's all.

Ibrahim's Responses

Card I: Scorpion; leaf; bat.

Card II: Sad face; cat; fear; can I say that? Someone feeling sorry for himself; also see a church there; top of the church.

Card III: Two people trying to carry an object; see two people in love; two people losing love; also see in that picture, two people fighting over evil; involved in evil; drugs, probably.

Card IV: I see the devil; Satan. I see two roads to nowhere, lead to nowhere; see, a . . ., I see a good path or bad path; or see angels.

Card V: This is basically the same picture I have seen before; yes, I see devil again; I see a path with two different roads: one good, one bad; I see the back of a horse; actually what I see is, two race horses running at each other.

Card VI: See something dangerous; something you should look at, not touch; see a desert; I also see a road to evil; I also see a path away from evil; I see something good in the future.

Card VII: I see, I see heaven; I see there is a world after drugs; I see a goal where I want to reach; I see my children playing and happy; I see myself rich; I also see road-blocks before I get there;

not relapses; but people trying to stop me from getting to my goal; evil; I see myself reach on top and going down.

Card VIII: I see evil all around me trying me to do bad; I see I have reached the top but people continue to try to drag me down again; I see it's very difficult to get away from evil; I'm having a hard time; I see frustration too; then, I see happiness.

Card IX: I see tears; I see a hand, reaching out trying to help me; help me with someone in my family; I see difficulty; I see evil and what should I call the good? Angel trying to break me into half again; I cannot make decision which way I go.

Card X: I see more happiness; I see my family together; I see some road-blocks, more difficulties; I'm able to break free from road-blocks; no problem; I see more road-blocks; more evil; I am sad but I'm sure of myself; I am laughing inside this evil.

Mary's Responses

Card I: A butterfly; a bug.

Card II: I don't know, a uterus?

Card III: I don't know; looks like, a lady and a man; got some video game going, or maybe, two people playing a video game.

Card IV: That looks like a big foot, or elf.

Card V: That'd look like a butterfly or a bat.

Card VI: A devil coming up in smoke.

Card VII: This is, like, two kids; two little girls; seesaw or something.

Card VIII: This is, like, rats; trying to eat something.

Card IX: I don't know; it's, like, like, animals on top of each other; two animals standing on top of each other.

Card X: It's like, some spiders, some spiders, or bugs.

In this chapter, as we said earlier, an attempt is being made to interface the Rorschach and literature. The first section provided a brief overview of three classic works (*Yey Kothey-waaliaan*, *Metamorphosis* and *Swami and Friends*) by three great literary figures, Amritlal Nagar, Franz Kafka and R.K. Narayan respectively. The second section presented three Rorschach protocols: Shakher, Ibrahim and Mary. Now, in the third and final section, we will make some observations about the similarities and differences between the two processes of creativity: generating Rorschach responses on the one hand and literary works on the other.

SECTION III: COMPARATIVE OBSERVATIONS

Creative writers possess multiple personalities. However, they indicate multiple personality *order* (MPO) rather than multiple personality *disorder* (MPD). They are capable of creating different personalities and then looking at the world through their eyes and developing a configuration of a 'good' figure by reconciling the incongruities.

A similar process occurs in the Rorschach experience. The testee looks at the inkblots, *creates* a narrative by making the blots *look like* objects that are meaningful for him/her, places them in a context and often makes them do things.

There are, however, two main differences: (*a*) creative writers intentionally create incongruities among characters and events. Rorschach testees also create incongruities but these are unintentional (often, some intentional contradictions may be created by some testees like malingerers), and (*b*) authors and poets reconcile the contradictions. Thus, at the end of the narrative, the reader does experience a sense of *closure* ('good figure', *Pragnanz*). Persons responding to the Rorschach cards are often not aware of the contradictions they come up with, and even if they are, they are not able to reconcile them. So, a lot of work needs to be done by the Rorschacher to get a sense of closure. In fact, this is precisely the challenge of interpreting a Rorschach protocol. It is not easy. It requires, among many other things (e.g., understanding of clinical dynamics), a theoretical orientation about human behavior in general and human personality in particular.

Nagar, for example, narrates the starvation, hardship and a genuine sense of embarrassment in Lulu's mother to reconcile herself to prostitution. On the other hand, Shakher in Card I, sees parents on each side and a child in the middle. Parents are 'trying to go away from each other' (and thus, abandoning the child). The child is mad. Shakher seeks reconciliation. He sees the child as someone with a split personality; as if saying the child belongs to both parents and instead of going with one, and disappointing the other, he would rather split himself and share one-half with each parent. It is a neat example of what Kernberg (1984) calls 'splitting' as a favored mode of protecting integrity, often found among patients suffering from borderline personality disorder. The cognitive sense of splitting is enriched by Shakher by feelings of uncertainty, '. . .colors are very dark' indicating anxiety.

Kafka concretizes and reconciles the experience of existential despair by making Gregor Samsa a beetle, a dung-beetle. Once you recognize (perhaps also experience) that the hero is indeed a *gobraila*, you tend to empathize with his helplessness and embarrassment, and perhaps wish that everything would end soon. On his death, his body is called 'the stuff' by the housemaid. In Hindu culture, a person is a human while he/she is alive. On death, the dead body is called *mittee* ('dirt'). (A comment. It is almost certain that Franz Kafka was not well versed in the Hindi language. However, describing Gregor's dead body as 'stuff' [as translated from Czech] arouses a word *associated* with a dead body in Indian culture, *mittee* ['dirt']. Jungian *racial/universal archetypes* at work?)

So much needs to be, and *possibly*, could be done—that unsettling sense of *niraashaavaadi ashaa* (pessimistic optimism), so typical of Kafka, comes to life in *Metamorphosis*. Contradictions are created. Also reconciled.

Let us flip the focus now on to, for example, the Rorschach protocol of Ibrahim. He starts with (*a*) scorpion, leaf and bat (Card I), (*b*) moves through sad face, cat, fear, someone feeling sorry for himself, top of church (Card II), (*c*) people trying to carry an object, two people in love, losing love, fighting over evil, drugs (Card III), (*d*) Satan, two roads (Card IV), (*e*) two race horses running at each other (Card V), (*f*) something dangerous, desert (Card VI), (*g*) heaven, world after drugs (Card VII), (*h*) evil, pressure to do bad things (Card VIII), (*i*) tears, angel trying to break me into half again (Card IX), and (*j*) ends up in Card X with seeing more happiness, my family together, laughing inside this evil, etc.

There is experiential agony in both Gregor Samsa and Ibrahim. They both feel trapped in a sea of helplessness. Emotionally intense. The incongruities are resolved in Greg's case by just dying and disappearing into space or merging with the *Purush*, the 'Ultimate Being', as we might say in Hindu philosophy. Ibrahim reconciles the conflict phenomenologically. He sees happiness, a family that is together; he is able to break away from road-blocks; he is sad but also sure of himself, and as a climax, laughing inside the evil! Literary writings and the Rorschach experience have a lot in common.

Finally, let us look at Narayan's *'Rorschach'* of Swami and Mary's protocol.

After much debate over how to get the bats and balls and wickets to play a competitive game of cricket with a rival team, Swami and friends draft a letter to a sports goods store in Madras requesting it to send, 'two junior willard bats, six balls, wickets and other things' immediately, and that the money will be sent 'afterwards'.

The whole narrative in *Swami and Friends* is such a benign, innocent world-view from the eyes of a ten year old and his four friends that you literally don't want to leave it, even at the end. Rajam's father (superintendent of police in Malgudi) is transferred to another city and Swami feels 'abandoned' by Rajam because he runs away from the angry head master and could not play for the M.C.C. (Malgudi Cricket Club). Swami goes to the railway station to say goodbye to Rajam and manages to give him a parting gift, Anderson's *Fairy Tales*, through Mani (the bully), and leaves with a sense of emptiness inside him.

'Swaminathan and Mani stood as if glued, where they were, and watched the train. The small red lamp of the last van could be seen for a long time, it diminished in size every minute, and disappeared around a bend' (Narayan, 1992, p. 178). The story ends. You wish it never ended though.

You are left with a sense of anticipation, guesses, wishes. You want to know what happened after that. Was Swami able to restore his friendship with Rajam? What about Mani? Did he ever finish school? How did Pea and Sankar do? And on and on. It seems the story ends at a point where it perhaps started. That's what good narratives are. You don't want them to end. Often, the same is true of a Rorschach protocol. You wish the testee continued seeing the inkblots and telling you *what might it be*?

Butterfly, bug; uterus?; lady and a man, some video game going on; big foot, or elf; bat; devil coming up in smoke; two little girls, [playing] seesaw or something; rats trying to eat something; animals standing on top of each other; spiders or bugs. That's Mary, and her story.

Swami's is the story of his friends, school and family; Mary's of bugs and people and the devil and rats and animals. It seems like Narayan's narrative has a continuity of themes: people, places, episodes. On the other hand, Mary's narrative is disjointed; like a telegram; a collage.

It is not easy to do good narratives. It requires a thematic perception of the world around you and then, more importantly, skills to translate these themes into a continuous, connected whole. Not so with the Rorschachs. You don't have to struggle for themes. The Rorschach cards do that for you. They hint at the possibilities. The vagueness and ambiguities of the blots (combined with some structure like symmetry, colors, shades) help you fluctuate between reality (of the cards) and fantasy (of your phenomenological views of the world).

The gaps in the Rorschach narratives are inherent in the nature of the task: ten cards and instructions. Everyone cannot write good narratives. Everyone cannot give 'good' Rorschachs either. But then, you interpret the narratives (novels, poems and the stories a subject tells you in response to the Thematic Apperception Test [Murray, 1938]); you interpret the Rorschachs. The concrete specifics are different. Not the process.

The element of the unknown is common in literature. This is also so in the Rorschach. Reading a Rorschach protocol is like reading a novel. You never can tell what you are going to get. Like what Forrest Gump says about life in the movie *Forrest Gump* 'My mamma always said, "Life is like a box of chocolates; you never know what you are going to get"'

SUMMARY

In this chapter, we have tried to 'connect' the Rorschach *experience* with the literary *experience*. This was done (*a*) by first describing three literary classics, Nagar's *Yey Kothey-waaliaan*, Kafka's *Metamorphosis* and Narayan's *Swami and Friends*, then (*b*) by presenting three Rorschach protocols: Shakher, Ibrahim and Mary, and finally (*c*) by making some comparative observations between the literary process and the Rorschach process.

Writers, poets and playwrights *experience* the world around them. They select a part of this world, their world, and then describe what it *looks like* to them. Similarly, a subject tries to select a part of his/her world and sees how the inkblots match with what he/she *carries* inside his/her world.

The test instruction, 'what might it be?', gives the testee some structure by providing the inkblots. At the same time, there is some flexibility insofar as he/she is free to 'match' the features of the inkblot to what he/she might have come across in the past. The objects seen on the different Rorschach cards capture a sample of the testee's world. The percepts are his/her creations, no less or no more than the percepts of creative writers in their plays, novels and poems. Nagar's story about the prostitutes, Kafka's novel about Gregor Samsa and Narayan's narrative about Swami and his friends appear to have gone through the same process of seeking and searching from a host of images and perceptions as the processes involved in Shakher's, Ibrahim's and Mary's attempts to produce the Rorschach responses. The differences are in the complexity and intensity, and in the cognitive and emotional integration. Literary writings tell us about the psyche of the authors. Rorschachs tell us about the psyche of the testees. Looking at a Rorschach protocol as a piece of creative writing enriches its potential for understanding personalities.

Before getting into the specifics of the Rorschach technique and the different systematic ways of looking at the responses, we want to give a brief, very brief, overview of the Rorschach test in the Indian context. This is done in the next chapter.

3   THE RORSCHACH TEST IN INDIA

The Rorschach test is very much alive, well and living in India. However, like any other event or movement, this too has had its periods of active and not-so-active phases. From the first publication (Prasad and Asthana, 1947) to the most recent study (that we were able to locate) by Kumar and Patel (1990), there are well over 150 papers on or about this test. Asthana (1994) in his search was unable to find any Rorschach related publication in Indian journals after 1990.

In our search through *PsycINFO* between 1966 (the year *PsycINFO* started keeping information) and 1990, we found 41 studies on or using the test. Actually 42; however, one study (Yadav, 1977a, 1977b) appears to have been published in two different journals.

Prabhu (1984) provides an excellent overview of the work in India from 1947 to 1983: about 130 studies. Raychaudhuri (1988) reviews Rorschach publications identifying publications in five-year intervals. He reports that after a spurt in the post-1955 period, the number of studies declined after 1970. He also surveyed 32 universities about the current status of the test and found that teachers favored training students in the use of the test. Most of the teachers in the universities, says Raychaudhuri, were trained Rorschach specialists.

This chapter is divided into three sections. Section I reviews four studies in detail (Prasad and Asthana, 1947; Mukerji, 1961; Asthana, 1963; Raychaudhuri, 1971). The reason we selected these studies is that they appear to focus on the theoretical and dynamic foundations of the Rorschach test, an area that needs further work, at least in the Indian context. Section II is an overview of the 41 studies generated by the *PsycINFO* search. Finally, Section III makes some general comments and suggestions for Rorschach research in India.

SECTION I: THE FOUR STUDIES

Starting with Prasad and Asthana's work (1947) on psychology of meaning, we move on to Mukerji's (1961) study of normal Indian personality as projected on the Rorschach, followed by a review of Asthana's normative study (1963). Then we mention an interesting study of creativity and the Rorschach by Raychaudhuri (1971); it is interesting because it generated a comment from Aronow (1972) and a rejoinder by Raychaudhuri (1972).

Prasad and Asthana (1947)

The Rorschach test was introduced in India in 1947. It was used in a study of meaning by Prasad and Asthana (1947). It is described in detail in Prasad (1949). It was reported that in perceiving inkblots, people usually attend to the global wholes, form is a major determinant, associations develop after the responses are given and that these continue to be elaborated.

Evidently, the focus on elaborating associative material in the test has been developed and described in detail by Aronow, Reznikoff and Moreland (1994)—the Association Phase of the Content Rorschach Technique. After a person has responded to all 10 cards, he/she is asked to associate the responses. 'There is one more part to the procedure', the instructions say, 'Sometimes what people see in the Cards brings to mind something that they remember . . . . When I read back your responses to you, I'd like you to tell me the first thing that comes to mind' (ibid., p. 141).

In their studies of meaning, Prasad and Asthana (1947), and Prasad (1949) noticed that meaningful configurations 'flash' after the initial responses have been given. 'There appears to be an irradiating quality which occurs as a *flash* at various levels of apperceptive organization. The parts of the blots are *never seen as parts at all*, but as foci in a field of remarkable stress and strain. The blots assume meaning according[ly] as these stresses develop in a fluid domain of [a] perceptive-imagined situation' (Prasad, 1949, pp. 163–64, emphasis in the original).

It is perhaps more than a coincidence that Prasad and Asthana's (1947) paper 'An Experimental Study of Meaning by the Rorschach Method' appeared around the same time as two other seminal works on the Rorschach were published in the West. One was a study by Arnheim (1947) and the other by Bruner (1948).

Arnheim (1947) places perceptual abstraction in art in the context of the laws of perception of the Gestalt school of psychology. 'Gestalt research suggests', says Arnheim, 'that such global characteristics are not only directly perceivable but must even be considered the primary perceptive phenomena. They seem to strike the eye even before the more specific detail of a visual object is grasped' (ibid., p. 68).

In the same vein, Annand K. Coomaraswamy (1939) points out that form is the first thing we notice in a piece of art; this is then followed by ornamentation or embellishment. 'To have thought of art as an essentially aesthetic value is a very modern development, and a provincial view of art', he says, adding, 'born of a confusion between the (objective) beauty of order and the (subjectively) pleasant, and fathered by a preoccupation with pleasure . . . in asserting that "beauty" has to do with cognition' (ibid., p. 382).

Coomaraswamy's comment about the confusion between objective beauty and the subjectively pleasant is often seen in the Rorschachs of schizophrenics, e.g., 'two angels making love to a headless woman' (Card I), or 'marriage being performed in heaven' (Card X).

Bruner's study (1948) also resembles the work of Prasad and Asthana (1947). Looking for a model of perception to answer the question why the Rorschach test works, Bruner argues in favor of using the test for studying perceptual processes. He points out that there are four different types of situations where the Rorschach cards could be used as stimulus material: (*a*) situational control (administering the test under varying conditions: hypnosis, elation), (*b*) group control (giving the test to special population groups with known features: scientists, schizophrenics), (*c*) case control (administering the test to persons whose life histories are known to us), and (*d*) facet control (comparing Rorschach responses with facets of personality like anxiety, depression and suicidality). He points out that Rorschach responses vary along a continuum of the rigid form determined on the one end, and the embellished ones on the other. According to Bruner,

. . .Rorschach methodology and the interpretation of Rorschach responses are closely linked to the development of perceptual theory. Perceptive theory, in the past so neglectful of personality dynamics, has on its part the task of contributing a fuller understanding of why such techniques as the Rorschach have been so successful. *The future will perforce witness the coalescence of research on perception and research on diagnostics. The two belong together* (Bruner, 1948, p. 167, emphasis added).

That was in 1948. Since then Schafer (1954), Schachtel (1966), Lerner (1991) and others have successfully integrated perceptual processes with psychodiagnostics in a dynamic, experiential and phenomenological framework. Thus, the first study on Rorschach in India (Prasad and Asthana, 1947) was well within the spirit of the times.

Mukerji (1961)

Maya Mukerji did a normative study of the Indian personality as reflected on the Rorschach test. This was her doctoral thesis under the supervision of Dr. Asthana. Mukerji points out that she wanted (*a*) to explore the personality pattern of a group of Indians and to relate these findings to the social–psychological forces in Indian society, (*b*) to assess the operational efficiency of the test in clinical and social research in a cultural context, and (*c*) to set up some reference frames for the Rorschachers in India.

The test was individually administered on '. . .a small but carefully selected sample of urban adult population from one of the biggest and the most heavily populated cities in India' (p. 62). Although Mukerji does not mention the name of the city from which the sample was selected in her work, it was taken from Calcutta. She also had a control group of psychiatric patients from the same city.

The main findings were that normals reflected 'constricted yet integrated personality . . . more abstract and theoretic than concrete, more idealistic than practical . . . logical and pedantic with a stolid determination and an assertiveness to pursue his path' (p. 62).

She observed that (*a*) ego structure, and (*b*) affect, as expressed in the content of the responses, differentiated normals from controls. 'These seem to be directly related to the processes of socialization in [the] family and in the community outside' (p. 63).

Among the normals, their '. . . emotional life is stable and mature. There is very little egocentricity of infantile outbursts; even impulsiveness seldom gets a chance to break through' (pp. 62–63). Affect was neutral rather than labile. Experience balance: introversive; affective ratio: high.

'The swing in a perceptive mode', says Mukerji, citing Rorschach, ' "*now chasing an abstract idea, now stuck on a tiny curious detail*" seems to reflect a highly impractical temperament' (p. 63; emphasis added).

'On the whole', she observes, 'there seems to be an overdevelopment of control and integration at the expense of emotional forces. This is how the Indian personality seems to structure out in terms of the Rorschach test pattern' (p. 63).

It is indeed unfortunate that Mukerji did not publish her important work. Fortunately, however, Asthana summarized most of her findings when he compiled normative data.

Asthana (1963)

Asthana compiled the findings from Mukerji's study as well as the data collected by the Late Promod Kumar (a psychologist at the mental hospital at Ranchi, Bihar) and published his work in 1963. Some of the main findings are given in Table 3.1.

Table 3.1
Selected Rorschach Indices for Normal and Clinical Groups*

Indices	Normals (n: 450)	Schizophrenics (n: 180)	Paranoids (n: 58)	Neurotics (n: 42)
R	33.00	14.91	16.87	17.45
W	9.33	5.06	6.80	7.47
D	16.97	7.63	9.63	9.71
Dd	6.70	2.22	0.44	0.27
S	1.61	2.30	–	–
F+%	83.14	58.00	68.00	86.00
A%	36.98	30.08	35.53	33.86
M	3.83	1.98	1.50	1.39
FC	3.08	1.33	1.56	–
CF+C	1.61	3.66	3.31	1.33
L	0.33	0.43	0.40	0.53

* Compiled by Asthana (1963). Reproduced here with author's permission.

R   = Total number of responses given by the subject.
W   = Number of responses in which the whole area of the inkblot was used.
D   = Number of responses in which a commonly used area of the inkblot was used.
Dd = Number of responses in which a not frequently used area of the inkblot was used.

Table 3.1 (continued)

S	=	Number of responses in which white area of the inkblots was used.
F+%	=	Number of responses in which the percept matched the blot area very well (F+), divided by the number of F+ responses and the number of responses in which the match was poor (F−), multiplied by 100.
A%	=	Number of responses in which the content was whole animal (A) or part animal (Ad), divided by the total number of responses, multiplied by 100.
M	=	Number of responses in which human or human-like movement was experienced.
FC	=	Number of responses in which both form and color were used as determinants, but form was more dominant than color.
CF+C	=	Number of responses in which both color and form were used as determinants, but color was more dominant than form, added to the number of responses in which only color was a determinant.
L (Lambda)	=	Number of responses in which only form was used as a determinant (i.e., F+, F, F−), divided by the total number of responses minus the number of responses in which only form was used as a determinant.

'The normal group', observes Asthana, 'appears to be intellectually well-endowed, but the intellect is less tuned to the obvious and the practical; an abstract theoretic mind seems to be operating. Emphasis on clarity of associations . . . and a methodologic-rigid succession reinforces this theoretic aspect . . . fantasy life is rich . . . *erlebinstypus* shows an introversive trend . . . a cautious propriety restricts the capacity to experience and enjoy life' (pp. 284–85).

Placing his observations in the cultural context of India, Asthana suggests that early childhood experiences in India are relatively satisfying. 'Weaning is slow and fairly late compared with western standards and much permissiveness is allowed to [the] child in toilet training . . . mother continues to be the most significant figure in the individual's later life . . .' (p. 285).

Although Asthana compiled the form frequency tables of the responses, he never published them. With his permission, an illustrative sample of these is being published here in this book for the first time. A few comments on Asthana's work.

1. *Timeliness*: The data, although very meaningful, seem to have 'aged' with time. Most of these were collected over almost 40 years ago. While some of the figures may still be valid, we should consider using these as general guidelines. We do,

however, need data that are current. Until then, this is the best
we have at this point.

2. *The 'Match'*: Although somewhat comparable, we need to
recognize that the cases in the categories of 'normals', 'schizophrenics', 'paranoids' and 'neurotics' are not 'matched' in the
rigorous sense of the term. The data were collected in different
settings, e.g., the normals were picked up in a metropolitan
town while the clinical groups were from a psychiatric hospital
in a small town in another state. While the differences may not
be dramatic, one needs to be aware of contaminating variables.

3. *Data Collection*: Finally, the data were collected by at least two
different testers in at least two different settings. In the absence
of specifics about, for example, administration procedures and
scoring variables, the comparative observations need to be
'corrected' for methodological issues.

Having pointed out these limitations, we do not intend to minimize
the value of the work. Asthana has done a commendable job of
putting a voluminous body of Rorschach data into a usable form
for Rorschach workers in India.

Raychaudhuri (1971)

Raychaudhuri studied human movement on the Rorschach in relation to creativity and sex roles. He hypothesized that:

1. females may see more movement than males,
2. human movement (M) among the creatives would be greater
than among the non-creatives,
3. creative females would give more M than creative males,
4. non-masculine males would see more M than normal males,
and
5. non-feminine females would give fewer Ms than normal females.

In a total sample of 100 cases, the female normals (n = 20)
included secretaries and telephone operators. The creative females
(n = 20) as well as males (n = 20) included painters, writers and
musicians. Two other groups, the non-feminine females (n = 20)
and the non-masculine males (n = 20), were so classified based on
test scores on the Welsh Figure Preference Test (Welsh, 1959)
and the Franck Drawing Completion Test (Franck, 1958).

Raychaudhuri found that:

1. the normal females produced more M than normal males. The median M values were 2.6 and 1.5 respectively and statistically significant,
2. creative females and creative males did not differ in the median M values: 4.80 and 4.40; they were statistically not significant,
3. the median values of M for the combined groups of creatives (both males and females) and the non-creatives (males and females) were 4.50 and 1.80 respectively and statistically significant,
4. non-masculine males gave more Ms than normal males: 2.25 and 1.15 respectively and were statistically significant, and
5. the difference in the Ms of non-feminine females (2.70) and normal females (2.60) was statistically not significant.

Aronow (1972) commented that perhaps the subgroups were inadequately matched and may have affected the findings. 'The methodological flaws in this article', he says, 'involve inadequate controls over relevant variables . . . Raychaudhuri's findings become difficult to interpret, and the results cannot be regarded as further proof of a relationship between creativity and sex and the Rorschach M response' (ibid., p. 303).

Responding to this comment, Raychaudhuri (1972) clarified that he did not intend to claim an infallible relationship between M, creativity and sex. He admitted the methodological flaws. He, however, also suggested that one of the things he wanted to point out in his work was the role of cultural factors in Rorschach research. He said,

By keeping their eyes closed to the practical problems of studying creativity that are always present in different cultures, critics can freely reject inferences drawn on cross-cultural Rorschach data. But that neither does justice to these researches nor helps to advance cross-cultural research. Aronow's criticism appears to suffer from such irregularities and, therefore, his statement, though theoretically interesting, is of little practical value (ibid., p. 306).

A few comments on Raychaudhuri's work.

1. *Cultural Perspective*: Although not fitting in with the so-called 'pure science' paradigm, this study provides a fascinating window, interfacing creativity and sexual orientation as reflected in the Rorschach data from a cultural frame of reference. It is all the

more exciting in the Indian context where the male–female dichotomy has been bridged by (*a*) the concept of *Ardhnareeshwar* (literally, 'half-feminine God') in Hindu religion, and (*b*) the concept of *hijra* ('effeminate man') in society at large. Unlike in the West, where for instance until the early 1970s the American Psychiatric Association considered homosexuality as pathological but later normalized it as 'sexual orientation', in India, attraction to the same sex has been considered as 'different' but not 'pathological'. The so-called 'feminine-men' (*zankha*) have been accepted by society as 'normals'. So have the so-called 'masculine-women' (e.g., *Khoob lari mardaani, woh toe Jhaansi-waali Rani thee* [Bravo for the manly lady; she certainly was the Queen of Jhaansi]).

2. *The Issue of Ill-matched Subgroups*: We may want to look at this issue in two ways: (*a*) yes, perhaps the groups indeed were not exactly matched; in which case other Rorschach workers could 'fine-tune' this problem and do another study of this problem, and (*b*) let us avoid masking the cultural–phenomenological focus of this study by stressing methodological concerns. Methodology is important. However, it should also be guided by the conceptual, pragmatic aspects of the problem under study. Sometimes, in our well-meant intentions to be 'scientific', we feel overwhelmed (overawed?) with the pure science model and perhaps unconsciously (?) modify the problem to suit the methods. Thus, maybe, Raychaudhuri did compromise the revered scientific model of physics in studying creativity, sex and the Rorschach. Just maybe. Assuming that, we may still want to look beyond this and focus on the clinical and cultural connotations of this important work.

SECTION II: *PsycINFO* STUDIES

A *PsycINFO* search of Rorschach related studies in Indian journals generated a total number of 42 studies from 1966 to 1990. As mentioned earlier, apparently one study (Yadav, 1977a; 1977b) seems to have appeared in two journals: the *Indian Journal of Clinical Psychology* and *Social Defence*. So, in fact, there were actually 41 unduplicated studies. A chronological listing of the studies, along with their authors and titles of the work, is given here. Specific citations for locating these publications are given in the References.

1. Pratap and Filella (1966). 'Rorschach correlates of Taylor's Manifest Anxiety Scale'.
2. Prabhu (1967). 'The Rorschach technique with normal adult Indians'.
3. Mukerji and Majumdar (1968). 'A comparison of direct and projective method of personality assessment'.
4. Pal and Chakravarty (1968). 'An enquiry on the construct of the schizophrenic pattern of ideas'.
5. Shanker (1968). 'Education and Rorschach affective factors of the Harijans'.
6. Majumdar and Mukerji (1969). 'Examination of certain Rorschach ratios: A factorial study'.
7. Mukerji and Raychaudhuri (1970). 'Assessment equivalence of clinical ratings, structured and projective measures of personality'.
8. Prabhu (1970). 'Clinical utility of Piotrowski's alpha diagnostic formula'.
9. Raychaudhuri and Mukerji (1971). 'Rorschach and Ktaguchi– Rorschach (Ka–Ro) ink-blot series'.
10. Malaviya (1973). 'A replication of Rorschach signs with suicide attempted schizophrenics'.
11. Upadhyaya and Sinha (1974). 'Some Findings on Psychodiagnostic Tests with Young Retarded Adults'.
12. Vagrecha and Mazumdar (1974). 'Relevance of Piotrowski's signs in relation to intellectual deficit in organic (epileptic) and normal subjects'.
13. Akhtar, Pershad and Verma (1975). 'A Rorschach study of obsessional neurosis'.
14. Dutta, Jha and Shukla (1976). 'A Rorschach study of peptic ulcer'.
15. Dubey (1977). 'Rorschach analysis of impotence cases and their response to psychotherapy'.
16. Gupta (1977). 'Rorschach Ranking Conformity Test: An evaluation'.
17. Pershad and Dubey (1977). 'A proposed statistical design for Rorschach indices'.
18. Yadav (1977a). 'Rorschach responses of the institutionalized offender'.

18a. Yadav (1977b). 'Rorschach responses of the institutionalised offenders'.
(Apparently, Numbers 18 and 18a are the same article. We are not sure, though.)

19. Sandhu (1978). 'Rorschach responses in schizophrenia'.

20. Dubey and Dosajh (1979). 'Rorschach responses in normal army personnel'.

21. Dubey (1979). 'Rorschach indices of psychiatric patients in the army'.

22. Dubey, Pershad and Verma (1981). 'An evaluation of Rorschach as a clinical tool'.

23. Minhas (1981). 'A factor analytic study of psychometric and projective indices of creativity and those of intelligence and personality'.

24. Arora (1982). 'A Rorschach study of alcoholics'.

25. Jindal and Panda (1982). 'Anxiety and achievement: A Rorschach study of high- and low-achievers'.

26. Mookerjee (1982). 'A Study of Rorschach's indices of intelligence'.

27. Kaur and Kapur (1983). 'Rorschach study of hysteria'.

28. Thapa (1983). 'Personality patterns of Nepalese people in two diverse social groups as portrayed by Rorschach ink-blot cards'.

29. Pratap and Kapur (1984). 'Rorschach study of literate manics'.

30. Singh and Kapur (1984). 'Psychometric and behavioral correlates of group Rorschach measure of .hostility'.

31. Banerjee (1985). 'A resolution on the epileptic personality: A psychodiagnostic approach'.

32. Mujtaba and Mujtaba (1985). 'Homosexuality and paranoid schizophrenia: A study through Rorschach ink blots'.

33. Joseph and Pillai (1986). 'Projective indices of creativity'.

34. Murthy and Ram (1986).'Impulse life, emotional reactivity, introversive and extratensive balance in criminals on Rorschach'.

35. Sinha, Singh and Singh (1986). 'Delinquents: An observation of their Rorschach protocols'.

36. Rao, Verma and Kulhara (1987). 'Rorschach responses of obsessive neurotic and schizophrenic patients'.

37. Shukla, Tripathi and Dhar (1987). 'Validation of Piotrowski's signs of "organicity" against Bender Visual Motor Gestalt test'.

38. Verma (1987). 'A case study of a withdrawn boy as measured through Rorschach'.

39. Raychaudhuri (1988). 'The Rorschach testing and the trend in teaching of the Rorschach in India'.
40. Gupta, Verma and Kulhara (1989). 'Expression of hostility on Rorschach cards'.
41. Kumar and Patel (1990). 'Rorschach study of women showing high and low adjustment in marriage'.

A few comments on these studies:

1. *Classification by General Area*: Broadly speaking, these may be divided into three groups: (*a*) studies dealing with so-called normals, (*b*) studies focusing on clinical categories, and (*c*) theoretical/methodological papers.

    (*a*) *The Normals*: A total of 15 articles could be classified in this category: Kumar and Patel (1990); Verma (1987); Joseph and Pillai (1986); Sinha, Singh and Singh (1986); Thapa (1983); Jindal and Panda (1982); Mookerjee (1982); Minhas (1981); Yadav (1977); Upadhyaya and Sinha (1974); Majumdar and Mukerji (1969); Shanker (1968); Prabhu (1967); and Pratap and Filella (1966).

    (*b*) *The Clinical Categories*: There were 18 papers that addressed various clinical groups: Gupta, Verma and Kulhara (1989); Shukla, Tripathi and Dhar (1987); Rao, Verma and Kulhara (1987); Murthy and Ram (1986); Mujtaba and Mujtaba (1985); Banerjee (1985); Pratap and Kapur (1984); Singh and Kapur (1984); Kaur and Kapur (1983); Arora (1982); Dubey (1979); Sandhu (1978); Dubey (1977); Dutta, Jha and Shukla (1976); Akhtar, Pershad and Varma (1975); Vagrecha and Mazumdar (1974); Malaviya (1973); and Pal and Chakravarty (1968).

    (*c*) *Theoretical/Methodological*: There were eight papers that could possibly be grouped in this category: Raychaudhuri (1988); Dubey, Pershad and Verma (1981); Pershad and Dubey (1977); Gupta (1977); Raychaudhuri and Mukerji (1971); Mukerji and Raychaudhuri (1970); Prabhu (1970); and Mukerji and Majumdar (1968).

2. *Classification by Sample Size*: Here the range is from a sample of 1 (Verma, 1987) all the way to a sample of 300 (Dubey, 1979).

3. *Classification by Setting*: The studies were done in academic institutions, prisons, the army and hospitals. The topics studied

spanned a wide range: homosexuality, peptic ulcer, creativity, hostility indices, intelligence, thought processes, impotence, and so on.

SECTION III: GENERAL COMMENTS AND SUGGESTIONS

In terms of any systematic programmatic research, it seems the works of Mukerji (1961) and Asthana (1963) stand out. Also significant are the reviews by Prabhu (1984) and Raychaudhuri (1988). There are, however, a few things that may be mentioned here.

1. There is a need for some large sample-based studies of personality patterns of people living in different states of India. The multifaceted cultural matrix of Indians in various states along with their lifestyles would be of interest and value not only for students of clinical psychology and cultural anthropology but also for mental health practitioners.

2. We need Rorschach data to help us in differential diagnostic work in clinical settings. While it may be helpful to develop Rorschach profiles of at least some major syndromes according to the Western nosology, e.g., thought disorders, affective disorders and personality disorders, it would be important for us to use large-scale data for identifying some culture-specific disorders in the Indian context like *bhoot/jinn* (possession) disorders, *poorv-janm* (reincarnation) related disorders, and *abhi-shapt* (curse) related disorders.

3. The rural-urban variable is culturally very important in the Indian context. Rorschach studies in the rural areas would, both clinically as well as culturally, be of great value in generating data about personality dynamics. The body of knowledge thus created would help develop relevant curricula for teaching and training clinical psychologists, social workers and cultural anthropologists in Indian academic settings.

4. Related to the rural-urban issue is the rich variety of cultural subgroups in India, e.g., Bengali, Gujarati, Maharashtrians, South Indians and Uttar Pradeshis (or *bhaiyaa-log*, as they are called in Bombay). An instrument like the Rorschach would be

optimal for studying the personality structure, dynamics and psychopathology of different sub-cultures.
5. Finally, the tribals. We did not come across any work on them. Their object relations, as reflected in the Rorschach data, would be a rich source of understanding their world-view.

SUMMARY

In this brief review of the Rorschach's status in India, we identified three areas:

1. the four studies,
2. the *PsycINFO* generated data, and
3. a few suggestions for Rorschach research in the Indian context.

Perhaps, some readers may feel this review is lean and sketchy. They may be so far right. Our intent, however, was to offer a brief glimpse of the work undertaken.

Having talked about the spirit of the times (Chapter 1), Hermann Rorschach and his times (Chapter 2) and the status of the test in India (Chapter 3), we move on to describe the procedures for administering the test and recording the data, that is, the Rorschach procedure.

4 THE RORSCHACH PROCEDURE

The Rorschach procedure includes specifics like context, rapport, seating arrangement, instructions, free association, inquiry and recording responses. In all, there are 11 areas that may be identified:

1. context,
2. rapport,
3. seating arrangement,
4. instructions,
5. free association phase,
6. inquiry phase,
7. recording responses,
8. coding responses,
9. placing responses in a format,
10. interpreting responses, and
11. writing the test report.

Brief comments on each of these follow.

CONTEXT

Context includes the purpose of the testing, the physical setting and the demographic characteristics of the tester and testee.

Purpose of Testing
Testing could be done for assessing the dangerousness of the testee to self/others, clarifying diagnosis, developing a treatment plan or assessing progress in treatment.

Physical Setting
The physical setting could be a hospital, prison, army barrack, office, classroom, under a tree in a village, or in a posh office in a big town.

Demographics of Tester and Testee

The demographics could range from a young college male testing an elderly woman; a pretty, sexually attractive female testing a person convicted of rape or a professor testing his/her student.

RAPPORT

Basically, rapport refers to the ease and comfort with which the tester and testee relate to each other. The factors mentioned under 'context' affect rapport too. One of the more important considerations for establishing and maintaining rapport is that the tester should avoid coming across from a position of power and authority. The reason is that usually the testee enters the testing/assessment situation in a state of anxiety. To aggravate this feeling of uncertainty by trying to impress him/her with grandiose gestures and behavior is going to make the subject all the more anxious; perhaps, also angry. The tester will be in control of the testing situation, and the genuineness and sincerity of the tester–testee dynamics would be greatly affected. It is, therefore, very important for the tester to assure the testee that the assessment/testing is being done *not* to pass judgement on his/her disabilities, but rather to identify his/her strengths that may be used to deal with stressful situations and to identify factors that may be limiting his/her ability to function at an optimal (*not* ideal) level.

A reasonable amount of mutual trust and respect is necessary for the tester and testee to feel comfortable in the testing situation. Some of the specific things that need to be considered include how the tester greets the testee, how the tester explains the purpose of assessment, how the tester addresses the testee (by first name or by last name with Mr/Ms) and how the tester describes the limitations of the tests (e.g., tests are *not* foolproof, crystal balls that probe the hidden secrets of the testee's mind). Complimenting the testee on his/her appearance is often helpful. Also helpful is an assurance to give the testee the feedback of the test results. It is also important to address the testee's curiosities, questions and concerns. This should, however, be done in a non-committal way. All this would help establish and maintain rapport.

SEATING ARRANGEMENT

The seating arrangement is an important element in the Rorschach procedure. Some Rorschachers (e.g., Beck, 1961) recommend that the subject sit with his/her back towards the tester. Others (e.g., Exner, 1993; Hertz and Klopfer cited in Exner, 1993) advise a side-by-side arrangement. Still others (e.g., Rapaport, Gill and Schafer, 1968) prefer sitting face-to-face.

In our opinion, the seating arrangement should be guided by the specific context. It may be a bit difficult for a tester to sit behind the subject if he/she were testing in an Indian village under say, a neem tree. It may cause concern, perhaps also suspicion, in the mind of the subject. In clinical settings, sitting behind an apparently paranoid patient may not be a good idea.

If it is possible, we would suggest a face-to-face seating arrangement. However, if the test is being done for individualized, clinical assessment, the seating arrangement is flexible. On the other hand, if you are using the test to collect data for clinical research, it would be necessary to have a uniform seating arrangement across the testing situations.

INSTRUCTIONS

Instructions create a set in the mind of the subject. They are also helpful in preparing the subject by saying something to the effect that you are going to show him/her a set of cards with inkblots on them and that you would want him/her to tell you what they look like to him/her. Then, present Card I right side up and say, 'What might this be?' You may want to translate the instructions into the subject's language/dialect, e.g.,

Hindi: '*Meharbaanee ker kay bataayen, yeh kyaa hoe sakta hai?*'
Bengali: '*Boloon toe, yayee taa kee hotay paray?*'
Gujarati: '*As shu chhe?*'
Kumaoni: '*Yoe ki hai sak choo?*'
Tamil: '*Idu yena vega erukalum?*'

FREE ASSOCIATION PHASE

The free association phase begins when the testee starts following the instructions. The subject is associating freely with the inkblots and telling you what they might be. The free association phase begins with Card I and ends when the subject has given the last response to Card X.

Often, the subject may ask questions during the free association period like, Do you want to know the first thing that comes to mind? Do I have to give only one response to each card? I see a bat on this card, what do you see? Are these blots supposed to mean anything? etc. All these, and similar questions, should be responded to in a non-committal way like, It's up to you; you may give as many responses as you like; I will tell you after we are done with all these cards; etc.

INQUIRY PHASE

During the inquiry phase, the tester tries to find out more about each response given during the free association phase. Specifically, the purpose is,

1. to find out where exactly on the card the subject saw whatever he/she saw (*location*), and
2. how he/she saw the object (*determinants*).

The tester then goes through each response and in a *non-directive* and *non-suggestive* way tries to find out what features of the blot helped the subject see the objects. Usually, *repeating the response in the subject's words* is enough to prompt him/her to tell you what blot-features (shape, color, texture, movement) played a role in shaping the response.

Sequencing Inquiry Phase

An important issue in the Rorschach procedure is the placement of inquiry. Should it be done after the subject has responded to all 10 cards? Should it be done following each card? Some Rorschachers recommend doing inquiry when all the 10 cards have been responded to (e.g., Beck, Exner); others recommend doing inquiry after each card while the card is taken away from the subject (e.g., Rapaport, Schafer, Lerner).

We recommend doing inquiry following each card. Take the card away from the subject and ask him/her to tell you how did he/she see the objects. While some may feel that this method 'contaminates' the responses and alerts the subject for the next card, we feel this procedure provides a freer range for understanding the role of fantasy in shaping responses. If one looks at the Rorschach as a problem-solving task (e.g., Exner), doing inquiry after all the 10 cards seemingly controls memory factor. However, if one looks at the test as a phenomenological, experiential interplay of the external environmen. on the one hand, and the subject's psyche on the other, doing inquiry after each card seems more meaningful.

RECORDING RESPONSES

Since the specific words used by the testee to give responses as well as the words used to explain *how* the objects were seen play an important role in coding and interpreting them, it is necessary to record them verbatim. And, since the testee often speaks too fast for the tester to be able to write down everything, it is important to do two things:

1. tell the testee that you are going to write everything and hence he/she should speak at a relatively slow pace; usually, this works; sometimes, however, a testee may not be able to do so or may not want to do it (to challenge you!), and
2. develop some standard or personalized shorthand language or a few signs/symbols to ensure that you end up with a verbatim record.

Here are a few suggestions.

1. *Card Position*: Use an inverted 'V' to indicate that the card was upside down for a given response, or use 'Λ'to indicate it was right-side up for the response.
2. *Card Turning*: If a testee turns a card many times before he/she responds, you may want to indicate the various positions through a series of signs 'Λ', 'V', '<', '>', 'V' and '>'. In such cases, the reader will know that the testee first looked at the card in the upright position (Λ), then turned it upside down (V), turned it

sideways with the top on the left hand (<), then turned it the other way, with the top on the right hand (>), then again turned it upside down (V), and then finally sideways with the top on right-hand side (>) before giving the response.

3. *Silences/Pauses*: Often, the testee may say something and then pause for a short while. You may want to indicate short pauses (say, of a few minutes) by drawing a line between words and phrases ('I think _____ it may be _____ no, wait a minute _____ maybe, it's a spinning top': Card II, middle white space). In case the testee waits for longer periods, you may indicate it by drawing long lines between the words/phrases ('Oh, that's pretty, It is _____ well, something out of a fairy tale, I don't know _____ may be, two bears trying to save a man in trouble on top of hill': Card VIII).

4. *Verbalizations*: Most Rorschachers with training and experience develop abbreviations (e.g., *Idk* for 'I don't know', *ll* for 'looks like', *ds* for 'deep sigh', *bf* for 'butterfly') to record a testee's responses and behavior, both during the free association period and during inquiry.

There is no standardized listing of such abbreviations. We all develop our own individual styles. It is, however, important to have abbreviations so that the responses as well as the clarifications during inquiry can be recorded verbatim. Exact words and phrases improve the chances for accurate coding (scoring) of the responses, and later for interpreting them to develop a personality profile of the testee.

While it is important to note and write down everything during the testing (for which shorthand signs and symbols are necessary), it is equally important that we be able to communicate the data to others. For this, it is necessary to write down the responses/inquiry in long hand after the testing is done: *fair kar lain* ('let us copy it neatly') as we used to say during school days!

The next step in the Rorschach procedure involves additional 'shorthanding' of the responses: coding.

CODING RESPONSES

Coding responses is important to summarize the data generated during the free association period and during inquiry. Two things are important to note in this context.

First, it is helpful to interpret on the basis of the summary. However, it is often necessary to go back to the unsummarized data to understand some of the clinical implications of the data, e.g., 'mountain' on Card VIII or 'lake' on Card VII could both be coded as 'nature' responses; however, in terms of the specific verbalizations of the testee, the 'mountain' could have been Kailash *Parvat* and 'lake' may have been Bhadkal Lake near New Delhi, India, or it could have been Lake Tahoe in California, USA. In interpretation, the connotations of these responses would make a difference.

Second, remember in coding responses that different Rorschachers have developed different (often, overlapping) ways for summarizing the data. For example, Beck would discourage coding for non-human movement: tiger *chasing* a deer or bear *climbing* a tree is not scorable as movement. Beck suggests scoring movement only if it is a human or human-like movement: two women *talking* is movement; two bears *kissing* is movement. But a duck *floating* on water is not.

Coding of responses is done in three-*plus*-one (a total of four) categories:

1. *Where* on the card was the object seen? Whole blot? Commonly used part of the blot? Rarely used part of the blot? White space?—*Location*,
2. *How* was the object seen? Form/shape? Color? Shading? Texture? Movement? Combination of all, or some of these?—*Determinants*,
3. *What* was seen? Animals? Humans? Household objects? Anatomy? Architecture? Blood? Sex?—*Content*, and
4. (Plus One): *Relationships* between where, how and what, e.g.,

   (*i*) relationship between the number of whole human figures seen to the part-humans (H:Hd),
   (*ii*) ratio of the number of responses given to the last three cards (VIII, IX, X) to the number of responses given to the first seven cards (I through VII)—*Affective Ratio*,
   (*iii*) ratio of responses in which only form or shape was used as a determinant to the responses in which at least one other determinant was used—*Lambda*, and
   (*iv*) number of responses in which the objects seen *matched pretty well* (Good Form) to the number of responses in which objects *did not match* the shape of the blots (Poor Form).

PLACING RESPONSES IN A FORMAT

If the coded responses, ratios and percentages are placed in an easy-to-read format, it makes the process of drawing inferences relatively easy. Different Rorschachers have developed their preferred ways of

1. recording responses, and
2. formatting structural summaries (that is, the structure of the subject's personality in a summarized form).

Formats for Recording Responses

The specific formats for recording responses vary from one end of the scale where you write down the responses according to each card along with the codes (scores) next to each response (Hermann Rorschach, 1975), all the way to a format in which one notes down the responses along with scores (Exner, 1991, 1993), to Ulett's (1994) system which incorporates Exner's Comprehensive System. Essentially, the form in which you write down the responses should include the following basic elements, namely,

1. card number,
2. response number,
3. location of the blot area to which the subject gave the response (one may use the location numbers [e.g., Beck's, Exner's] and also the area on the location sheet [miniature reproductions of the Rorschach cards] to indicate exact location),
4. verbatim responses given by the subject in the free association phase, and
5. verbatim responses given by the subject in the inquiry phase.

These are the essentials of a Rorschach response record. Additionally, for the section on the inquiry phase, you may also consider writing down your specific questions as well as the subject's answers verbatim; at least in the initial stages of training it would be a good idea to do that.

As far as recording of scores is concerned, you may prefer to write these against each response, or alternatively, write them on a separate sheet.

Format for Structural Summaries

The form in which you organize your response codes (scores) is guided by the level of simplicity (or complexity) with which you have coded your responses. Again, on the one extreme we have a simple format used by Hermann Rorschach (1975) and on the other, Ulett's (1994).

Rorschach's Format

1. Total number of responses at the top center of the sheet.
2. Column 1 on the extreme left indicating number of responses classified by the areas of the blot used, e.g., whole blot (W), commonly used areas (D) and less commonly used areas (Dd).
3. Column 2 in the center containing the features of the blots involved in seeing the blots (determinants), e.g., human movement (M) (note: Rorschach did not score animal and/or inanimate movement), form (F), color (C), combinations of form and color. Again, Rorschach used only these three determinants in his book (1975). However, in his interpretation of a patient of his colleague Oberholzer, published after Rorschach's death by Oberholzer in 1923, Rorschach introduced an additional determinant—light and shading. He called this 'chiaroscuro' and coded it as F(C).
4. Column 3 on the extreme right side containing contents of the responses.
5. Lower left-hand side containing

  (*i*) percentage of good form responses (F+ %),
  (*ii*) percentage of responses with animal content (A %),
  (*iii*) percentage of original response (Orig. %),
  (*iv*) relation between number of whole and detail responses (apperceptive mode), and
  (*v*) the sequence of responses, that is, (*a*) did the subject move from W to D or D to W, and (*b*) was this movement methodical or irregular (sequence).

Note 1: Rorschach also did not write down experience type (*erlebinstypus*) on the computation sheet. He did, however, start interpretation with this index.

Note 2: Rorschach also did not use the number of popular (or what he called 'vulgar') responses in his calculations. He introduced it in his interpretation of Oberholzer's patient (published posthumously by Oberholzer in 1923, in a German journal *Zeitschrift fur die die gesamte Neurologie und Psychiatre*, 82 and reprinted in English in the 1975 edition of *Psychodiagnostics* [Rorschach, 1975]).

From this original simple structural summary format we jump to the most recent one by Ulett (1994) based on Exner's system.

Ulett's Format

George Ulett's format is in the form of a circle, a pie, sliced into three big pieces and 10 smaller pieces. The three big slices are (alphabetically):

1. affect,
2. cognition, and
3. object relations.

Each of these big pieces contain smaller pieces.

Affect Segment: (*a*) affectional needs, (*b*) deep affects, and (*c*) emotions.

Cognition Segment: (*a*) reality testing in neutral situations, and (*b*) general reality testing.

Object Relations: (*a*) originality, (*b*) content, and (*c*) imagination.

Ulett's (1994) AutoScore Form is given in Figure 4.1.

As we mentioned earlier, the nature and extent of formats for recording and organizing Rorschach responses are guided by the way one theorizes about the responses and what they indicate, for on that depends the next important step in the Rorschach procedure, namely, interpretation.

For instance, Paul Lerner (1991) considers administration, scoring and interpretation as integral parts of the whole Rorschach process. Based on his psychoanalytic object relations theory, he describes the Rorschach procedure as a five-step process:

Step 1: data gathering,
Step 2: quantitative analysis,
Step 3: first order inferences,
Step 4: transformation, and
Step 5: the psychological report.

Based on his theoretical orientation, Lerner does *not* do complicated computations. Essentially, he counts only (*a*) the number of responses in terms of form quality (F+, Fo, etc.), and (*b*) all responses having movement as a determinant (kinesthesias).

Figure 4.1
Rorschach AutoScore™ Form

WPS Rorschach AutoScore™ Form
Interpretation Chart

Published by

WPS WESTERN PSYCHOLOGICAL SERVICES
Publishers and Distributors
12031 Wilshire Boulevard
Los Angeles, California 90025-1251

George Ulett, M.D., Ph.D.

Client's Name: _____
Examiner's Name: _____ Date: _____
Comments: _____
_____
_____
_____

$R =$ _____ (15 to 25)
(Total no. of responses)

$\blacksquare =$ _____ (.45 to .75)
(Lambda = Pure F + [R minus pure F])

$Afr =$ _____ (.40 to .75)
(Affect Ratio = [No. of responses to Cards VIII to X]
+ [No. of responses to Cards I to VII])

Special Scores

FABCOM =	_____	(0)
DV =	_____	(0)
INCOM =	_____	(0)
DR =	_____	(0)
ALOG =	_____	(0)
CONTAM =	_____	(0)
CONFAB =	_____	(0)
SUM, =	_____	(0 to 1)

(sum of the preceding
seven Special Scores)

AG =	_____	(1)
MOR =	_____	(0)
PER =	_____	(1)
PSV =	_____	(0)
COP =	_____	(2)
CP =	_____	(0)
Other =	_____	(0)

Note:
Numbers in parentheses
are average values.

Reality Testing

$X+\% =$ _____ (.70 to .90)
$F+\% =$ _____ (.70 to .90)
Blends + R = _____ (0 to .30)
$Zf =$ _____ (9 to 15)

Apperception

$W\% (W + R) =$ _____ (.20 to .30)
$D\% (D + R) =$ _____ (.50 to .70)
$Dd\% (Dd + R) =$ _____ (.10)
$S =$ _____ (0 to 1)
$DW =$ _____ (0)

Content

H:(H) =	_____	(3:1)
Hd + Ad =	_____	(0 to 3)
H + A =	_____	(6 to 15)
$M^a:M^p$ =	_____	(3:1)
P =	_____	(5 to 9)
m:FM =	_____	(1:4)
m:M =	_____	(1:4)

Affective Functioning

FC: (C + CF + C/F) = _____ (2:1)
C = _____ (0)
FT: (TF + T) = _____ (0:0 to 1:1)

Ego Functioning

EB =	_____	(3:3 to 5:5)
EA =	_____	(6 to 10)
eb =	_____	(3:5)
es =	_____	(7 to 9)
Stress Tolerance =		
Adjusted Stress Tolerance =	_____	(-2.5 to + 2.5)

When the responses have been coded and various ratios and percentages computed, we move on to the next step involved in the Rorschach process, namely, interpretation.

INTERPRETING RESPONSES

Interpretation involves examining both the protocol and structural summary. They constitute the *elements* for the body of interpretation. The way these elements are analyzed and synthesized for generating the final *product*, namely, the test report, depends primarily on the theoretical orientation of the Rorschacher.

A Jungian, for instance, may want to look at the responses in terms of persona, shadow, anima, animus, archetypes and individuation (e.g., McCully, 1971).

A person with a psychoanalytic ego psychology orientation may prefer to view responses in terms of unconscious, impulses, Oedipal conflicts, ego defenses and adaptation (e.g., Schafer, 1954).

Clinicians favoring the psychoanalytic object relations approach (e.g., Lerner, 1991) would look at the protocols in terms of character structures (hysterical, depressive, narcissistic, etc.) and levels at which personality structures are organized (instinctual, ego weaknesses, ego defenses, object relations, object representations, etc.).

Behaviorists may just want to focus on various Rorschach indices, ratios and percentages, and look for relationships between them on the one hand and the specific behavioral manifestations on the other. This approach is well illustrated in Exner's Comprehensive System (1991, 1993) where the clinician has access to over 300 variables to describe the subject's behavior.

Whatever the theoretical orientation of the clinician interpreting the test protocol, the final report does need to describe the subject in a meaningful (usable) way. This is the final step in the Rorschach procedure.

WRITING THE TEST REPORT

The Rorschach test report, explicitly or implicitly, contains some assumptions about human behavior in general and about human personality in particular, or else, there would be no internal consistency and coherence in the observations made about the testee's personality and/or behavior and/or treatment recommendations. In other words, in the absence of these guiding principles, the final report may look like a guava tree with bananas hanging from the branches!

Putting together an integrated report is complicated, not only by the theoretical orientation of the report writer, but also by factors like (a) the audience for whom it is written (court, lawyers, psychiatrist, police), (b) access to the report by the subject and/or family, and (c) length, style and language of the report.

There are variations in addressing each of these and other related issues. However, here are a few suggestions.

1. The report should be *brief* (say, no more than three to four double-spaced typed pages).
2. It should be divided into main and subheadings (e.g., *purpose of testing*: diagnosis, differential diagnosis, dangerousness to self/others; *assessment*: cognitive functioning, emotions, conflicts; *treatment recommendations*: short-term and long-term goals; and *summary*: overview of the report's contents, and most importantly, the specific responses to the specific referral questions).
3. Regarding *style*, you may want to illustrate your observations by (a) giving examples from everyday life, and (b) by quoting comments and statements made by the testee during the initial rapport-building phase and/or during testing.
4. Regarding the *language*, please avoid using big words and technical jargon. Judges and attorneys do not want to spend time figuring out technical terms. Also, other members of the treatment may have backgrounds and training in non-psychology disciplines. If we want our report to be useful for the testee and for those who are trying to help him/her, we should make it as simple as we possibly can.
5. Regarding the issue of sharing the report with the testee and significant others, we feel if the testee wants a copy of the report, by all means, give it to him/her. After all, you have found out some things about his/her personality. He/she has a right to know. However, if you have good clinical reasons that the testee may unintentionally misinterpret your observations, you should consider asking him/her to designate another person

(parent, sibling, therapist) to whom you may then give a copy of the report.

SUMMARY

In this chapter, we have described the Rorschach procedure by identifying the main steps involved in the procedure from the context in which testing is done to preparing the final test report. We discussed 11 steps: context, rapport, seating arrangement, instructions, free association phase, inquiry phase, recording responses, coding responses, placing responses in a format, interpreting responses and writing the test report. We now move on to outlining four different systems of doing and interpreting the Rorschach test in the next four chapters.

5 EXNER'S COMPREHENSIVE SYSTEM

Exner's Comprehensive System (Exner, 1991, 1993), or the ECS as it is called in short, attempts to include most of the elements in the Rorschach procedures developed around the forties and fifties by Beck, Hertz, Klopfer and Rapaport. Having introduced the ECS in 1974, Exner has consistently been refining and fine-tuning his approach.

There are at least three important features in the ECS that deserve a special mention: (*a*) computerization, (*b*) training non-clinicians, and (*c*) structuring interpretation.

Computerization: Exner has quite successfully harnessed computer technology for processing the Rorschach data. Analyzing hundreds of protocols and thousands of responses, he has identified (*a*) 11 key variables (e.g., schizophrenia index greater than 3, coping deficit index higher than 3, Lambda greater than 0.99), and (*b*) seven clusters (e.g., affect, self-perception, mediation) for developing a testee's personality profile.

Training Non-clinicians: By standardizing the procedures for administration (both free association and inquiry phases), Exner has expanded the potential for generating large-scale Rorschach data. He points out that one does not have to be a psychologist to be able to administer the test. Exner has successfully trained a musician, a high school student, a homemaker and a secretary to administer the Rorschach.

Our examiners have included many professional psychologists and psychology graduate students, but nearly half come from more varied backgrounds, ranging from a professional musician and a retired tailor to an extremely talented high school senior, homemakers, and a few very adept secretaries . . . . The ability of these laypeople to learn to administer and score the test in a standardized format has been among the very reassuring aspects of the system (Exner, 1993, p. ix).

Structuring Interpretation: If 'p', then 'q'. Based on computerized data processing, Exner has developed a range of what he calls *interpretive strategies* for developing personality profiles from the Rorschach data. The 'p' involves examining the key variables for the critical cut-off points. The 'q' is the sequence in which clusters are approached for formulating interpretive statements about the testee's personality. For example, *if* the coping deficit index (CDI) is greater than 3, *then*, the recommended cluster sequence is: controls—affect—self-perception—interpersonal perception—processing—mediation—ideation. In another protocol, however, *if* Lambda is higher than 0.99, *then*, the sequence in which clusters should be reviewed is: processing—mediation—ideation—controls—affect—self-perception—interpersonal perception. The 'If "p", then "q"' approach tends to make the process of interpreting Rorschach data relatively objective.

The flip-side. While ECS is empirical and apparently minimizes the bias factor of the clinician, it also tends to ignore the ideographic focus of the test and, in turn, valuable 'qualitative' insights of the clinicians in examining a protocol. By stressing the psychometric aspects of the test, Exner has indeed made a significant contribution towards re-gaining the respectability of the test from its critics who are seemingly obsessed with the issues of *psychometric reliability* and *validity* of any assessment procedure.

There still, however, remains a significant chunk of data that is just not amenable to numbers, ratios and percentages. It is important to be able to integrate these data for developing an integrated personality picture. We want to caution against an overly undue reliance on quantification of the Rorschach data (and, for that matter, any data).

Section I in this chapter briefly describes the system. The format is similar to the one in the previous chapter on the Rorschach Procedure—the 11 steps. In Section II, we present two protocols: (*a*) Seema, a twenty-two year old Indian female, and (*b*) Roberts, a twenty-three year old African–American male to illustrate the ECS.

SECTION I: THE COMPREHENSIVE SYSTEM

Context

Exner (1993) stresses the importance of issues like preparing the subject for the assessment process through a brief interview, reassurance, and answering and clarifying the subject's questions.

A cultural issue. In Western countries, testing is embedded in day-to-day routine. A child grows up taking tests. This is not so in many (if not all) developing nations. The concept of test anxiety operates at different levels in various cultures. Preparing the subject may require different degrees and levels of preparation in say, India, than in, for example, the USA. Thus, what Exner calls the 'test-wise' subjects do not 'exist' in India. One difference that seems to stand out is between what may be called 'achievement anxiety', on the one hand, and 'approval anxiety', on the other. It may be conjectured that while 'achievement anxiety' is more a Western phenomenon (Misra, 1976/1977, 1980; Misra and Kilroy, 1992), it is 'approval anxiety' that characterizes a typical Indian. For a variety of reasons, an Indian looks up to authority figures more often than his/her American counterpart. Thus, preparing a subject for assessment/testing in the US seems to be much easier than in India.

Rapport

Reassuring the subject by addressing his/her concerns is necessary to establish a comfortable level of trust.

Seating Arrangement

Exner recommends a side-by-side arrangement.

Instructions

The instructions in the ECS are the same as used by Rorschach: 'What might this be?'

Free Association Phase

The subject is shown the cards one at a time. The responses are written exactly as he/she verbalizes them.

Inquiry Phase

Unlike the system of Rapaport and his collaborators (e.g., Gill, Schafer), who suggest doing inquiry *after* each card, in the Exner system, inquiry is done after the subject has responded to *all* 10 cards.

Exner cautions against using inquiry without preparing the subject. 'It is *critically important* that the subject be prepared for the Inquiry' (Exner, 1993, p. 75; emphasis in original). The tester, he suggests, should explain that the intent now is for the subject to help him/her (that is, the tester) see what he/she (that is, the subject) saw on the inkblots. The three areas to be identified in inquiry are *location, determinants* and *content. Repeating the response*, says Exner (ibid.), usually enables the subject to elaborate on the responses and thus help the tester identify the three inquiry elements.

Recording Responses

'*All responses*', says Exner, '*must be recorded verbatim*' (1993, p. 72, emphasis in original). For doing this, he has developed a listing of abbreviations, e.g., *mayb* for 'maybe', *ll* for 'looks like', and *y* for 'why'.

Coding Responses

In ECS, each response is coded in terms of seven categories: (*a*) location, (*b*) developmental quality, (*c*) determinants including blend responses, organizational activity and form quality, (*d*) content including unusual content and special content categories, (*e*) populars, (*f*) special scores, and (*g*) special response features.

Location

The area of the blot where the testee sees the object. There are four codes for location:

1. whole blot (W),
2. commonly used part (D),
3. rarely used part (Dd), and
4. white space (S).

To help facilitate identification of locations, Exner has adopted the numbering system used by Beck (e.g., the raised hand-like area in the middle of Card I as D1; the white space in the center of Card II as DS 5). In case a testee responds to an unidentified area, Exner suggests designating it as Dd 99.

Developmental Quality

Location code of each response is further sub-coded in terms of its developmental quality (DQ). It denotes the level of integration of the response elements: (*a*) simple (e.g., butterfly), or (*b*) complex (e.g., large Indian butterfly hovering gently over a cute, red little flower). There are four codes for DQ:

1. *Clearly Synthesized Developmental Quality* (+): Two objects are seen as separate (at least one has a commonly accepted form/shape—'form demand') and in relation to each other ('Two monsters pulling a woman in two opposite directions'—Card I),
2. *Vague/Synthesized Developmental Quality* (v/+): Objects are seen separate and related, yet none has a form demand ('Thunder and lightning'—Card VII),
3. *Ordinarily Articulated Developmental Quality* (o): Objects are seen to have a common form demand ('Bunch of islands from an airplane'—Card VII), and
4. *Minimally Articulated Developmental Quality* (v): ('Fire in a forest'—Card IX).

Determinants

Determinants indicate the specific features of the blots that appear to have *determined* the objects seen by the testee, namely,

1. *Form* (F): 'bat [Card I] shaped like a bat; wings, body, antennas',
2. *movement*: Human (M): 'Two women talking about their day's work' (Card III); animal movement (FM): 'two bears fighting' (Card II); inanimate movement (m): 'rising sun' (Card IX),
3. sub-coding of movement response in terms of *active* (fighting, dancing) and *passive* (looking, sleeping),
4. *chromatic color* (e.g., C, CF): 'Blood' (Card II); 'green forest' (Card IX),
5. *achromatic color* (e.g., C', C'F): 'Storm' (Card IV); 'black butterfly' (Card V),
6. *shading-texture* (T): *Mrig-chhalaa* ('deer-skin') (Card VI); *komal, mulayaam baadal* ('gentle, soft clouds') (Card VII),

7. *shading-dimension* (V): *Woe door, dhundhlee imaaret* ('far off, fuzzy, building') (Card II, center, top); *Door say, aag kee laptain dekhaee day raheen hain* ('flames, far off') (Card IX),
8. *shading-diffuse* (Y): 'Thunderstorm' (Card IV); 'man in a grey overcoat' (Card IV),
9. *form dimension* (FD): 'Door to an ancient cave' (Card VII, lower middle); 'paratrooper getting ready to jump' (Card X, lower, center, green),
10. *pairs/reflections* (2): 'Two women' (Card III); 'two bears climbing a mountain' (Card VIII),
11. *blends* (.): 'Two women, wearing a black dress, talking' (Card III); 'vampire with a cape' (Card V),
12. *organization* (Z): 'Two boxers, fighting' (Card II); 'two witches, casting spell' (Card IX), and
13. *form quality*: FQ+: 'Pretty woman, looking in a mirror, trying to fix her hair' (Card VII); FQo: 'Bat' (Card V); FQu: 'Two people in a pose' (Card IV); FQ−: 'Something very solid, falling apart' (Card IV).

Content

The specific object seen on the blot, e.g., angel, tree, fire, flower and giant. There are 26 content categories such as whole human (H), mythological whole human (H), clothing (Cg), geography (Ge), nature (Na), and so on. It may be mentioned here that there is no separate category for coding architectural responses in this system.

1. *Unusual Content*: Unusual contents with individualized significance are to be written as stated by the testee and coded as *Id* (Ideographic): 'Evil; this is evil' (Card IX), and
2. *Special Content Categories*: These are aggressive movement: '*fighting*' (Card II), 'killing' (Card IX); cooperative movement: 'two women dancing' (Card III), 'two girls, talking' (Card VII); and morbid content: 'piece of human flesh, floating on water' (Card X, middle, blue part), *zindaa laash* ('live, dead body') (Card III, top, red parts).

Populars

There are 13 populars in the ECS, e.g., bat, butterfly (Card I), animal forms (Card II), butterfly, bat (Card V) and animal skin (Card VI).

Special Scores

There are four specific types of special scores:

1. *Deviant Verbalizations*: Responses using neologisms and/or redundancies—*Hindlish auret* ('Indlish woman') (Card I).
2. *Inappropriate Combinations: Haathee kay pankh* ('Elephant wings') (Card I).
3. *Inappropriate Logic: Doe ulloo haanth milaa rahay hain* ('Two owls, shaking hands') (Card VIII, upper, middle part).
4. *Perseveration and Integration Failure*: 'It is the same bat I saw earlier' (Card I), 'only now, it is smaller and prettier' (Card V).

Other Special Response Features

There are three codes under this category:

1. *Abstraction*: sadness (Card II); happiness (Card X).
2. *Personalized Answers*: 'Bat, like the one I saw in Ajanta caves' (Card V).
3. *Color Projection* (color seen in black-and-white area): *Haree kaai* ('Green scum') (Card IV).

Placing Responses in a Format

Once the responses have been coded into various categories, there are numerous computations to be done including frequencies (e.g., total number of responses—W, D, Dd, S, M, FM, m), percentages (e.g., F+, A) and ratios (e.g., M, sum C, Af r, Lambda). All these are then written in a certain format.

The *structural summary format* is divided into two parts. The top part contains frequencies, developmental quality, form quality, determinants (both frequencies of responses with single as well as blends [more than one determinant] contents), the suicide constellation and special scores. The lower half of the structural summary contains ratios, percentages and derivations.

Interpreting Responses

The process of interpretation, recommends Exner, should follow a certain specific sequence:

1. Start by examining the suicide constellation (namely, FV + VF + V + FD > 2; color shading blend > 0; ego strength < 0.31 but > 0.44; MOR > 3; Zd > ± 3.5; es > EA; CF + C > FC; X + % < 0.70; S > 3; P < 3 or > 8; Pure H < 2; and R < 17),

2. look at the indices in key variables to see if any one is above the cut-off point, and
3. finally, go step-by-step through each of the seven clusters in the sequence as indicated by the critical key variables.

In the ECS, interpretation is a three-step process:

1. propositional statements are developed based on key variables and clusters,
2. statements are integrated to form an overall picture of the testee's personality, and finally,
3. the test report is written addressing the referral questions (diagnosis, dangerousness to self/others, treatment recommendations, etc.).

In addition, there are two specific points in the ECS about the interpretive process: (*a*) while developing statements, the focus is to be on indices, *not* on the content of the responses, and (*b*) Rorschach protocols with fewer than 14 responses need not be processed; in fact, Exner says one does not even need to conduct inquiry in these brief protocols.

Unlike many other Rorschachers who base their interpretations on distinct theoretical foundations, namely, Psychoanalytic Approach (e.g., Beck, Rapaport), Jungian Archetypal Approach (e.g., McCully), Psychonalytic Ego Psychology Approach (e.g., Schafer), or the Psychoanalytic Object Relations Approach (Paul Lerner), Exner does not seem to subscribe to any specific theory. His system appears to imply an empirical, behavioral approach to the Rorschach data—If 'p', then 'q'.

Rorschach interpretation, according to Exner (1991, p. 28),

. . . should create a picture of the individual that is broadly encompassing . . . [identifying] liabilities, [and] assets . . . [focusing] on the integrity and balance of internal operations . . . in the context of environmental exchange. It should not be a description that consists of a collection of glib, overgeneralized phrases. Instead, it should capture the psychological substance of the subject, as a person who is similar to others in some ways but, in reality, is different from everyone else.

Writing the Test Report

In Exner's system, the test report describes the subject in terms of key variables and clusters. Once this is done, the report addresses the specific diagnostic and/or treatment issues raised by the referral source.

Following this brief review of Exner's system, we now present two protocols illustrating the ECS. The first is Seema, a twenty-two year old Indian female; the second, Roberts, a twenty-three year old African–American male.

SECTION II: ILLUSTRATIVE PROTOCOLS

The statements made during the free association period are given following each card. The statements made during the inquiry phase are given in italics.

Protocol 1: Seema

Card I, Response 1: Two creatures trying to hold on to something for stability; for support—there is a hint of desperation, for, they are trying to hold on—it is the struggle of daily life—trying to hold on to an ideal.

Because one can see them trying to hold on, to clutch on to something—may be, an ideal; it is not concrete; something abstract which is the focal point of existence.

Score: W+; FM,a,u; (2); A, Id; 4.0; AB, MOR.

Card II, Response 2: Could be a new butterfly—a product of modern genetics; it is a cross between a bug and a butterfly—lacking the usual beauty of a butterfly.

Looks somewhat like a butterfly.

Score: Wo; Fo; A, Sc; 4.5; INC, Level 1.

Card II, Response 3: Two people holding hands—could be a dance—put one foot forward and holding hands type of dance.

Two people with legs put forward and a vague body structure—enlarged than the head which is smaller.

Score: D+; Ma−; (2); H; 3.0; COP.

Card III, Response 4: Two women who have gone to fill water, pot in hand; they are filling water from the river and talking; could be pose for a dance; they are in positive mood.

Women because of face, body parts; hands, legs—I can see the ripples in the water—it is a dance pose because they are exactly in the same pose which is not otherwise possible; but it looks like two women standing near a well.

Score: D+; M,a,o; (2); H, Hh, Na; P; 3.0; COP.

Card IV, Response 5: Two people in a pose, ambivalence, one foot forward indicates defiance; also head down indicates depression; they are doing this for some ideal which isolates them from the rest of the world; both defiant and depressed.

Two people bound together by some ideal; the foot indicates defiance which is greater than depression; the depression may be momentary; defiance involves putting the foot forward; the foot is much bigger and enlarged than the head which is smaller.

Score: W+; M,p,u; (2); H, Id, Na; 4.0; AB, MOR.

Card IV, Response 6: Something very solid which is cracking and falling apart—some great structure.

A great structure with a central part—the other parts are cracking— it is like a kingdom; the main people are there but others are moving away—somewhat like the fall of the movements; like the fall of Communism.

Score: Dv; m, a−; Sc, Id; AB, MOR.

Card V, Response 7: A bat—going down—something pessimistic; (V) it is also going up.

Small head; large wing-span; small feet; the bat is going up and down.

Score: Wo; FM,a,o; A; P; 1.0; MOR.

Card VI, Response 8: Explosion; after the explosion it is very beautiful—clouds rising up, colors taking expression; it rises from a small point and covers a wide area; focal point is the midline from which it spreads.

Focal point is the midline from which it is spreading out; it is an atomic nuclear explosion; riot of colors; there is a certain aesthetic beauty in destruction; it is like a black-and-white photograph and I can fill in the colors; could be an oil well suddenly coming up.

Score: Wv, m, a, u; Ex; CP.

Card VII, Response 9: Two dancers; acrobats; heads towards each other; body focused on the other side; graceful movement.

Head, hand up; other hand is down; they are in a pose which is difficult to perform; beauty in posture but no beauty in face.

Score: W+; M,a,u; (2); H; 2.5; COP.

Card VIII, Response 10: Design seen in kaleidoscope; very beautiful iceland.

Ice mountain with many different colors; you can see from the top and all the colors are visible.

Score: Do; CFo; Ls; P.

SEEMA

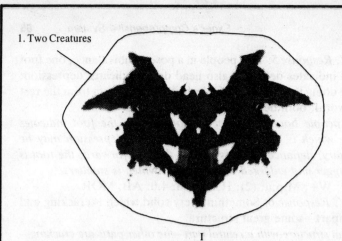

1. Two Creatures

I

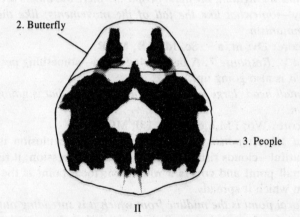

2. Butterfly

3. People

II

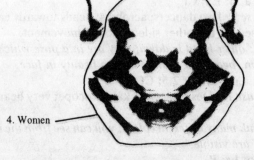

4. Women

III

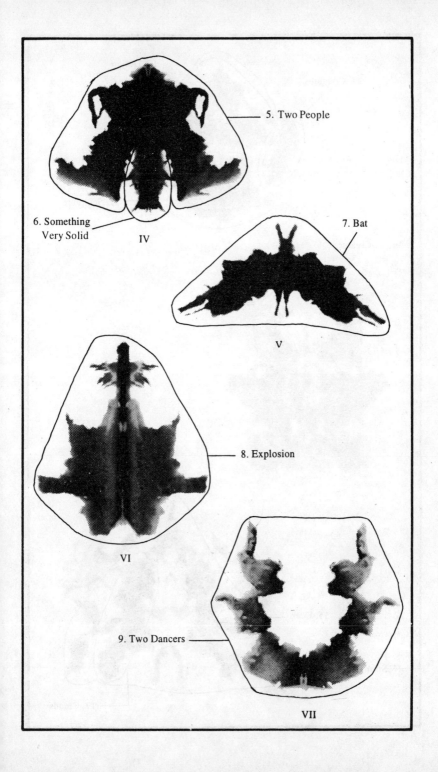

5. Two People

6. Something
Very Solid

IV

7. Bat

V

8. Explosion

VI

9. Two Dancers

VII

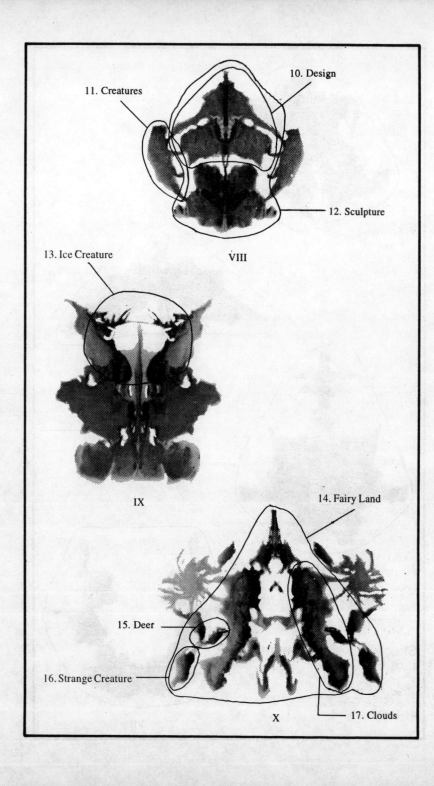

11. Creatures
10. Design
12. Sculpture

VIII

13. Ice Creature

IX

14. Fairy Land
15. Deer
16. Strange Creature
17. Clouds

X

Card VIII, Response 11: Two creatures trying to climb up; it is a 90° climb which is being done with ease.

Practically, straight climb; I can see the body, tail, feet, and mouth.

Score: D+; FM,a,o; (2); A; P; 3.0.

Card VIII, Response 12: Sculpture which is built around a central something.

Sculpture which is built around a central point; modern art; it is architecture which is difficult to construct; there are no links; therefore, it is a sculpture.

Score: Dv; F−; Sc, Art.

Card IX, Response 13: Ice creature or someone dressed up in white and showered with confetti; cannot see the face, only eyes; the creature is not very happy; maybe scared.

Snowman showered with confetti; similar to the Japanese festival of ice in which snowman is showered with things; looking very scared; eyes can be seen; pondering on the ways of human beings; like, the figures seen in Grid Blyton's books.

Score: DS+; M,p,u; Ay, (H); 5.0; MOR.

Card X, Response 14: A fairyland with lots of creatures; two goblins.

Goblins are remembered from childhood stories; grey signifies naughtiness; they are not positive.

Score: Do; FC',u; (2); (H); AB.

Card X, Response 15: Deers.

Deers; pose and antlers; they are running.

Score: Do; FM, a, o; (2); A.

Card X, Response 16: A very strange creature.

Dragons; they are very cute; as featured on Japanese kimonos.

Score: Dv; F−; (2); (A); Ay.

Card X, Response 17: Colored clouds; something from a childhood book.

Pink, brown and yellow colored clouds.

Score: Dv; CF, u; (2), CI.

Structural Summary

1. R = 17.
2. Location: W = 6; D = 11; S = 1.
3. Developmental Quality: DQ+ = 7; DQ o = 5; DQ v = 5.
4. Form Quality: FQ, o = 6; FQ, u = 7; FQ, − = 4.

5. Determinants: F = 3; M = 5; m = 2; FM = 4; CF = 2; FC' = 1; active movement = 9; passive movement = 2.
6. Content: H = 4; (H) = 2; A = 5; (A) = 1; Art = 1; Ay = 2; Cl = 1; Ex = 1; Hh = 1; Id = 3; Na = 1; Sc = 3 (Note: All the contents are counted here; thus, although R is 17, the contents total is 25. In nine responses there is single content. In the remaining eight there are two or more contents).
7. Special Scores: AB = 7; COP = 3; CP = 1; MOR = 5; INC = 1.
8. Ratios/Percentages: F + % = 33; X + % = 35; Xu % = 41; EB = 5:2; EA = 7.0; eb = 6:1; es = 7; Adj es = 6; D = 0; Adj D = 0; Z sum = 30; Zd = +2.5; FC:CF + FC = 0:2; Ma:Mp = 3:2; a:p = 9:2; An + Xy:R = 0:17; Isolate/R = 0.29; 2AB + Art + Ay:R = 11:17; H + A:Hd + Ad = 12:0; (H) + (Hd):(A) + (Ad) = 2:1; H:Hd + (H) + (Hd) = 4:2; W:M = 6:5; L = 0.21; Af r = 0.89; Ego = 0.59; (2) = 10; W:D = 6:11.
9. Indices: DEPI = 4; SCZI = 1; SCON = 4; CDI = 2.

Interpreting Seema's Protocol

Interpreting Seema's structural summary data within the context of the ECS poses a big challenge. As per the ECS, the interpretive statements are made based on a comparison of the structural values with the normative data. We do not as yet have any recent large-scale normative data in India. The best approximation we have is the compilation by Asthana. Comparing Seema's Rorschach values with Asthana's (1963) norms (on 450 normals in India) would be perhaps as relevant as comparing them with Exner's (1993) norms (on 700 cases in the USA). For example, let us take the number of R responses. Asthana reports an average R of 33 for Indians. Exner's figure is 22.67. Seema's R is 17. Seema's responses were coded using Exner's system; Asthana's data were coded using Beck's system. So, where does Seema fit in this scheme? Comparing her R with Indian norms makes her overly inhibited. Compared with US norms, she is only slightly inhibited. And, since in Rorschach data we look at the total picture and not at any datum in isolation, let us pick up yet another figure, Lambda (the ratio of all pure form determined responses to all other responses in which determinants in addition to form, e.g., color, shade, texture have been used). Asthana reports an L of 0.33. Exner found an L of 0.58. Seema's L is 0.21. Compared with

Exner's norms, Seema is much less affected by stimulus complexity than most people. As per the Indian norms, however, she is not.

The point is, until we have Indian norms within the guidelines of the ECS, we may not want to use the structural summary of the ECS data for an Indian population. However, we do not have to go from one extreme (to wait for the ECS Indian norms) to the other extreme (of comparing with Asthana's [dated] norms). Probably, a compromise could be considered by using Exner's approach as a 'crude' guideline for looking at the data. With this caution, we would interpret Seema's protocol in terms of Exner's (1991, 1993) formulations, namely, (*a*) suicide constellation, (*b*) key variables, and (*c*) clusters.

Suicide Constellation: There are 12 indices of suicide constellation (more than three morbid responses, more than three white space responses, less than two H responses, etc.). If a testee scores positive on eight or more out of these 12 indices, he/she may be a suicide risk. However, cautions Exner, absence of positives on these indices does not automatically make him/her low risk.

Seema's positives on the suicide constellation are four. She seems to be well within the so-called, suicide-free zone.

Key Variables: There are 11 key variables. Each of these has a critical cut-off point. These are:

1. SCZI > 3
2. DEPI > 5
3. D > Adj D
4. CDI > 3
5. Adj negative
6. Lambda > .99
7. Reflection Responses 0
8. EB Introversive
9. EB Extratensive
10. p > a + 1
11. HVI positive

The first five of these key variables, says Exner, focus on pathology. The remaining six reflect personality styles.

If a testee's scores on any one of these indices reach/exceed the cut-off score, it should be used as a starting point for interpreting his/her personality in terms of the seven clusters (namely, affect, controls, information processing, cognitive mediation, self-perception and interpersonal perception). For each key variable, Exner recommends a specific cluster-sequence. For example, if EB is introversive, the cluster-sequence should be ideation—processing—mediation—controls—affect—self-perception—interpersonal perception.

In Seema's case, EB seems to be an appropriate key variable to start looking at her personality. A global comment seems to be that just on the basis of the fact that the first five variables are not significant for her, interpreting her Rorschach indices is more indicative of her personality style rather than psychopathology. She appears to be within the normal range of people.

Clusters: As mentioned earlier, based on EB being the key variable, the recommended cluster-sequence is ideation—processing—mediation—controls—affect—self-perception—interpersonal perception.

Based on this sequence and reminding ourselves that in the absence of Indian norms, we are only making some tentative observations, let us see how Seema's personality is reflected on these clusters.

Ideation indicates how we conceptualize our world, 'the procedures of conceptualizing the information that has been translated' (Exner, 1991, p. 204). *Information processing* includes the way we process incoming stimuli. *Mediation* refers to translation of input information. *Control* is '. . . the ability to draw on available resources to formulate and implement deliberate behaviors designed to contend with demand situations' (ibid., p. 161). *Affect* indicates emotional features. *Self-perception* focuses on self-image. Finally, the seventh cluster, *interpersonal perception* includes, '. . .some needs, attitudes, sets, and coping styles that often exist in people' (ibid., p. 182). Exner emphasizes that this cluster (interpersonal perception) *does not* represent self-image or self-value.

Describing Seema's personality within the framework of these seven clusters in the sequence (as indicated by the key variable EB being introversive) would then mean commenting on how she conceptualizes her world (ideation), how she processes incoming information (processing), how she translates incoming information (mediation), how she deals with situations demanding specific behaviors (controls), what her emotional features are (affect), how she sees herself (self-perception), and finally, what are some of her needs, attitudes, sets and coping styles (interpersonal perception).

Seema is introversive (EB, 5:3). She is, what Rorschach calls, an M-person. Sorting out problems and solutions within herself before putting the most appropriate one into action is her way of dealing with situations. Is it her pervasive style? Yes (EB Per, 2.5). She does not let her emotions influence her decision making. This essentially seems to be the case because in her information processing Seema gets overly involved with situations around her (Lambda, 0.21) and oversimplifies them (maybe because that reduces the demand on thinking about them). There is nothing *remarkable* in her capacity for control and stress tolerance (Adj D is 0 and CDI is 2). Emotionally, Seema is rich. Her Afr is 0.89; also, she tends to focus on emotions with little effort to modulate them (FC:CF + C is 0:2). Seema's self-perception appears to be somewhat exaggerated (egocentricity index, 0.59); however, the exaggeration is negative (MOR, 5). She, thus, seems to be overly under-estimating herself. Finally, in terms of her needs, sets, attitudes and coping styles, she is liked by others (COP, 3), actively interacts with others (a:p is 9:2) and does not tend to isolate herself (Isolate/R = 0.29).

We may want to give a human form to these statistics. Seema is Paro, the main female character in Sarat Chandra's novel *Devdas* (1990). Paro and Devdas loved each other. Paro expressed her feelings towards him to her friend Manorama, before saying anything about it to Devdas. She liked to rebel when his father refused to approve of the marriage (mainly because they belonged to different castes). Paro visits Devdas in his home at night; begs him to marry her. Devdas cannot oppose his parents. He refuses. Paro goes along with her parents' wishes who arrange her marriage with an elderly zamindar (a widower with three grown-up children). Paro fulfils all her social obligations as wife, stepmother, homemaker. She, however, cannot stop loving Devdas in her heart. She is rich in emotions as well as self-pride. She is compliant and conforming with social standards and values. An M-person. So is Seema.

As mentioned earlier, we wanted to illustrate Exner's system with two protocols. Having described Seema's protocol and having made a few interpretive statements about her personality, we now look at Roberts' protocol in the same sequence, namely, (*a*) his responses, (*b*) scores, (*c*) structural summary, and (*d*) interpretation. A major difference is that for interpreting Roberts' responses we would be able to use the US norms of Exner's system.

Protocol 2: Roberts

Card I, Response 1: Somebody; looks like, somebody; looks like, got ran over.
> *This whole thing looks like, something ran over it.*
> Score: Wv; F−; H; MOR.

Card I, Response 2: This could be the vertebrae; when doctors open you, you see the insides.
> *These here are the vertebrae; they are like your insides.*
> Score: DdSo; F−; An.

Card I, Response 3: This here, may be the spot of cancer.
> *The spot here looks like cancer; just the way it looks.*
> Score: DdSv; F−; An.

Card II, Response 4: This here looks like a jet; it is blasted off with fire.
> *Looks like, it is taking off; you see fire here at the tail.*
> Score: DdS+; ma. CFo; Sc, Fi. 4.5

Card II, Response 5: This here, looks like, volcano top.
> *This is just like, volcano top.*
> Score: Do, Fu, Ls.

Card III, Response 6: This is fish here; this could be, like, a water; and sun is shining; this guy might be; this may be angel falling; all this is taking place on the water; these are two creatures on the water.
> *This looks like fish; this is all water; sun here; these are creatures; they are on water; the whole thing is on water.*
> Score: W+; mp, Mp, FDu; (2); H, (H), A, Na; P; 5.5.

Card IV, Response 7: It's a monster.
> *This whole thing; he has hurt somebody. This is, kind of, evil.*
> Score: Wo; Mao; (H); Hx; P; 2.0; AB.

Card V, Response 8: It's a moth.
> *Just looks like a moth; the way a moth looks.*
> Score: Wo; Fo; A; 1.0.

Card VI, Response 9: It's like a cat that got ran over; like, he got ran over by something; splattered.

ROBERTS

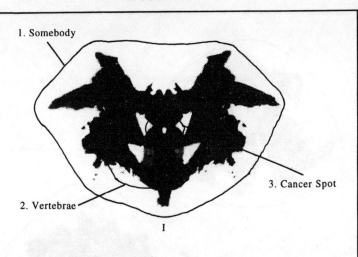

1. Somebody
2. Vertebrae
3. Cancer Spot

I

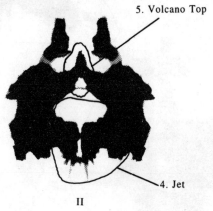

5. Volcano Top
4. Jet

II

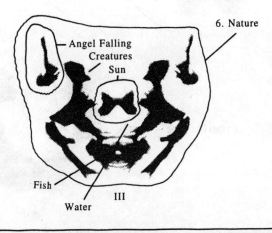

6. Nature
Angel Falling
Creatures
Sun
Fish
Water

III

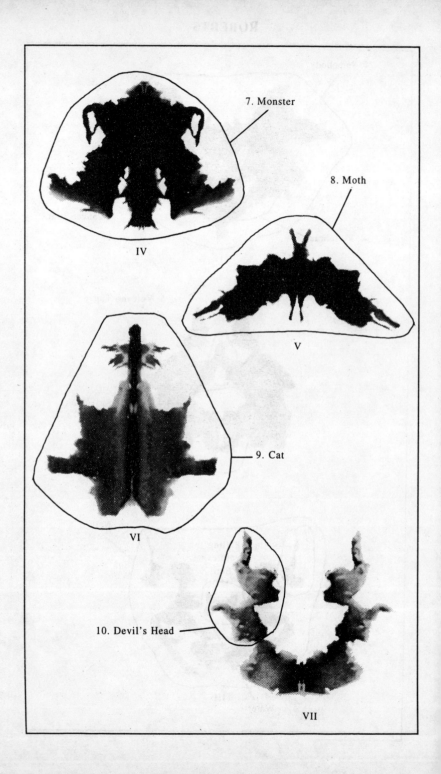

7. Monster

IV

8. Moth

V

9. Cat

VI

10. Devil's Head

VII

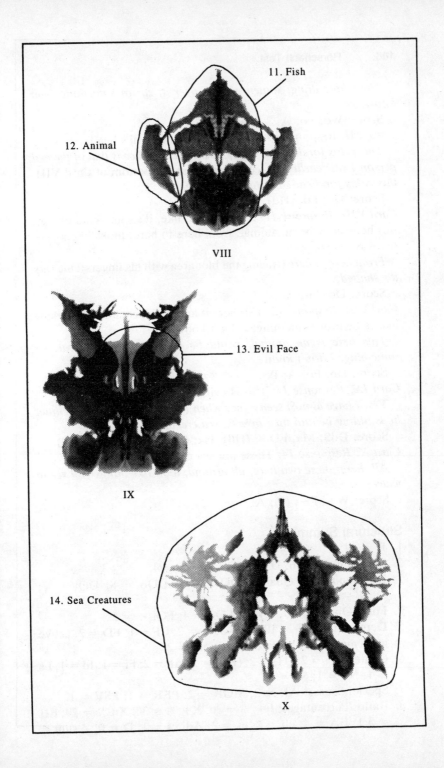

11. Fish

12. Animal

VIII

13. Evil Face

IX

14. Sea Creatures

X

The whole thing; something ran over it; car or something, you know.

Score: Wo; Fo; A; 2.5; MOR.

Card VII, Response 10: It's the top of the devil's head.

This is his forehead and face goes here; his face is that of the evil person I saw earlier (placed Card IX at the bottom of Card VII), *this is his forehead and this is his face.*

Score: Do; Fu; (Hd).

Card VIII, Response 11: It looks like, like, it's some kind of fish; this here, may be an animal; from here to here, looks like a fish; the way it's shaped.

From here to here (tracing the blot area with his fingers); *the way it's shaped.*

Score: Do; Fu; A.

Card VIII, Response 12: This here is an animal; could be something like, a bear or something; I don't know.

This here is an animal; could be something like a bear, or something, I don't know.

Score: Do; Fo; A; P.

Card IX, Response 13: This is evil; evil.

Yes, I have almost seen a face when I look into mirror sometime; he is hiding behind this; insects; sea creatures.

Score: DdS; Ma; FD−; (Hd), Hx, Id; 5.0; PSV; PER; AB.

Card X, Response 14: These are sea creatures.

All these; these two here; all around; look like things you see in water.

Score: W+; F−; (2); A.

Structural Summary

1. R = 14.
2. Location: W = 6; D = 4; Dd = 4; S = 4.
3. Developmental Quality: DQ+ = 3; DQo = 8; DQv = 2; DQv/+ = 1.
4. Form Quality: FQ, o = 5; FQu = 4; FQ, − = 5.
5. Determinants: F = 10; M = 3; m = 2; CF = 1; FD = 2; active movement = 3; passive movement = 2.
6. Content: H = 2; (H) = 2; (Hd) = 2; An = 2; Fi = 1; Id = 1; Ls = 1; Na = 1; Sc = 1.
7. Special Scores: AB = 2; MOR = 2; PER = 1; PSV = 1.
8. Ratios/Percentages: F+ % = 30; X+ % = 36; Xu % = 29; EB = 3:1; EA = 4; eb = 2; es = 2; Adj es = 1; D = 0; Z sum =

26.0; Zd = +5.5; FC:CF + FC = 0:1; Ma:Mp = 2:1; a:p = 3:2; An + Xy:R = 2:14; Isolate/R = 0.20; 2AB + Art + Ay:R = 4:14; H + A:Hd + Ad = 2:4; (H) + (Hd):(A) + (Ad) = 4:0; H:Hd + (H) + (Hd) = 2:4; W:M = 6:3; L = 2.50; Afr = 0.40; egocentricity index = 0.14; (2) = 2; W:D = 6:4.

9. Indices: DEPI = 5; SCZI = 4; SCON = 3; CDI = 3; HVI = 3.

Interpreting Roberts' Protocol

As mentioned earlier, in the ECS, the interpretation is a three-step process:

1. propositional statements based on (*a*) suicide constellation, (*b*) key variables, and (*c*) clusters,
2. integrating these statements to describe a testee's personality, and
3. addressing the referral questions.

Propositional Statements: Out of the 12 indices comprising this constellation, a concern about the testee's suicide risk is indicated if he/she scores positive on eight or more of them. The 12 indices are:

1. Sum V + FD > 2
2. C − SBl > 0
3. Egocentricity Index < 0.31 or > 0.44
4. MOR > 3
5. Zd > ± 3.5
6. es > EA
7. CF + C+ > FC
8. X + % < .70
9. S > 3
10. P < 3 or > 8
11. Pure H < 2
12. R < 17

In Roberts' case, there are only three positives, namely, egocentricity index (0.14), Zd (+5.5) and R (14). Based on this, he does not appear to be a suicide risk.

The 11 key variables are used to determine the sequence in which the seven clusters are to be examined. The 11 key variables (with their cut-off points) are:

1. SCZI > 3
2. DEPI > 5
3. D > Adj D
4. CDI > 3
5. Adj negative
6. Lambda > 0.99
7. Reflection 0
8. EB Introversive
9. EB Extratensive
10. p > a + 1
11. HVI Positive

In the case of Roberts, Lambda is 2.5. Based on this, the recommended cluster sequence will be: information processing—cognitive mediation—ideation—controls—affect—self-perception—interpersonal perception.

Let us now examine a few of the indices in each of the above clusters and see what kind of interpretive statements can be made about Roberts' personality. A note: The comments under each cluster are *not* meant to be exhaustive. They are just *illustrative* of the intepretive process. We encourage readers to consult Exner (1991, 1993) for a complete and thorough picture of the scoring, computation and interpretive procedures.

> *Information Processing*: A very high L (2.5) indicates that Roberts tends to oversimplify the stimulus field. If Dd is 4 or higher, says Exner (1991), and Zf is less than 13, it indicates discomfort with decision making. Roberts has 4 Dd responses and his Zf is 7. Just based on these two indices (L, relation between Dd and Zf), Roberts' information processing is not in the normal range. Roberts is not an average 'processor'. He avoids complexity.
>
> *Cognitive Mediation*: Again, Lambda is critical. High Lambda (2.5) coupled with low number of popular responses (3) suggests that Roberts not only oversimplifies the stimulus field but also tends to engage in unconventional modes of behavior. He is, what Exner would describe as someone who makes '. . . more individualistic responses, even in situations that are simple and/or precisely defined' (1991, p. 211).
>
> *Ideation*: Constricted EB (3:1) does not suggest that Roberts has a pervasive style of conceptualizing his environment. A low

EB (2.0) in conjunction with high Lambda (2.5) indicates that Roberts avoids complex stimuli and is usually in a hurry to react. This is more likely says Exner, '. . . if the FM value is 0 or 1, and suggests that the subject is able to minimize or avoid many of the natural stimulus irritations that are common among most people' (1991, p. 221). That is Roberts.

Controls: Most important indices of control reported by Exner include EA and/or es, and Adj D values. Roberts' EA is 4.0, es 2.0 and Adj D + 1.0. Customarily, an Adj D value in the positive range suggests good controls. However, if Adj D is positive and EA is below average, it implies poor controls. Thus, Roberts appears to have good controls; however, it is precisely that: an appearance. In fact, his controls are poor.

Affect: Affective Ratio, DEPI, S, FC:CF + C, CP, EB, EB Per, are some of the indices of emotionality in Exner's system. In Roberts' case, Afr is 0.40, DEPI is 5, there are four Ss and the FC:CF + C ratio is 0:1. He is highly emotional (depressed). In fact, if his DEPI value were 6, he could be considered clinically depressed and may be recommended to be evaluated for medication. A high index of depression when seen against an introversive EB and an FC:CF + C value of 0:1 indicates that his emotions are not well modulated. He is possibly impulsive.

Self-perception: How does Roberts see himself? What does he think of himself? In the ECS, indices of self-perception include reflection responses, egocentricity, morbid responses, form dimension responses, etc.

There are no reflection responses in Roberts' case. His egocentricity index is 0.14, 2 MOR and 2 FD responses. Evidently, he has a fairly negative self-perception. An FD value of 2, in the absence of any vista responses, suggests that he is overly critical (vigilant) in evaluating his self-worth.

Interpersonal Perception: For assessment of interpersonal perception issues, Exner recommends looking at HVI, CDI, a:p, PER, AG, COP, etc.

For Roberts, HVI is 3 (cut-off is 4), CDI is 3 (cut-off is 4), a:p is 3:2, PER is 2, AG is 0 and COP is 0. Apparently, there is not much of significance to report in his interpersonal perception. Exner warns that the indices in this cluster *do not* relate to self-image or self-worth; rather, these are suggestive of sets, attitudes and coping styles. All the indices in Roberts' structural summary relating to interpersonal perception are below the critical cut-off points. There seems to be a tendency in him to be somewhat alert while interacting with others (HVI, 3) and to some extent he is not very effective in coping with demanding social situations (CDI, 3).

Having made a few *sample* propositional statements about Roberts in terms of suicide constellation and clusters (the sequence of which was guided by the key variable, in this case Lambda), we may now want to integrate these statements to describe his personality.

Integrated Summary: Roberts is an introversive person. His inner resources, however, are less than most people. As a result, he tends to oversimplify situations and thus makes it easier for himself to react. He is emotional—depressed. Associated with this sense of depression is a poor self-image. Under stress, he tends to get impulsive. Denial of complexity in situations encourages him to conceptualize objects in an almost child-like, simple, straight forward cause-effect relationship.

SUMMARY

In this chapter, we started with mentioning three special features of Exner's Comprehensive System: (*a*) computerization, (*b*) training non-clinicians to administer the Rorschach, and (*c*) structuring interpretation. Then, Section I described the main elements of the Rorschach procedure, e.g., context, rapport, instructions, inquiry, recording responses, coding responses and personality theory. In Section II, we illustrated the ECS by discussing two protocols—Seema and Roberts.

It needs to be emphasized that here we have presented only the bare essentials of the ECS. The intent is to arouse enough interest in readers to make them go to the primary sources (e.g., Exner, 1974, 1991, 1993) to fully appreciate the complexity and comprehensiveness of the system. There are over 300 Rorschach variables in the ECS. Exner (1991) provides a step-by-step guide for examining various indices in each of the seven clusters as well as the suicide constellation for developing specific propositional statements and then integrating them for profiling a synthetic picture of the subject's personality.

There are two major limitations in the ECS. One, at least at the present time, is that it is not practically possible for an average Indian student to use this system because he/she may have quite a 'project' to manually compute and cross-check various statistics in the structural summary. Maybe, with increasing access to computers, a small town/rural student will have computer facilities in the near future.

A second limitation of the ECS seems to be its impracticality in clinical settings. Even if one were able to crank out the statistics, there still remains the difficult task of articulating about 300 variables to come up with an integrated personality picture of the testee. It is not easy to be able to do that in a relatively short period of time. From that point of view, ECS appears to be heavily loaded in favor of research rather than clinical practice. Hopefully, Exner may come up with an abridged version which would be helpful for practitioners.

Until that happens, we may want to use statistically less cumbersome, although clinically more complex, methods of looking at Rorschach data, namely, the systems developed by Schafer (1954), McCully (1971), and most importantly, Paul Lerner (1991). The next three chapters describe these three systems.

6 McCully's (Jungian) Archetypal Approach

The mirror does not flatter, it faithfully shows whatever looks into it; namely, the face we never show to the world because we cover it with the *persona*, the mask of the actor. But the mirror lies behind the mask and shows the real face.

—Jung, 1990, p. 20, emphasis in original.

Kyaa koyee nai baat nazar aatee hai mujhmen?
Ayeenaa hamain daikh kay, hairaan saa quon hai?
(Is there something new in me?
How come, the mirror, kind of, looks confused?)
—A song from the Hindi film, *Gaman*, released in mid-seventies.

Asking someone to look at his/her face in the mirror is often used sarcastically in India when the other person seems to be coming across as grandiose.

'*Haan, haan, barey aaye wahan say. Film actor (professor/ governor) baney gain. Jaayeye pahlay sheeshay main mooh daikh aayeye*' ('You want to be a film actor [professor/governor]. Sure! Why don't you go and check out your face in mirror' [the implication being that the mirror will honestly tell you that you are just not capable of being an actor, or professor, or governor]).

Carl Gustav Jung (1875–1961) commented on the honesty and authenticity of the mirror in his paper 'Archetypes of the Collective Unconscious' back in 1934 (republished recently in Jung, 1990). The Hindi film song appeared in the mid-seventies; the Indian idiom has been there for almost ages. The idea is separated in space (Switzerland, India) and time (1934, seventies, for ages). Still, the theme is common. Of course, Jung was greatly influenced by India and its rich culture. He did visit India in 1938 (on invitation by the British government) to participate in the twenty-fifth anniversary of Calcutta University; he also traveled a lot including Allahabad (where he received an honorary doctorate at the University), Benares (now Varanasi), Bhubaneshwar, Madras, etc. But he wrote about the mirror as the de-masker of the persona in 1934. The Indian proverb has been in existence long before Jungian observations, and *Gaman* was released in the seventies. Thus, Jung's exposure to India was before he made the aforementioned comments. It is highly unlikely that he was aware of Indian thought. And, it is equally unlikely that the late Shahariyaar (the poet who wrote the song for *Gaman*) was influenced by Jung's writings. Yet, the three comments have a common theme—archetypes.

Then, there are stories. A poor person in love with a rich person. A princess in trouble and being saved by a commoner. A man leaving his home in search of something of value—*gyaan* (knowledge), *dhan* (wealth), *sukh* (happiness)—but eventually finding it right within himself.

Niraakaar, jub tumhain diyaa aakaar, Swayum saakaar hoe gayaa ('O, the Formless!, when I finished giving you a shape, I realized that in fact, I ended up shaping my own self') (Gopal Das 'Neeraj', 1961, p. 75).

Heinrich Zimmer (1890–1943) in his classic work *Myths and Symbols in Indian Art and Civilization* (1992) narrates the story of Rabbi Eisik, son of Rabbi Jekel of Cracow, Poland.

Eisik had a dream. He was asked to go to Prague to get hidden wealth buried under a bridge that led to a castle of the Bohemian kings. The first time he dreamt about it, he ignored it. Then, after the third time, he decided to go to the directed location.

The bridge was guarded by security forces. Eisik kept staking it out, hoping one day he would be able to get to the spot and dig the buried treasure out. Many days passed. He had no luck. Meanwhile, the officer in charge of security became curious seeing Eisik there everyday.

He asked Eisik if he had lost something. Eisik replied that he was there in response to a dream he had had back home that there was treasure hidden somewhere there under the bridge. He would like to dig it out. The officer counseled Eisik that he also had had a dream and '. . . it spoke to me of Cracow, commanding me to go thither and to search there for a great treasure in the house of a Jewish rabbi whose name would be

Eisik son of Jekel. The treasure was to have been discovered buried in the dirty corner behind the stove . . .' (Zimmer, 1992, p. 220).

Rabbi Eisik heard this carefully. He did not disclose his identity to the officer. But he did hurry back to his home in Cracow. He dug under the dirty corner behind the stove. And, lo and behold, he did indeed find the hidden wealth. With it, Rabbi Eisik put an end to his poverty; he also built a prayer-house. And, he lived happily ever after.

'Hindu myths and symbols, and other signs of wisdom from afar', says Zimmer (1992, p. 221), describing the moral of this story, 'in just such a way will speak to us of the treasure which is our own. And we then must dig it up from the forgotten recesses of our own being'.

There is an individual psyche; an individual unconscious. Freud talked about it in his writings. Corresponding to this individual unconscious, said Jung, there is a collective unconscious; a collective psyche. The contents of the individual psyche are the repressed wishes of the person. The contents of the collective psyche are archetypes. Archetypes are the repressed wishes of a culture.

Archetypes are common to human beings all over the world. These are the themes of life, death, love, fear, hope, anger, honesty and trickery experienced in all countries—primitive and modern.

The Rorschach test not only uncovers the individual unconscious but also the collective unconscious. It unfolds the testee's repressed wishes, impulses and desires. It also unfolds a part of his/her personality that contains elements of the collective unconscious—archetypes. This is the thesis of Robert McCully (1971).

'Dr. McCully's brave, novel, and unconventional book,' says Piotrowski in the Foreword to McCully's book (1971, p. ix) 'is a determined step not only toward enriching the Rorschach test but also toward that high aim of objectivity in a very difficult and arresting area of personality research'.

In the present chapter, we shall describe McCully's (Jungian) archetypal system of looking at the Rorschach protocols. As in the case of Exner's Comprehensive System in the previous chapter, we will follow the format outlined in the Rorschach procedure: (*a*) context, (*b*) rapport, (*c*) seating arrangement, (*d*) instructions, (*e*) free association, (*f*) inquiry, (*g*) recording (*h*) coding, (*i*) for-matting, (*j*) interpreting, and (*k*) writing the report.

In Section I, we will describe McCully's system. In Section II, we will present two protocols to illustrate his system. In describing McCully's system, we will digress a bit while discussing the personality theory underlying his approach. Since McCully has focused on the Jungian theory of personality, we will present an overview of Jungian thought and philosophy and connect them to McCully's system.

In essence, observes McCully, the Rorschach cards have the potential to activate archetypes. In many cases, responses to the cards indicate that archetypes have been aroused. Looking at these archetypal responses provides an additional, meaningful insight into the personality of the testee.

SECTION I: McCULLY'S APPROACH

Interpreting Rorschach imagery in terms of archetypes and looking at the Rorschach experience in order to understand psychic structure are the two major dimensions of McCully's system. 'Some years ago', says McCully in his Preface, 'while studying the *Dhammapada*, a collection of Buddhist teachings, the author was astonished at the correspondence between the stages in the Buddhist thought and stages of Jung's individuation process' (McCully, 1971, p. xi).

The specific Jungian concepts that McCully finds relevant to the Rorschach experience include: self, ego, collective unconscious, archetypes, persona, anima, animus, individuation and symbols.

About the Rorschach experience, McCully has to say,

Rorschach data are not dream data. They are not just conscious activity and do not contain a symbol that came from a dream. *They are something new and something different, carrying their own uniqueness.* They are a product of what happens when [the] conscious and unconscious are provided with the opportunity to react with each other (McCully, 1971, p. 26, emphasis in original).

Within the context of the contributions of Hermann Rorschach (1975) and Roy Schafer (1954), McCully examines the Rorschach imagery beyond the pathological focus and re-directs our attention to the value of understanding symbols inherent in Rorschach responses from a non-pathological perspective.

The Rorschach experience is a creative process. It offers an understanding of not only a pathologically affected psyche but also a healthy psyche. McCully talks about identifying *sources* of Rorschach imagery: collective unconscious, archetypes, culture at large.

Archetypes include such prototypal experiences as food gathering, elimination, fertility, father, mother, authority, self, feminity, goddess, eternity, childhood, circle, square, devil (evil), god (good), maleness, and sleep. If we look at the core or essence of a symbol, according to laws pertaining to subjective processes, we will find evidence for archetypal influences (McCully, 1971, p. 51).

Each Rorschach card has the potential to arouse archetypes in the mind of the testee as follows:

- Card I: Archetype of matriarchal power; feminine functioning.
- Card II: Archetype of opposites.
- Card III: Archetype of persona.
- Card IV: Archetype of patriarchal power.
- Card V: Archetype of good and evil.
- Card VI: Archetype of masculine power.
- Card VII: Archetype of feminine structure.
- Card VIII: Archetype of interpersonal bonds.
- Card IX: Archetype of karma and experience type.
- Card X: Archetype of *sansara* (Hindu notion of vast wheel of life on which all things turn).

With this brief introduction, let us look at McCully's system in terms of the Rorschach procedure categories.

Context

McCully's focus in terms of context is not only to look for pathology but also for growth-oriented trends in the protocol. The purpose may or may not be to assess dangerousness or to make a diagnosis, it is also to examine for trends of individuation—the archetypal influences.

Rapport

As in any clinical (as well as non-clinical) situation, a trusting, non-threatening relation between tester and testee is critical to have a meaningful experience. In the context of the Rorschach test, it is all the more important because the tester needs to empathize with the testee in order to understand his/her symbolization and its archetypal roots.

Seating Arrangement

There are no specific suggestions. One can be flexible depending on specific situations.

Instructions

There is nothing rigidly specific about instructions in McCully's approach. However, the original Rorschach instructions 'What might this be?' are implied. We are not sure, though.

Free Association Phase

Again, no specific suggestions.

Inquiry Phase

McCully gives nothing exclusive, except focusing on non-suggestive methods for finding out locations and determinants.

Recording Responses

Recording the responses (in free association as well as inquiry phases) verbatim is implied.

Coding Responses

In McCully's system, the responses may be coded in terms of conventional systems (Beck's, Exner's, Hertz's, Klopfer's, Rapaport's or Lerner's).

Placing Responses in a Format and Interpreting Responses

McCully recommends placing and interpreting responses within the overall Jungian frame of reference. Specific areas to be examined include,

1. pragmatic schema,
2. Rorschach experience,
3. laws governing the Rorschach process,
4. archetypal influences, and
5. Rorschach process quadrants.

A brief description of each of these follows.

Pragmatic Schema

McCully reminds us that Jungian analytical psychology addressed not only the pathological but also had a growth-oriented approach to human personality. Under the area of pragmatic schema, McCully has developed a conceptual framework of Jungian theory of understanding Rorschach responses. He identifies specially a set of concepts, namely,

Ego: Ego includes 'psychic elements that are in awareness at any given time' (McCully, 1971, p. 11). It is to be understood through persona. Relating ego to karma and *erlebinstypus*, McCully describes ego as something that observes, 'momentary manifestation of psychic processes in us' (ibid.).

Unconscious: 'The ego is like a coral reef, and the vast area that surrounds it represents the source, the unconscious, from which unknown material may wash up' (p. 12). It incorporates personal unconscious (similar to, but not identical with, Freudian id) and shadow.

Collective Unconscious: This contains things that exist in the culture and society of the individual. These are not traceable to the development of the person. As a result, there exists an element of mystery to collective unconscious. Its contents are archetypes. Myths, folklores, fairy tales, rituals, superstitions—all symbolize contents of the collective unconscious. Identifying archetypes in the Rorschach responses and de-coding the symbols representing them is one of the most important aspects of Rorschach analysis in McCully's system.

Self: Self is broader (may be also bigger) than ego. Ego facilitates in the discovery of self. In life's first half (up to age 50?), ego acts as an intermediary between the person and his/her environment. In the second half, post-50, self takes control. McCully observes that self develops in opposition to ego. 'If one extends one's contact with one's potentials that are not directly related to outer affairs and the concerns of the moment, one builds onto a psychic structure that emerges opposite to the ego. We call it the self' (McCully, 1971, p. 15).

Individuation: Through individuation, a person becomes aware of the self. In a way, self replaces ego. It seems, we start our life with ego (the process by which we become aware of what is going on around us including pre-Oedipal processes) and later on, as we grow and mature, we tend to become increasingly aware of our self: the bigger picture of our personality that relates to the world at large. The mask (persona) starts thinning out; shadow starts getting diluted. We start becoming more and more aware of ourselves. We move closer and closer to our real being. *Isthiti-pragya awasthaa* (the stage of cognition of self).

Let us digress a bit here and comment on this self-cognition stage at two levels: (*a*) conceptual, and (*b*) concrete.

At the conceptual level, we learn about it in the *Shrimad Bhagvat Geeta* (the Divine Song of dialogue between Lord Krishna and Arjun), one of the most erudite expositions of cognitive psychology.

In answer to one of the many questions from Arjun, What are the features of an *isthiti-pragya* person? How does he talk, sit and walk? says Lord Krishna: *Prajaahaati yadaa kaamaan, servaan Paarth manoegataan, Aatmannayvaatmana tushtha isthipragyaast-dochyatay* ('O Arjun! When a person becomes indifferent to all of the desires and wishes inside him, and is fully contented from his soul with his soul, that's when he realizes who he is; that's when he becomes *isthiti-pragya*') (*Bhagvat Geeta*, Chapter 2, Verse 55).

At the concrete level, we may illustrate self-awareness by recalling the story of Vilvamangal (Poddar and Goswami, 1939).

Vilvamangal was infatuated with a pretty prostitute, Chintamani. He would visit her regularly, religiously. One day, when his father died, the family was offering gifts and prayers to the gods of the dead (*pitra*). This involved performing specific rituals (*shraadh*). Vilvamangal was becoming restless. He was not able to visit Chintamani. He went through the ceremonies hurriedly. As soon as it was over, he rushed to her house. It was late at night, raining heavily and pitch dark. Chintamani lived across a river. Vilvamangal was obsessed. He had to visit her. He rushed out, but could not find any boatman to take him across. He decided to swim across the river in spate. He did so. Chintamani was fast asleep. He did not want to wake her up. He decided to climb the wall of the courtyard. He noticed a rope hanging along the wall. Holding it, he climbed up. The 'rope' was, in fact, a long, dark, poisonous snake. Vilvamangal did not notice the difference. He knocked on the door. Chintamani saw him, looked at him, all drenched and disheveled, and asked 'How did you get inside?' 'I got hold of that "rope"', replied Vilvamangal. Shocked and angry, Chintamani admonished Vilvamangal, 'You Fool! You swam through a flooded river on a dark night on the day of your father's *shraadh*, used that poisonous snake to climb the wall; you did all this to see me, a body of flesh, which is going to end up in the dust one day. You know what, if you had taken all that trouble to seek God, you would have found Him and thus, would have freed yourself from the painful cycle of birth—death—rebirth!' (Poddar and Goswami, 1939, p. 611).

An embarrassed and humiliated (perhaps also re-awakened) Vilvamangal immediately decided to punish himself for his infatuation with an earthling, Chintamani. He touched her feet, expressing his gratitude to her for awakening him. He left her house. Then, he picked up two sharp nail-like thorns. Telling himself that the eyes that had been 'blinded' to the point of disrespecting his father and getting infatuated with a human body which had but a short life had no business to see, he then pierced the thorns through both eyes and literally blinded himself.

Watching him stumbling and bumping against objects on the street, a little boy came up to him. He asked Vilvamangal to hold one end of a stick while he held the other end and said, 'Here, Baba [a common form of address in India for a helpless, saint-like, often also, elderly man] hold on to this stick. I will help you walk around'. And then, with the help of this little boy, Vilvamangal spent the rest of his life singing devotional songs in praise of the Lord. That little boy? He was God Himself who had assumed the form of a boy to help Vilvamangal!

Let us translate this story into the Jungian ego and self. With his ego, Vilvamangal was able to live his routine, daily life; he participated in his father's *shraadh*; met and got infatuated with Chintamani. With his self, he was able to experience a much bigger world. Ego is just a part of the self. Self is bigger, wider, more meaningful, and thus, more satisfying than ego.

Having described the Jungian concepts used by McCully and the idea of individuation at conceptual and concrete levels, we will add one more Jungian concept that McCully finds helpful in understanding personality through the Rorschach test: the anima and the animus.

Masculine and Feminine Principles: Anima and animus are two components of the same being. They, says McCully, determine our experiential modes. Masculine and feminine principles are not identical with the masculine and feminine psyche. Socially and culturally, males and females relate to their environment differently. However, it is a matter of relative dominance of both these principles within us. Our 'selves' have both these dimensions of experience. The concept of *ardh-naareeshwar* in Hindu mythology emphasizes the unitary complementarity of the masculine and feminine aspects of our selves.

According to McCully, 'As the only forms of human beings, men and women have a great collective archetypal heritage together as one . . . sexes strive for union physically, and psychically too . . .' (1971, pp. 16–17).

To recap, the first component in McCully's system of coding Rorschach responses, namely, pragmatic schema, describes the Jungian concepts that are helpful in looking at the responses. We listed and described six of these (ego, unconscious, collective unconscious, self, individuation and masculine and feminine principles). We now move on to the next category of coding responses, that is, the Rorschach experience.

Rorschach Experience

What happens to a testee when he/she is shown Rorschach cards? Often, a spontaneous comment comes out, 'Oh, my God!'. 'What are these?' 'You mean, these blots signify something?' 'I'm supposed to tell you what these are?' and so on. *Something* happens to the subject when he/she sees the cards. This *something* is the Rorschach experience.

Phenomenologically, Rorschach cards are *experienced* differently by each subject. Spontaneous comments provide a glimpse of this experience, more like a mask for the underlying emotions: anxiety, fear, anger, depression. At another level, the specific responses provide further insights into the cognitive imagery that may be arousing specific emotions. At yet another level, there may be the contents of the collective unconscious (archetypes) associated with the percepts.

Rorschach responses are symbols. They represent something, namely, the contents of our psyche (both individual psyche as well as collective psyche). Percepts mean something to the subject. Decoding personal and cultural archetypal symbolism in the percepts provides insights into the forces that may have been at work in forming the percepts.

Understanding the Rorschach experience requires 'fitting' the percepts into the subject's individual and collective psyche. There are certain identifiable processes influencing this experience. McCully calls them laws of Rorschach experience. These are different from the laws of logic that direct our normal thinking. The Rorschach experience is more akin to dreams than the real world. It is not an *as if* kind of experience. Things look and feel real in dreams. It is only after you wake up that you realize they were fantasy. Like reality, fantasy too has its logic. Laws of Rorschach experience illustrate this logic.

Laws Governing Rorschach Experience

Law of Excluded Awareness: We may perceive a symbol but may not have an awareness of its meaning, e.g., the kind of experience an Indian and a non-Indian may have looking at a picture of Goddess Kaali. The Indian's psyche may be activated by archetypal sources of sustenance, destruction and killing of the demon *Mahishaasur*. For the non-Indian, it is a picture of an Indian goddess.

Law of Altered Visual Perception: Perceptual distortion is a subjective phenomenon. When the same inkblot is seen differently by different people, it may often be caused by archetypal forces. Subjective consciousness determines perception. Seeing a child being split into two halves and shared by two parents in Card I is an example of perceptual distortion influenced by subjective consciousness. The percept seemingly is activated by the archetypal sources of parental power.

Law of Symbol Formation: The Rorschach experience provides a unique opportunity for symbol formation. Ego is somewhat restricted by the features of the Rorschach cards but at the same time there exists enough ambiguity to facilitate flights of fantasy. The synaptic points of fantasy and reality, unique in each case, evolve into ideographic symbols which are meaningful in the context of subjective consciousness, e.g., 'two owls shaking hands' (Card VIII); 'a strong structure crumbling' (Card IV); 'Communist revolution' (Card X).

Law of Psychic Correspondence: Often, features of the inkblots may not match the objects seen. There may not be a physical correspondence between what is realistically possible and what is perceived. It is an 'incorrect' perception. Not so in apperception. Guided by subjective consciousness, objects seen may not have physical correspondence, but there may be a psychic correspondence. There is something in the subjective psyche of the subjects which corresponds with the features of the inkblots and is articulated symbolically into 'owls shaking hands', 'strong structure crumbling', and 'Communist revolution'.

Psychic correspondence is usually guided by archetypes. Each Rorschach card has the potential to arouse archetypes, although it may or may not. All responses do not contain archetypal influences. It is, however, necessary to examine responses for archetypal influences.

Archetypal Influences
Archetypal sources appear in Rorschach responses according to these laws of altered perception. Whether we subscribe to the Freudian view that symbols represent repressed libidinal impulses or to the Jungian view that symbols reflect the collective unconscious, symbols do cushion the exposure of the unconscious from the conscious. They bypass cognition; symbols are perceived. Awareness of what they mean is not necessary. According to McCully,

'. . .one of the conditions peculiar to the emergence of a symbol is that of blocked off awareness while perception remains open, *so that symbols may appear*' (1971, p. 35, emphasis in original).

Archetypal influences in the various Rorschach cards have been described in great detail by McCully (1971). A few examples are given below.

Card I: Archetype of early man; cave; Paleolithic fertility.

Fifty-four year old male: *Taantric jaisaa lag rahaa hai* ('Looks like a Taantric' [a person who knows *Tantra*, the science of mystical words and procedures to influence events; a psychic]).

Seventy-five year old female: *Shamshaan kaa Bhairav; kaalaa, kaalaa* ('God Bhairav of cremation grounds; all black').

Card II: Archetype of opposite forces.

Fifty-nine year old female: *Yeh Bhagwaan kee moorti jaisee lag rahee hai; bahut sunder dikh rahha hai* ('This looks like an idol of god; very pretty').

Twenty year old male: *Doe saadhoo haanth say haanth milaa kar baithay huay hain* ('Two saints, holding their hands together, sitting').

Card III: Archetype of persona and shadow.

Fifty-two year old male: *Mujhay aisaa lag rahaa hai ki raastaa hai; beech main payer hain; stagnated water hai; road straight hai; baree door tuk jaa rahee hai* ('To me it looks like, there is a road; along the road are trees; there is stagnated water; it is a very long, straight road').

Thirty-six year old male: *Yeh chiriyon kaa human skeleton hai; yeh haanth main kuch uthaa rahaa hai; yeh do aadmiyon kaa skeleton hai, yaa dinosaur kaa avashaish hai* ('This is a human skeleton of birds; he is picking up something with his hands; this is a skeleton of two persons; this is the remains of a dinosaur').

Card IV: Archetype of patriarchal world.

Twenty-three year old female: *Bahut grand-saa Maseehaa; donoe haanth phailaye khara hai; kaafee powerful lug rahaa hai; baadaloen kay beech main say aayaa hai; human race koe bachaanay kay liyey yaa khatm karnay kay liyey; kuch daraawana hai* ('A, kind of, grand Christ; standing with his hands spread out; he has emerged from the midst of clouds to save the human race, or maybe, to destroy it; kind of, scary').

Twenty-five year old male: 'Two boots of ancient days'.

Card V: Archetype of myths

Fifty-nine year old female: *Ismay Shiv jee kaa jaaisaa dikh rahaa hai* ('In this, looks like the Lord Shiva').

Twenty-two year old female: *Doe jaanwar ek doosray koe jhaankna chaah rahay hain, laykin beech main unkoe koee hataa rahaa hai* ('Two animals trying to peek at each other, but there is someone in the middle who is trying to keep them away from each other').

Card VI: Archetype of authority; phallic worship.

Twenty-four year old female: Eruption leading to destruction.

Twenty-two year old female: *Hinduoen kay ghar main puaa bantaa hai; usee kaa design hai* ('This is like the design of *puaa* [sweet, round, deep-fried bread, usually made on auspicious festive occasions], made in homes of Hindus').

Card VII: Archetype of feminine containment; protection.

Fifty-nine year old female: *Ismay Bhagwati kaa roop dikh rahaa hai* ('I see the form of Bhagwati in this one').

Twenty-three year old female: *Ander-waalee profile say aik bahut sunder-saa burtan; antique-type* ('The inside part here looks like, a very pretty pot; kind of, antique').

Card VIII: Archetype of functioning through principles of masculinity and femininity.

Twenty-two year old female: *Aisay jeevan main kaee rung aatay hain, chalay jaatay hain* ('It's like, various colors of life, they come and then go away').

Twenty-three year old female: *Oopur-waalee cheez: koi pahaar, jis per doe aadmee baithay hain; puraanay zamaanay kay auzaar haanth main liyay huyay* ('This top part: Looks like, two persons are sitting atop this mountain; they are holding tools of ancient days').

Card IX: Archetype of karma (*erlebinstypus*); individuation; movement toward goals.

Twenty-four year old female: *Shivling* ('Phallic symbol of Lord Shiva').

Twenty-two year old male: A man being attacked by two pythons.

Card X: Archetype of source of life; *sansara (kaal-chakra?)*.

Twenty-two year old female: *Bahut colorful hai; jaisay Holi kisee nay khaylee hoe; deewaar per color hoe jaataa hai pichkaaree maarnay per, colors aa gaye hain; yay zaadaa baltee say maaraa ho gaa* (It's really colorful; like, someone celebrated Holi [Hindu festival celebrating victory of good over evil; people throw colored water, usually through big syringe-like objects; often, also pouring buckets of colored water on each other]; walls are splashed with colors from Holi-syringes; although, looks like this one was done more using buckets').

Twenty-four year old male: Saintly, *rishi jaisee* [like a sage] figure, who is praying.

The last element in McCully's system of coding (conceptualizing) Rorschach responses is placing responses in the Rorschach process quadrants.

Rorschach Process Quadrants

Instead of forcefully trying to frame Rorschach data within a rigid diagnostic system (which apparently is a by-product of our focus on pathology in understanding human personality), McCully recommends that we should use the Rorschach not only for understanding pathology but also for normal, growth-oriented aspects of human behavior. For this, he suggests placing Rorschach responses along two dimensions: (*a*) withdrawal–expansion (Axis A–B), and (*b*) conscious–unconscious (Axis C–D).

The horizontal axis A–B, the vertical axis C–D and the corresponding quadrants provide a framework for conceptualizing the nature and extent of normalcy and pathology in Rorschach responses. Formal scores are an important way of understanding relationships between various areas and levels of personality (e.g., what was apperceived on which parts of the inkblots and what features of the blots contributed towards developing that percept). Equally (maybe more) important is to have a grasp of the connections between these various percepts. Says McCully (1971, p. 169) '. . .process is what links happenings, and neither scores nor content alone provides us with a sufficient grasp of them'.

Rorschach process analysis involves looking at the responses and estimating their best location in the quadrants of the psychic processes, namely, Axis A–B (withdrawal–expansion) indicating extent of adaptiveness (something similar to pure color determined responses versus the responses in which emotions have been modulated by use of form—C:CF + FC) and Axis C–D (conscious–unconscious) which reflects influence of psychic processes involving the level of awareness on the part of the subject.

The last item in the format for presenting McCully's system before presenting illustrative protocols is personality theory.

Personality Theory

The theory of personality underlying McCully's system is to a great extent based on Jungian thought and philosophy. As described in the preceding section, McCully has focused on the Jungian concept of archetypes as an important source of influencing the formation of percepts in the Rorschach test. He has extended it further by conceptualizing psychic processes in terms of two specific dimensions: withdrawal–expansion and conscious–unconscious. In order to appreciate the complexity of McCully's approach, we need to place it in the context of Jungian theory.

Jungian Theory of Personality

Jungian theory of personality is contexed in his world-view. Developmentally he worked with Eugen Bleuler on schizophrenia, was closely associated with Freud, and worked in mental hospitals. Away from these concrete connections, he looked at man on a giant canvas of creation. He was able to conduct word association studies, and diagnose and treat mental disorders. On the other hand, he was also able to look at the concepts of culture, religion, mythology, faith and miracles. His theory of personality is more like a philosophy of personality rather than a bunch of cut-and-dried statements. We will attempt to summarize his views here in order to link them with McCully's system. Interested readers are encouraged to start with Joseph Campbell's (1971) excellent overview of the Jungian system of thought.

In an over-simplistic way, Jungian ideas may be described in five areas:

1. concept of man in the East and the West,
2. anatomy of psyche,
3. archetypes,
4. phenomenological self, and
5. literature and psychology.

Brief comments on each of these follow.

Concept of Man in the East and the West: Eastern man is intro-verted. The world outside of us is *maayaa*. For the West, whatever is here, is real. Mind is more important than matter for the East. The idea of *kaal-chakra* ('Wheel of Time') makes man as someone passing through this illusory world. The Eastern mind recognizes an Universal Mind. The extroverted Western mind discourages a person from recognizing an 'inner man'.

Anatomy of Psyche: Psyche helps us grasp our world, the world as we *experience* it. This is done through four processes: sensing, thinking, feeling and intuiting. Sensing brings stimuli in contact with our sense-organs. Objects are sensed. Thinking helps us recognize the object (perception, apperception). We name it. Feeling makes us like or dislike the object. Perceiving (guessing, apperceiving) possibilities in an object is intuiting.

Archetypes: Archetypes are primordial concepts of human experi-ences spanning thousands of years. They are not based on individual experiences. They are not person-specific; some of them may not even be culture-specific. The individual unconscious contains our personal experiences (complexes). The collective unconscious contains universal experiences (archetypes).

Phenomenological Self: Self incorporates ego. Self also includes persona, anima and animus. Ego is a connector. It links us with reality. Persona presents our self to the outside world. It is a sublimated, socialized, adaptive and modulated part of our self. The self also has bi-sexual features in it. Man's self has a feminine component (anima). A woman's self has a masculine component (animus).

Literature and Psychology: Psychological processes generating a work of art and neurosis are similar. An artist and a neurotic both undergo the same kinds of environmental experiences: father–mother complex, myths, rituals, folklores, fairy tales, etc. Individual neurotics may be influenced more by one or other of these experi-ences. The same is true of artists, poets and authors.

Underlying the creative process is a primordial idea. Products of creativity (paintings, poems, plays) represent these primordial, archetypal thoughts. The creative process, says Jung, is a 'living thing implanted in the human psyche . . . this living thing is an *autonomous complex*' (Jung, cited in Campbell, 1971, p. 313, emphasis in original).

In summary then:

1. Life is a wandering journey.
2. The purpose of life is to seek individuation; becoming aware of one's self—self-awareness. Self is everything that we may or may not be aware of. Specifically, self includes,

   (*i*) persona (mask); the part that others see,
   (*ii*) shadow (the 'real hidden' self),
   (*iii*) impulses (contents of individual unconscious),
   (*iv*) archetypes (contents of the collective unconscious),
   (*v*) anima (femininity), and
   (*vi*) animus (masculinity).

Individuation, in other words, is seeking self-hood.

3. Seeking self-hood means becoming aware of one's persona, shadow, impulses, archetypes, anima and animus. This aware-ness would result in eliminating the boundaries between (*a*) persona–shadow, (*b*) impulses–archetypes, and (*c*) anima–animus.
4. There are two ways in which a person seeks this self-awareness: (*a*) attitudes, and (*b*) functions. Attitudes determine the direc-tion of psychic energy. Functions, on the other hand, determine the concrete ways in which a person relates to the world.
5. There are two types of attitudes: an introverted attitude and an extroverted attitude—*introversion* and *extroversion* respectively.

   Introversion implies that

   (*i*) psychic energy is turned inwards,
   (*ii*) interest moves *away from* objects, and
   (*iii*) persons, *not objects*, are important.

   Extroversion implies that

   (*i*) psychic energy is turned outwards,
   (*ii*) interest moves *towards objects*, and
   (*iii*) objects, *not self*, are important.

The attitude of extroversion may be active or passive. In an *active extroverted attitude*, a person attends more to the object than to him/herself. In a *passive extroverted attitude*, a person does not consciously attend to objects; on the other hand, he/she feels *attracted* towards the objects.

6. There are two types of functions: (*a*) *rational* functions, and (*b*) *irrational* functions. Rational functions are of two types: *thinking* and *feeling*. Irrational functions also are of two types: *sensation* and *intuition*.

7. Thus, a person seeks *individuation* through the methods of:

    1. attitudes (namely, introversion or extroversion; in extroversion, a person's attitude may be active or passive), and
    2. functions (namely, rational, that is, thinking and feeling; and irrational, that is, sensation and intuition).

    Through these attitudes and functions, we seek individuation (namely, becoming aware of our persona, shadow, impulses, archetypes, anima and animus).

8. In *jeevan yaatra* ('life's journey'), up to the age of 40, if we are predominantly introverted in our attitude, we tend to use the function of thinking more than the function of feeling. Or, as an alternative, we may use the function of sensation more than the function of intuition.

    On the other hand, we may have an attitude of extroversion. In that case, we may use the function of feeling more than the function of thinking, or the other way round. Similarly, we may use either *sensation* or *intuition* as primary or secondary.

    That is, we have various options—introverted attitude with thinking/feeling and sensation/intuition functions, or extroverted attitude with thinking/feeling and sensation/intuition functions.

9. Developmentally, our attitude reverses after we turn 40. A person who was dominantly introversive up to the age of 40 may reverse to being an *extroverted* personality in his/her post-40 life. Similarly, a pre-40 *extroverted* personality could become a predominantly *introverted* personality after attaining the age of 40.

Essentially, the Jungian theory of personality focuses on the self as the critical concept. When a person becomes aware of him/herself, ego is no longer the integrating concept. Instead, it is self. Self-awareness is somewhat similar to Maslow's term self-actualization. Becoming aware of one's self is an ongoing process. You never become aware of yourself. With every effort (e.g., meditation; prayer; learning from and listening to saints, priests, *mullahs, fakeers, saadhoos* and *mahaatmaas*) you get one step closer to the goal of self-awareness. You never attain complete self-awareness though. If you did, you would become the Being. You keep trying to figure out answers to that age-old question: *Who am I?*

All religious systems address this question. In Hindu philosophy, 'Who am I?' is answered with, *You are That.* And what is *that*? The Sun? Moon? Thunder? River? Mountain? Fire? *Neti. Neti* ('No'. 'No'). You are not this, not that. You are Absolute Truth. And what is Absolute Truth? It is not this, it is not that. It is not any object in particular. It is the Ultimate: *Prakrati* ('Nature').

On a more mundane level, our attempt to answer these questions (Who am I? Who is he/she? What is love? What is death? etc.) involves use of similes and metaphors. 'I am God' (*Uham Brhamaasmi*), 'You are my life' (*Tum mairi jaan hoe*), 'Life is an exciting journey' (*Zindgee ik safar hai suhaanaa*).

The key concept in McCully's way of using Jungian thought for understanding a person through the Rorschach is deciphering the symbols used for apperceiving his/her world of objects. Often, these symbols can be traced back to archetypal sources in the collective unconscious. Two points need to be emphasized in this context:

1. The Rorschach process illustrates creativity. The subject is asked to 'create' an object out of a set of ambiguous inkblots. 'What might this be?' structures the situation by having him/her figure out what those inkblots could be. Yet, the freedom implied in the instructions has the potential to stir up culturally, historically developed images (archetypes).

2. In some subjects, the cards may arouse primordial symbols. In others, they may not. It is important to know whether a response could have formed out of archetypal imagery; if so, what kinds of insights does it provide into the subject's psyche? It helps us understand how the process of individuation is operationalized in the subject in terms of sensing and thinking, and feeling and intuiting.

Following this very, very brief overview of McCully's system placed against the broad Jungian theory of personality, we may now articulate the steps involved in looking at a Rorschach protocol using McCully's approach. Essentially, there are three steps:

1. identifying archetypal influences,

2. placing responses in the Rorschach process quadrants, and
3. describing the subject's personality in terms of the pragmatic schema.

A few lines about each of these three steps follow.

Identifying Archetypal Influences Using the Framework of the Laws of Rorschach Experience: As a general guiding principle, there is a high possibility that if the subject gives an unusual response, it was perhaps influenced by archetypal forces. For example, 'Foreign forces attacking a helpless girl' (Card I); 'Some kind of crime; just a crime' (Card II); or 'Two roads to nowhere, lead to nowhere' (Card IV).

In identifying archetypal influences, we may also want to look for the laws of Rorschach experience at work, e.g., laws of excluded awareness, altered visual perception, symbol formation and psychic correspondence.

Placing Responses in the Rorschach Process Quadrants: Responses indicating archetypal influences are placed along the Axis A–B (withdrawal at one end and expansion at the other) and Axis C–D (conscious at one end and unconscious at the other). Axis A–B (horizontal) indicates movement away from environment at the left-hand-side (withdrawal) and movement towards environment (expansion) at the right-hand end. Axis C–D (vertical) indicates the level of awareness on the part of the subject: unconscious (at the bottom-end) and conscious (at the top-end). Thus, Quadrant AC would have responses indicating conscious, withdrawal; Quadrant AD suggests withdrawal operating at the unconscious level. Responses indicating expansion at the conscious level would be placed in Quadrant CD, while those suggesting expansion at the unconscious level go in Quadrant BD.

As may be expected, laws of symbol formation are at work in the Rorschach process quadrants. The symbols are more likely to be archetypal in source if the response is unusual, original and ideographic, than if responses are 'normal' and mundane.

Following these two steps of (*a*) identifying archetypal influences, and (*b*) placing responses in the Rorschach process quadrants, we move on to the third and final step of articulating the subject's personality in terms of the pragmatic schema.

Pragmatic Schema: This is the toughest part in McCully's system. What it means is to translate the subject's personality in terms of the Jungian concept of individuation. At this stage, we examine responses and infer the nature and extent to which the subject is able to evolve his/her self-awareness. The goal here is to observe how far and how much has the subject been able to reduce and/ or eliminate the barriers between (*a*) persona and shadow, and (*b*) anima and animus. It is through reducing the split between what he/she *looks like on the surface* (persona) and what he/she is *really like deep down* (shadow) on the one hand, and between the way he/she feels about femininity (anima) and about masculinity (animus), on the other, that we are able to guess his/her growth along the dimension of individuation.

An important thing to remember here in the context of examining individuation is the fact that there is a developmental sequence in the 10 Rorschach cards. McCully states the first seven cards are more critical than the last three in understanding personality: '. . .there is some kind of psychological progression connected with the succession of the Rorschach plates . . . they may correspond in a rough way to the stages Jung described as individuation' (McCully, 1971, p. 145). In fact, Cards VIII, IX and X, in a way, recapitulate the earlier Cards I through VII. 'The last three plates', observes McCully, 'may offer no more than a summary, or additional information about the psychology of the subject which has already been suggested' (ibid., p. 146).

Having described the three-step coding and interpretation process in McCully's (Jungian) Archetypal Approach, we will illustrate it by two protocols—a twenty-two year old Indian female, Anu; and a thirty year old Indian *hijra*, Sharda.

Writing the Test Report
In line with his theoretical framework, the Rorschach test report describes the nature and extent of archetypal influences in the subject's personality and the extent of individuation achieved by the subject.

SECTION II: ILLUSTRATIVE PROTOCOLS

Protocol 1: Anu
Card I, Response 1: Bat.

Shareer: beech-waalaa hissaa; punkh phailay huay hain ('The middle part; spread wings').

Card I, Response 2: Girl in the center; conflicting thing; girl caught between clouds or trying to rise through these wings; caught between two opposing things.

Sir aisay lug ruhaa hai; maang bhee hai; two plaits; long skirt yaa frock pahnay huay hai ('Looks like her head; there's parting in the hair; two braids; she has a long skirt or a dress on').

Card I, Response 3: Giants or may be clouds: *giants iskoe kheench ruhay hain* ('giants are pulling her'); the girl is caught helplessly between them.

Profile say giants lug ruhay hain; koi unearthly figure hai; vaisay, clouds ke tureh bhee lug ruhay hain; yey giants larkee koe upnee turuf kheench ruhay hain; ek upnee turuf, doosera upnee turuf ('The profiles look like those of giants; some kind of unearthly figures; although, in a way, they also look like clouds; the giants are pulling the girl towards them; one in one direction, the other in opposite direction').

Card II, Response 4: *Doe aadmee baithay hain; ek aadmee nay yuun haanth kiyaa hai; game saa hoe rahaa hai* ('Two men sitting; one has his hands up; a kind of, game is going on').

Ek aadmee hai; ooper red uskaa sir hai; neechay knees bent hain, aur uskay pair hain; punjaa laraa ruhay hai; ek haanth say doosraa haanth roekay hai; saamnay table hogaa; jaisay, 'Shatranj kay Khilaaree' film main aamnay-saamnay baith kay khailtay hain ('Here is a man; this up red here is his head; bent knees and these are his legs; they are arm-wrestling; one hand holding off the other; may be, a table in front; like, they sit opposite each other and play chess in the film *Shatranj kay Khilaaree* ["Chess Players"]').

Card III, Response 5: *Yay doe cheezain juree hain: iskoe doe loeg mil ker alug ker ruhay hain* ('These two things are joined together; two persons are trying to separate them').

Aadmee mil kar kuch kaam kar rahay hain; Hammer throw main jis discus kaa upyog kiyaa jaata hai, woh jur gayaa hai; forcefully alug kar rahay hain ('Two men are doing something; the discus used in discus throw is stuck; they are trying to pull it apart, forcefully')

Card III, Response 6: Butterfly; *shaayad butterfly hee hai* ('Butterfly; maybe, it indeed is a butterfly').

Doe pankh phailay huay hain ('Two widespread wings').

Card III, Response 7: *Yey cheez kuch signify kar rahee hai; putaa naheen chal raha hai; shaayed larkiyaan frock pahnay hain* ('This thing here signifies something; I cannot figure it out; maybe, the girls have a dress on').

Doe. larkiyaan hain joe sir jhukaaye kharee hain; dance kartay-kartay thuk gayee hain; shaayad yeh phaansee walaa posture hai ('Two girls standing with their heads down; got tired, dancing; looks like, it is the noose-pose').

Card III, Response 8: *Bahut bara darwaaza lug ruhaa hai; ander kuch mysterious hai; kuch oor kay jaa ruhaa hai; ander kee cheez samujh main naheen aa rahee hai* ('Looks like a huge door; there is something mysterious inside; something entering inside flying; I can't figure out the thing inside').

Card IV, Response 9: *Bahut grand-sa Maseehaa; dono haanth phailaye kharaa hai; kaafee powerful lug rahaa hai; baadlone kay beech main say aayaa hai; human race koe bachaanay yaa khatm karnay kay liyae; kuch daraawanaa hai* ('A big, grand Savior [Christ] with widespread arms; looks quite powerful; has emerged out of the clouds; maybe, to save or destroy the human race; kind of, scary').

Sar hai; haanth phailaye huyay hai; neechay baadal hai; aur yeh baddlone main say urtaa hua aa ruhaa hai; baadloen main say avatarit hoe ruhaa hai; per baadal as such dikhayee naheen day ruhay hai ('This is the head; widespread arms; clouds down below; and he is emerging, flying, out of the clouds; however, the clouds, per se, are not visible').

Card IV, Response 10: *Candle-stand main candle lugee huyee hai* ('Candle in the candle-stand').

Ooper-waalaa bhaag candle kee aakrti kaa hai ('The upper part is shaped like a candle').

Card V, Response 11: *Chimgaadar; achchee chiriyaa dikhnee chaahiay; per lug naheen ruhaa hai* ('Bat; should look like a nice bird, but it doesn't').

Punkh phailay huyay; yuun pair, sir, kaan; lug ruhaa hai ur ruhaa hai ('Has got its wings spread; legs, head, ears; looks like, it is flying').

Card V, Response 12: *Doe baadal achaanuk say takraa gaye hain* ('Two clouds; suddenly crashed into each other').

Yey doe baadal hain joe forcefully aa ker takraa gaye hain, isee kaaran kuch oooper hain, kuch neechay; itnee density nahee rah gayee hai ('These two clouds here; crashed into each other force-fully; that is why, some parts are up here and some down below; there is a loss in density').

Card V, Response 13: *Bone-structure; jaisay accident say hoe jaataa hai* ('Bone-structure; something you get as a result of accidents').

Accident kay baad pair toot gayaa hai; ghutnay kay neechay waala hissa hai ('There's a broken leg following an accident; the part below the knees').

Card V, Response 14: *Bull-fighting; bhee kah saktay hain* ('We may also call it, bull-fight').

Doe bulls hain; hump can be seen; structure say lug ruhaa hai; dono takraa ruhay hain; gulay kay neechay kaa hissa bhee aisaa hai; aur unkay pair bhee ('There are two bulls; you could see their humps; structures are like those of bulls; both hitting each other; indicated by the part below the neck and also, legs').

Card VI, Response 15: *Divine figure; fairy punkh phailaaye kharee hai; base say; shoot up ker kay gayee hai* ('Divine figure; a fairy standing with her widespread wings; she has shot [flown] up from the base').

Fairy, light shade waalay bhaag main dikh ruhee hai; punkh phailaye huye say divine lug ruhee hai; yahaan [base] say uth ker aayee hai; continuity-see lug ruhee hai ('Looks like a fairy due to this lightly shaded part; kind of, looks divine because of the wing spread; she climbed up from here [base]; kind of, gives an impression of continuity').

Card VI, Response 16: *Iskay ander seeds lug ruhay hain* ('These inside, look like, seeds').

Doe seeds; germinate kartay huye alug-alug hoe gayee hain ('Two seeds; gotten separated while germinating').

Card VI, Response 17: *Do polar bears yaa Santa Claus; opposite direction main jaa ruhay hain yaa dance ker ruhay hain* ('Two polar bears or Santa Claus; either they are going in opposite directions or may be, dancing').

Haanth phailay hain; dance ker ruhay hain yaa bhaag ruhay hain; Santa Claus bhee hoe saktaa hai kyon ki side-face say beard aur annya features dikhaee day ruhaa hai ('Widespread hands; dancing or may be running away; could also be Santa Claus because you may see beard from the side-view and some other facial features').

ANU

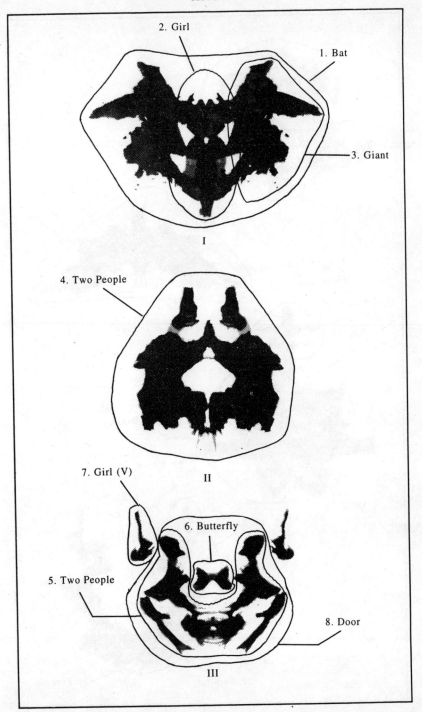

2. Girl

1. Bat

3. Giant

I

4. Two People

II

7. Girl (V)

6. Butterfly

5. Two People

8. Door

III

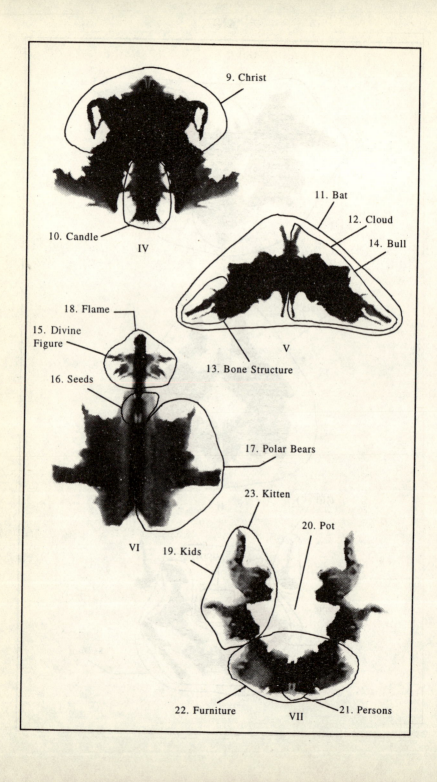

9. Christ

10. Candle

IV

11. Bat

12. Cloud

14. Bull

13. Bone Structure

V

18. Flame

15. Divine Figure

16. Seeds

17. Polar Bears

VI

23. Kitten

20. Pot

19. Kids

22. Furniture

21. Persons

VII

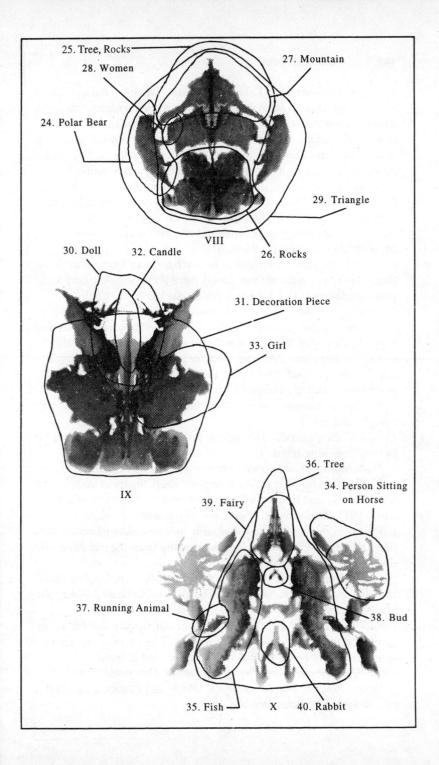

25. Tree, Rocks
28. Women
27. Mountain
24. Polar Bear
29. Triangle
VIII
30. Doll
32. Candle
31. Decoration Piece
33. Girl
26. Rocks
IX
36. Tree
34. Person Sitting on Horse
39. Fairy
37. Running Animal
38. Bud
35. Fish
X
40. Rabbit

Card VI, Response 18: *Yahaan per flame jul ruhee hai aur inkee intensity say dhuaan jaa ruhaa hai; flames zyaadaa hai aur dheeray-dheeray kum hoe ruhee hai; laykin dhuaan zyaadaa hai; volcano nahee kah suktay hain* ('This here is a flame; smoke going up because of its intensity; intense flame; gradually fading away; however, smoke is pretty thick; no, can't call it a volcano').

Flame kee intensity dheeray-dheeray kum hoe ruhee hai aur dhuaan jaa ker shape banaa ruhaa hai; iskee continuation main dhuaan lug ruhaa hai ('Flame is gradually losing its intensity and there is smoke going up converting form into shapes; smoke, kind of, is in continuation [to flame])'.

Card VII, Response 19: *Doe cute say bachchay khel ruhay hain; dance ker ruhay hain; mustee kertay huye* ('Two cute-looking kids; playing; dancing; just having a good time').

Dress, top pahnay huye hain; haanth niklay huye hain; peechay ghoom ker ek doosray koe daykh ruhay hain ('They have skirts and tops on; extended hands; turned around, looking at each other').

Card VII, Response 20: *Ander waalee profile say ek bahut sunder-saa burtun; antique type* ('The inside profile looks like a really pretty pot; kind of, antique').

Buraa-saa burtun; shape aisaa hai ('Kind of, huge pot; it's shaped like one').

Card VII, Response 21: *Do aadmee haanth milaa ruhay hain* ('Two persons, shaking hands').

Donoen kay sir aur pooraa shareer dikhaee day ruhaa hai; kaala pair bhee peechay hai ('You could see their heads as well as the whole body; and there is also a black tree in the background').

Card VII, Response 22: *Furniture lug ruhaa hai; gaddee, pair; puraanay zamaanay kaa; aaj-kul aisay naheen miltay* ('Looks like a piece of furniture; cushion, legs; something from the old days; you don't get them anymore').

Ooper kaa bhaag headrest lug ruhaa hai aur neechay kaa bhaag sofa kay paaye lug ruhay hain ('The part up here looks like, the headrest; the parts down here look like legs of the sofa').

Card VII, Response 23: *Ooper koi cheez hai aur yey doe billee kay bachchay uchul ker khail ruhay hain* ('This up here, looks like some thing and these kittens are jumping and playing').

Card VIII, Response 24: *Doe polar bear* ('Two polar bears').

Payr, chehraa, shareer, poonch, shape hai ('Legs, face, body, tail; shaped like polar bears').

Card VIII, Response 25: Pair dikhaai day ruhay hain; neechay rocks hain ('I see trees; down below are rocks').

Pair aur rocks; shape hain, aur rung bhee ('Tree and rocks; it is the shape; also, colors').

Card VIII, Response 26: Rocks bhee hain; something, kind of, soft; shape say rough per texture say soft ('Also rocks; something, kind of, soft; shape makes it look rough but it has a soft texture').

Neechay walaa bhaag hai; rocks; shape oobur-khaabur saa bunaa hai; pink kee wajah say softness lug ruhaa hai ('The part down below, rocks; uneven surface; pink makes it look soft').

Card VIII, Response 27: Ooper-waalee cheez: koi pahaar jis per doe aadmee baithay hoen; puraanay zamaanay kay auzaar haanth main liye huay hain ('The top part here, looks like some kind of mountain; two men sitting on top; they are holding in their hands, some implements, of historical times').

Aadmee kay payr dikhaai day ruhay hain aur auzaar haanth main hain; chultay-chultay sustaanay kay liye baithay hain; auzaar apnay bachaav kay liye hain ('You may see the legs of men; they are holding the tools in their hands; like, they got tired after a long walk; they are taking a brief rest; they have got the tools for their protection').

Card VIII, Response 28: Doe aurat bhee lug ruhee hai ('Also, looks like two women').

Ghutnay moer ker dono baithay hain ('Both are sitting down, with knees bent').

Card VIII, Response 29: Total jaisa triangle lug ruhaa hai; more, chiriyaa; haree-bharee plain hai joe ki toot ruhaa hai, prithvee summit kaa usar hai ('The whole thing looks like a triangle; peacocks, birds; green landscape; kind of, crumbling down as a result of earth summit').

Yay plain beech say crack hoe ruhaa hai; pooraa green-waalaa portion hai ('This plain is cracking down in the center; this whole green portion').

Card IX, Response 30: Mushqil-saa hai ('Kind of, difficult'). *Beech main Bandura kaa doll lug ruhaa hai* ('Looks like, Bandura's [Albert Bandura, the experimental psychologist] doll here in the center').

Bandura nay apnay experiments main isee turah kay dolls use kiyay thay: eyes, shape iskee turah round-saa hai; overall shape kay kaaran ('Bandura had used the same kind of dolls in his experiments;

the eyes and shape were round, like this one; overall because of the shape').

Card IX, Response 31: *Pink color kaa base, decoration piece hai; abstract-saa; pink aur green kaa combination achchaa hai* ('This pink colored base; it's a decoration piece; kind of, abstract; color combination of pink and green looks good').

Pink base hai is decoration piece main; pink aur green kaa combination hai; symmetrical hai; achchaa-saa hai ('Pink is the base in this decoration piece; a combination of pink and green; symmetrical; kind of, pretty').

Card IX, Response 32: *Church kee koi candle beech main lug ruhee hai* ('Looks like a church candle, here in the middle').

Candle hai; hulkaa-saa flame hai ('This is the candle; kind of, light flame').

Card IX, Response 33: *Green color: lurkiaan daur ruhee hain, yaa, doe aadmee car main, opposite direction say ek doosray koe chase ker ruhay hain* ('Green color: girls running, or two men chasing each other in a car from opposite direction').

Is jugah per car lug ruhaa hai; ek yaa opposite direction main jaa ruhay hain ('This here, looks like a car; they are going either in the same or opposite direction').

Card X, Response 34: *Is blue bhaag main lugaa ki koi ghoray per baithaa hai; first glance per aisaa lugaa* ('In this blue part, at a first glance, looks like, someone sitting on a horse').

Ghoray per koi baithaa hai: payr, haanth main kuch liye huye hai ('Someone sitting on a horse; carrying something in legs, and hands').

Card X, Response 35: *Pink-waalaa bhaag: muchlee-type kee cheez yaa jaisay baadlone main bun jaatay hain; doe larkiyaan* ('This pink part here: a fish-like object; the way shapes are formed in clouds; two girls').

Muchlee kaa shape yaa, larkiyon kaa chehraa ('Shape of a fish or faces of girls').

Card X, Response 36: *Ooper koi pair hai; nayaa-saa per bahut fragile naheen; keerayn hain joe iskee jaron koe khaa ruhee hain; khatm ker ruhay hain* ('Up here, there is some kind of tree; kind of new, yet, not fragile; there are insects eating off its roots; destroying it').

Pair aur pattiyaan hain; keeray bugal main ('This is a tree, and these are its leaves; the bugs are on the sides').

Card X, Response 37: *Bhaagta huaa jaanwar* ('Running animal').
Pair aagay peechay dikhaai day ruhay hain; running ('You can see
the legs, in front and back; running').

Card X, Response 38: *Koobsoorut-saa bud yaa patti; alug hoe
gayee hai yaa gir gayay hain* ('Kind of, pretty bud or leaves; has
been separated or fallen down').

*Bud alug hoe gayaa hai; iskay tukray alug paray hain; ooper kaa
seed dikhayee day ruhaa hai; doe pattiyan hain per gir gayee hain*
('The bud is off the leaves; its pieces are lying away from it; you
can see the top seed; there are two leaves, they have, however,
fallen down').

Card X, Response 39: *Baadal per paree yey sub cheez apnee peeth
per lay ker aa ruhee hai* ('A fairy is bringing down all these objects
carrying on her back').

*Paree joe haanth main aagay-waalee blue cheezain, dono koe lay
ker aa ruhee hai; paree kee slender-see body hai; punkh chipkay hain*
('Fairy is bringing these two blue things down; her body is, kind of,
slender; wings are stuck on the back').

Card X, Response 40: *Khurgoesh-jaisaa lug ruhaa hai* ('Looks,
kind of, like a rabbit').

Khurgoesh; cartoon kee turah ('Rabbit; like in a cartoon').

Anu gave the following two additional responses during the inquiry
phase.

Muchlee: shape, ooper chehraa hai ('Fish, shape; up here is the
face').

Moer: punkh, baray feathers; shareer muree hui position main
('Peacock; feathers; big feathers; body is in a bent-down position').

Coding and Interpreting Anu's Protocol
As mentioned earlier, we will look at Anu's protocol in terms of
(*a*) identifying archetypal influences, (*b*) placing responses into the
Rorschach process quadrants, and (*c*) pragmatic schema. But first,
a few general comments.

Anu is struggling to individuate. The boundaries between persona
and shadow and also between anima and animus are still strong.
Her persona is in the formation stage. Shadow is stronger than
persona. A tug-of-war is on between them. A similar tension is
visible between her femininity (anima) and masculinity (animus).
She appears to be more under the influence of collective unconscious

(archetypes) than individual unconscious (impulses). Developmentally, Anu is a 'normal', young adult.

Identifying Archetypal Influences: There are many responses indicating archetypal influences in Anu's personality. We may point out that more than one archetype may be involved in a response. Also, many responses may indicate only one archetype. A few examples are given here.

1. Archetype of Opposites:
   Response 2: Girl in the center; conflicting thing; girl caught between clouds, or trying to rise through these wings; caught between two opposing things.
   Response 12: Two clouds; suddenly crashing into each other.
   Response 14: Bull-fighting.

2. Archetype of God/Goddess:
   Response 9: A big, grand savior (Christ); with widespread arms; looks quite powerful; has emerged out of clouds; maybe, to save or destroy human race; kind of, scary.
   Response 15: Divine figure; a fairy standing with her widespread wings; she has shot up (flown) from the base.
   Response 39: A fairy is bringing down all these objects carrying on her back.

3. Archetype of Mystery:
   Response 8: Looks like a huge door; there is something mysterious inside; something entering inside flying; I can't figure out the thing inside.

4. Archetype of Childhood:
   Response 19: Two cute looking kids; playing, dancing; just having good time.
   Response 30: Looks like Bandura's doll here in the center.

5. Archetype of Femininity (anima):
   Response 2: Girl in the center . . . (inquiry), there is parting in the hair; two braids; she has a long skirt or dress on.
   Response 11: Bat; should look like a nice bird, but it doesn't.
   Response 15: . . .a fairy standing with her widespread wings, (inquiry) looks divine because of the wing-spread.
   Response 19: Two cute looking kids; playing; dancing; just having good time.

Response 20: The inside profile looks like a really pretty pot; kind of antique; (inquiry) huge pot.

Response 30: Looks like, Bandura's doll here in the center.

6. Archetype of Masculinity (animus):
   Response 3: Giants . . . the girl is caught helplessly between them.
   Response 9: A grand big savior (Christ) with widespread arms; looks quite powerful; has emerged out of clouds; maybe, to save or destroy human race.
   Response 14: Bull-fighting.

On the basis of the archetypal material in her responses, it seems Anu is fairly intensely under the grip of archetypal forces. There is a lot of collective unconscious in her personality. She is not able to separate herself away from parental authority. Wanting to please both parents, she feels torn between the two (Response 1). She is wishing for some magical solution ('girl caught between clouds, or trying to rise through these wings . . . two braids . . .'). What comes to mind is the archetype of the damsel-in-distress. Also implied is the myth of Icarus (in Greek mythology, Icarus, the son of Daedalus, flew so high with his wings made of wax that when he reached near the sun, the wings melted and he fell down to his death).

The overpowering, ambivalent force of patriarchal power is evident in Response 9 ('A big grand savior [Christ] with widespread arms; looks quite powerful, has emerged out of the clouds; maybe, to save or destroy human race'). Inability to achieve a separate existence makes her identify with the human race which is vulnerable. This powerful, scary savior may end up saving the human race or may destroy it! In folklores and fairy tales, someone in trouble is eventually saved by a powerful person. The protector–destroyer dichotomy depicts the 'force' as someone who is expected to 'save' and may also go to the other extreme and destroy the person. Goddess Kaali is both protector as well as destroyer. The Hindu trilogy of Brahma, Vishnu and Mahesh depicts a three-in-one image—Brahma, the Creator; Vishnu, the Sustainer and Mahesh, the Destroyer.

At a more mundane level, this duality (savior–destroyer) has filtered down in romance and literature: *Maar daaloe mayree jaan* ('Come on my Life, kill me!'). This superficially funny-sounding paradox contains the archetype of opposites. Someone whom you love as much as your own life is being urged to kill you! At an equally intense level is the song from an Indian film *Jab Jab Phool Khile* released in the late sixties—*Naa, naa kurtay, pyaar tumhee say ker baithay; karnaa thaa inqaar, magur ikraar tumhee say her baithay* ('I kept on reminding myself not to love you, yet still, ended up loving you; I was supposed to say no; instead, I ended up saying yes').

The duality of good and evil is universal in most of cultures. Anu's response of seeing the Savior as someone who may save the human race or may destroy it seems to be influenced by the archetype of God and of opposites.

Another influential archetype in Anu's responses seems to be of anima and animus. She is experiencing femininity as well as masculinity. However, the boundaries separating anima and animus appear to be in a primordial state. For example, ' . . .girl caught between two opposing things . . .she has a parting in her hair; two braids . . .has a long skirt or a dress on' (Response 2), 'These two things are joined together; two persons are trying to separate them' (Response 5), 'Butterfly; maybe, it indeed is a butterfly' (Response 6), 'Divine figure; a fairy standing with her widespread wings; she has shot [flown] up from the base' (Response 15), 'This inside profile looks like a really pretty pot; kind of antique' (Response 20), and 'Looks like, Bandura's doll' (Response 30). It seems as if she wants to experience femininity separately from masculinity, but is unable to detach herself from parental authority.

Placing Responses into Rorschach Process Quadrants: The four quadrants in which responses could be placed are:

1. Quadrant AC: Withdrawn–conscious.
2. Quadrant AD: Withdrawn–unconscious.
3. Quadrant CB: Expansion–conscious.
4. Quadrant CD: Expansion–unconscious.

In case of Anu, the responses may be placed as follows:

Response 1: Quadrant CB.
Response 2: Quadrant CB.
Response 3: Quadrant AD.
Response 4: Quadrant CB.

Response 5: Quadrant CD.
Response 6: Quadrant CB.
Response 7: Quadrant AC.
Response 8: Quadrant AD.
Response 9: Quadrant AD.
Response 10: Quadrant AD.
Response 11: Quadrant AD.
Response 12: Quadrant AD.
Response 13: Quadrant AC.
Response 14: Quadrant CB.
Response 15: Quadrant AD.
Response 16: Quadrant AC.
Response 17: Quadrant AD.
Response 18: Quadrant CD.
Response 19: Quadrant CB.
Response 20: Quadrant AD.
Response 21: Quadrant CB.
Response 22: Quadrant AD.
Response 23: Quadrant AC.
Response 24: Quadrant AC.
Response 25: Quadrant AC.
Response 26: Quadrant AD.
Response 27: Quadrant CB.
Response 28: Quadrant AC.
Response 29: Quadrant AD.
Response 30: Quadrant CD.
Response 31: Quadrant CB.
Response 32: Quadrant AD.
Response 33: Quadrant CD.
Response 34: Quadrant CB.
Response 35: Quadrant AC.
Response 36: Quadrant AD.
Response 37: Quadrant AC.
Response 38: Quadrant CD.
Response 39: Quadrant CD.
Response 40: Quadrant AC.

Anu's processing of objects is more withdrawn and unconscious than expansive and conscious. She tends to move away from, rather than move towards, environment. That is, on the A–B axis (withdrawal–expansion), she is closer to the withdrawal-end than expansion-end of the continuum. On the C–D axis (conscious–unconscious), she appears to be functioning more at an unconscious, rather than conscious level, that is, Quadrant AD. Out of 40 responses, 14 (35 per cent) are in the AD quadrant. Among the remaining three quadrants, AC (withdrawn–conscious), CB (expansion–conscious) and CD (expansion–unconscious), Anu's responses are almost equally distributed: AC 9 (22.5 per cent), CB 9 (22.5 per cent) and CD 8 (20 per cent).

Based on the placement of her responses in the Rorschach process quadrants, Anu looks at her world more from an introverted perspective and at an unconscious level. She also processes her experiences in an expansive way and at a conscious level. However, her preferred mode seems to be one of unconscious withdrawal.

Having examined Anu's protocol in terms of archetypal influences and the Rorschach process analysis, we now move on to the third and final step in McCully's approach, namely, looking at her personality in terms of the pragmatic schema.

Pragmatic Schema: We have looked at the responses indicating archetypal sources. We also did a process analysis identifying the position of responses along two dimensions, namely, withdrawal from and expansion towards environment (Axis A–B), and the conscious and unconscious sources of the responses (Axis C–D). Process analysis was done by estimating the location of the responses in the quadrants (AC, AD, CD and CB). How do these two sets of data (archetypal effects and process analysis) then help us understand Anu in terms of the Jungian system, that is, self-awareness? How does she appear in terms of thinning/eliminating barriers between (*a*) persona and shadow, and (*b*) anima and animus. How much and how far has she moved towards the goal of individuation? Answers to these questions are sought in this third and final step, namely, articulating the personality profile within a pragmatic schema.

It appears that Anu is experiencing difficulty in separating her persona from her shadow. She is also not able to integrate her anima with her animus. We must stress that this does not mean that she is 'abnormal' or that she is exhibiting maladaptive responses. All that it means is that she is at a relatively, lower-end along the dimension of individuation. She is only twenty-three years old. In terms of life-experiences, she has a long way to go. We give here a few examples in support of our observation.

Persona and Shadow:

Response 2: A helpless girl is being pulled in two opposite directions (persona is pulling her in one direction; shadow, in the other).

Response 4: A negotiation is in progress between persona and shadow to decide who is more powerful ('Two men sitting; one has his hands up, a kind of, game is going on [inquiry] . . . they are arm-wrestling . . . like . . .play chess in the movie Chess Players').

Response 8: 'Looks like a huge door; there is something mysterious inside; something entering inside flying; I can't figure out the thing inside'—is significant. The term 'I' (persona) cannot figure out 'the thing inside' (shadow).

Response 11: She sees a bat (shadow), but is disappointed that it is not pretty (shadow). 'Bat; should look like a pretty bird; but it doesn't'.

Response 12: 'Two clouds [one being persona, the other, shadow] suddenly crashed into each other'.

Response 16: 'These inside, look like, seeds; [inquiry], two seeds gotten separated while germinating'. Apparently, the seeds of persona and shadow are separated while germinating. There is growth; however, it is in its nascent stages.

Response 18: 'This here is a flame [persona], smoke [shadow] going up because of its intensity; intense flame [strong personal], gradually fading away [persona giving in to shadow]; however, smoke is pretty thick [what else could persona do other than giving in]; no, can't call it a volcano'; [yes, shadow is strong but it is not going to overpower persona]; [inquiry] flame is gradually losing its intensity [persona becoming weak]; and there is smoke going up and converting form into shapes [shadow becoming more distinct and identifiable although, in many forms and shapes]; smoke is in continuation [shadow is an extension of persona].

Response 27: Two men (persona and shadow) are sitting atop a mountain, holding historical implements in their hands for protection and are taking a break to catch their breath. Interesting. Symbolizes constant battle between persona (ego, mask) are repressed, unconscious impulses and archetypes (shadow).

Response 30: Doll used in Bandura's experiments. A trial and error process in progress between cute, playful, doll-like persona on the one hand, and an awareness that although, it is a cute doll, it still is an experimental doll; implying, at the end of the experiment, it may be modified and changed or may even be shelved for record and/or later use. The shadow of experiment has overwhelmed the persona of doll.

Following these examples of the ensuing 'fight' between persona and shadow, let us look at the other critical element in self-awareness, namely, functioning of anima (femininity) and animus (masculinity).

Anima and Animus: Although, Anu is more influenced by anima than animus, she is still in the initial stages of development of experiencing anima and is trying to separate it from animus. Here are a few examples from her responses.

Response 6: 'Butterfly; maybe, it indeed is a butterfly; [inquiry] two widespread wings'. Delicate, feminine. Not sure, though. With wings spread, that is, apparently ready to take-off to explore the world outside.

Response 15: 'Divine figure; a fairy standing with her widespread wings . . . [connected with supernatural power]; she has shot up here from the base [archetype of parental authority] . . . kind of, gives an impression of continuity' [although she is standing on her own feet but still, she has come out of the base].

Response 19: 'Two cute-looking kids; playing, dancing; just having a good time'. Femininity–masculinity is experienced together in an innocent, playful way.

Response 26: 'Rocks . . . shape makes it look rough, but it has a soft texture'. As if, saying, I may look rough but deep down I am soft (feminine).

Response 31: 'This pink-colored base; it is a decoration piece; kind of, abstract; color combination of pink and green looks good'. She seems to be identifying with maternal power ('pink-colored base') and sees herself as a decoration piece (recall, 'two little kids playing', 'Bandura's doll'). She is part of her mother, evolved out of it, but still is not a separate entity.

Response 32: Church candle; lighted, but a faint flame. She feels firmly rooted in the supernatural ('church, candle'), but is also weak ('faint flame'). As if, although soft and gentle (femininity), she still feels fragile; willing, yet unable to provide nurturance: weak flame (recall 'The inside profile looks like a really pretty pot; kind of, antique').

Response 38: 'Kind of, pretty bud or leaves; has been separated or fell down; [inquiry] the bud off the leaves; its pieces are lying away from it; you can see the top seed; there are two leaves; they have, however, fallen down'.

'Bud' (daughter) has separated from 'leaves' (parental figures) and its pieces are lying away from the bud (yearning for close-ness with mother?); the seed on the top is archetypal (roots of origin); there are two leaves which have fallen down (experiencing isolation from parents?).

Thus, in terms of anima and animus, Anu seems to be wanting to be both, at least at this point in her life. She is passing through a period where her need to be feminine is almost as strong as her need to be masculine. Culturally, it is significant; also normal. In India, a twenty-two year old girl in an urban setting is at a devel-opmental crossroad. The biggest goal for her parents is to be able to get her married. Following a series of complex search missions for bridegrooms, including dowry negotiations, climaxed by numerous ceremonies and rituals, she is often forced to jump from being a daughter to being a wife. However, the wifely role is often peripheral and also short-lived. She is expected to provide a son to the family. After a brief stint as a wife, she becomes a mother. And, in between, she is 'thrown' into the roles of daughter-in-law and sister-in-law. Thus, femininity and masculinity for a young, unmarried, Indian girl are pretty stressful processes to go through. Anu is no exception. Her struggle between anima and animus is marked by strong ambivalence. She seems to be seeking a com-promise by retaining her childhood. As we mentioned in the beginning of presenting her protocol, Anu is struggling to indi-viduate. Boundaries between persona and shadow are still relatively firm and shadow is stronger than persona; she is still under the influence of the collective unconscious.

Protocol 2: Sharda

Let us begin by understanding the concept of *hijra*. Literally, *hijra* in Arabic means 'separated'. The origin of this term goes back to the year 622 AD when the Muslim prophet, Hazrat Mohmmad with a view to avoiding opposition to his message in Mecca, moved to Medina. *Hijra* (spelled also as Hegira and Hejira) means escape or any journey made for safety.

Within the Jungian framework, *hijra* reflects a fusion of animus with anima. A male feels that he is in fact a female in the body of a male. A fusion is symbolized (climaxed) by undergoing a surgical procedure of castrating genitals. He is a male who has decided to live like a female either because of deformed genitals or because of an urge to be a female. In both cases, he usually undergoes a surgical procedure to get rid of genitals. Often, male children born with deformed genitals are 'adopted' by *hijras* and raised as females. *Hijras* earn their living by singing and dancing at births of male children and also at their weddings.

Psychoanalytically, *hijras* may be seen as castrated males. Their genitals are literally severed from their body. However, instead of feeling helpless and weak, *hijras* take a sense of pride in being females. They wear make-up, dress in feminine clothes and adopt feminine mannerisms.

In India, they have local and national associations and meetings to discuss their concerns. Once a year, in April, they hold an all-India gathering in Kovagam village, 300 miles south of Madras. It is about a week-long festival. They re-live the myth of their origin: marrying in the evening and then becoming a widow the next morning. Evening is marked by rejoicing; morning by grieving. In one version of the mythology, *hijras* believe that they are actually Lord Krishna in the guise of a woman. Thus, metaphorically and mythologically, *hijras* are male–females. Those interested in more detailed discussion may want to consult scientific, literary works, e.g., Nanda, 1990; Shetty, 1990; Kant, 1993.

Sharda is a *hijra*. In our interview, she alternated between feeling proud of being a *hijra* on the one hand, and feeling like being neither man nor woman on the other. In Jungian terms, a fused-individuated blend of anima and animus.

Card I, Response 1: *Yey toe insaan kaa shareer hai; yey shareer kay under nus aayee hai; ismain doe nassain hotee hain; kinaaray kee ek ner kee; ek maadaa kee; ek nus motee hotee hai; ek patlee hotee hai* ('This is actually a human's body; this here is a vein inside [the] body; there are two veins here; the one at the end is the male vein; another is female vein; one vein is thick; another, thin').

Yey ling kay paas hotee hain; ek idhur, ek udher; eskay dabaanay say maloom hoe jaataa hai ki yey hijra hai ('These are near the genitals; one on this side; another on the other side; when you apply pressure on them, you'd find out whether the person is a *hijra*').

Card II, Response 2: *Ismay bachchay-daani kee koi jugah naheen hai; aur bachchaa hoe naheen saktaa ismay jub tuk bachchaa-daani naa hoe jaai; chaatee barabar aa saktee hai* ('This has no place for uterus; and one can't conceive a baby unless one has uterus; one may, however, grow breasts').

Yeh peshaab kee jugah hai; yey bachchay-daani kaa muh hai, usmay jhillee charhee hotee hai; jub muh bund nahee hogaa to bachchaa kaisay rukay gaa? ('This is the part for urinating; this is entrance to the uterus; it is covered with a membrane; how can the baby be held inside unless this entrance is kept closed?').

Card III, Response 3: *Yey grahan partaa hai tab bachchay kaa ung kharaab hoe jaataa hai; bachchay kaa muh ghoom jaataa hai* ('Whenever there is an eclipse it affects the shape of a child's organ; the child's turns upside down [is born with legs, not head, first]').

Jab grahan partaa hai toe pait main bachchaa ruhtaa hai toe woh terhaa hoe jaataa hai; yeh bachchay kaa ung hai; ek payr loolaa hoe gayaa hai; ek payr sahee hai ('Whenever there is an eclipse and the child is inside the womb, his shape gets crooked; these are the child's organs; one leg is lost; the other one seems alright').

Card IV, Response 4: *Hijroen main jub kisee murd say naheen milayen gay toe uskee sehat khoob phool jaatee hai aur uskay ander kaa beej niklay gaa toe uskay ander ladies-pun aa jaaye gaa; seena nikel aayay gaa* ('Among the *hijras*, if one did not sleep with a man, one would grow to be fat, and the semen inside one's body would not be eliminated, and one would develop effeminate features').

Aisaa hai jaisay yeh hijra hai; hijray kaa shareer hai; ismayen say yeh beej naheen niklay gaa toe badan phool jaaye gaa ('Like, this is a *hijra*; hijra's body; now, his body would swell if the semen inside did not get out').

Card V, Response 5: *Joe murd say milay gaa woh ekdum dublaa hoe jaaye gaa; haddiyan jhalukanay lagayen gee toe pait main dublaa-pun aa jaaye gaa; vaisay hijroen koe murd kee zaroorat naheen hotee hai* ('If a [*hijra*] sleeps with a man, he would grow to be very thin and would start to show his bones; his stomach would shrink; well, actually, a *hijra* does not need a man').

SHARDA

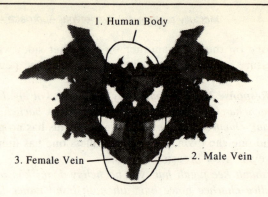

1. Human Body

3. Female Vein   2. Male Vein

I

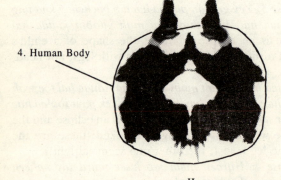

4. Human Body

II

5. Infant with
Deformed Organs

III

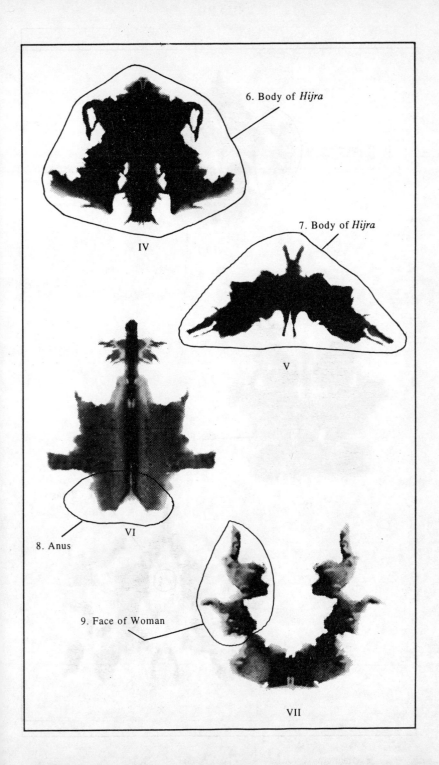

6. Body of *Hijra*

IV

7. Body of *Hijra*

V

8. Anus

VI

9. Face of Woman

VII

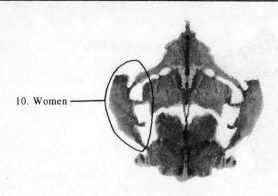

10. Women

VIII

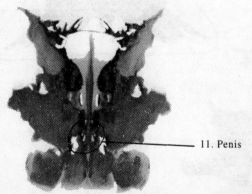

11. Penis

IX

12. Girl's Breasts

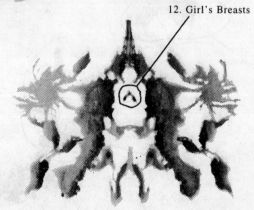

X

Jub murd say milay gaa toe haanth sookh jaayen gay; pindliyann sookh jaayen gee ('Sleeping with a man, [a *hijra*] would cause his hands and calves look like he were suffering from polio').

Card VI, Response 6: *Hijray murd say miltay hain toe murd kaa semen naheen ruktaa; woh latrine kay zariye say beej sub nikul jaataa hai* ('When *hijras* sleep with men, their [men's] semen is excreted through the anus').

Yeh latrine kay raastay beej baaher aa jaaye gaa ('This is anus; through it is excreted the semen').

Card VII, Response 7: *Yeh aiyaash aurat aiysee hotee hai; shaql kharaab hoe jaatee hai joe yaar yaa murd rukhtee hain; unkay ander kay ang main kharaabiyan paidaa hoe jaatee hain* ('This is how a wanton woman looks; the face is contorted among those who "keep" a "master" or a man; the insides of their body develop ailments').

Yeh bachchay-daanee kaa muh terhaa hoe jaaye gaa; chehraa ekdum kharaab hoe jaaye gaa ('This opening of the uterus gets crooked; face turns completely out of shape').

Card VIII, Response 8: *Yeh aurat hai joe murd say miltee hai; uskay pait main bachchaa rah jaataa hai; jub bachchaa gir jaataa hai toe pait main soojun aa jaatee hai; bachchay-danee dheelee hoe jaati hai* ('This is a woman who sleeps with a man; she conceives and carries a baby inside her uterus; when she has an abortion, there develops swelling in her stomach; uterus becomes loose').

Yeh kum umra kaa bachchaa hai; pait kay ander hai; jub doe-chaar murd say roez milay gaa toe bachchay-daanee say gir jaaye gaa ('This is a baby in its early stages; when he'd come in contact with two to four men every day, it would abort').

Card IX, Response 9: *School main chotay bachchay, fifteen-sixteen saal kay, aapus main lownday-baazee kurtay hain toe unkaa ang kharaab hoe jaataa hai; ling terhaa hoe jaataa hai* ('Young, fifteen-sixteen year old kids in school; when they engage into homosexual acts, their organ is damaged; penis becomes crooked').

Yeh hai ('These are [crooked penises]').

Card X, Response 10: *College kee larkiyaan lurkoen say chaatee chubhatee hain toe unkay seenay lutuk jaatay hain* ('College girls; their breasts sag down when they press them against boys').

Coding and Interpreting Sharda's Protocol
As in the case of Anu's protocol, we would code and interpret Sharda's responses in terms of (*a*) archetypal influences,

(*b*) placement in the Rorschach process quadrants, and (*c*) pragmatic schema.

Archetypal Influences: Sharda's responses indicate evidence of being influenced by at least three archetypal forces: archetype of opposites, archetype of birth, and archetype of morality.

Archetype of Opposites:
   Response 1: This is actually a human body; this here is vein inside body; there are two veins here; the one at the end is the male vein; another is female vein; one vein is thick; another, thin.
   Response 2: This has no place for uterus; and one can't conceive a baby unless one has uterus; one may, however, grow breasts.
   Response 5: If a *hijra* sleeps with a man, he'd grow to be very thin . . . actually, a *hijra* does not need a man.

Archetype of Birth:
   Response 3: Eclipse affects the shape of a child's organ; he's turned upside down.
   Response 8: . . .she conceives and carries a baby inside her uterus . . . .

Archetype of Morality:
   Response 7: This is how a wanton woman looks . . . .
   Response 9: When adolescents engage into homosexual acts, their penises get crooked.

Placing Sharda's Responses in the Rorschach Process Quadrants:
   Response 1: Quadrant AC.
   Response 2: Quadrant AC.
   Response 3: Quadrant AD.
   Response 4: Quadrant AD.
   Response 5: Quadrant AC.
   Response 6: Quadrant AC.
   Response 7: Quadrant CD.
   Response 8: Quadrant CD.
   Response 9: Quadrant CD.
   Response 10: Quadrant CD.

Out of 10 responses, four are in the Quadrant AC (withdrawn–conscious), two are in the Quadrant AD (withdrawn–unconscious), and the remaining four are in Quadrant CD (expansion–unconscious). Sharda tends to process her world as much at a conscious–withdrawn level as at an unconscious–expansion level. She likes to withdraw from, as much to expand towards, environment. And this processing is done almost equally intensely at the conscious and unconscious level. Her perspective is as much introverted as it is extroverted. She likes to approach others; she also likes to avoid them. She lives at the crossroads. Unlike Anu, whose preferred mode of relating is unconscious withdrawal, Sharda's preferred mode alternates between a withdrawal–unconscious and an expansion–unconscious mode. Anu's processing is more stable than Sharda's.

Pragmatic Schema: Let us now place Sharda's personality in the pragmatic schema. This would help us see how she is individuating, that is, how she is handling the boundaries between (*a*) persona and shadow, and (*b*) anima and animus.

Persona and Shadow:

Sharda has not been able to separate persona from shadow. Sometimes it is persona; at other times, it is shadow that controls her; more often, however, it is a mix of both. The same is true of her anima–animus. In fact, the blurring is more apparent in the anima–animus dimension than on the persona–shadow continuum. Logically, it makes sense. Her need to project herself in terms of her social role (a male turned into female) conflicts with her awareness that she was, perhaps, meant to be a man but is living her life as a woman. She is sure of what she is *not*, namely, she is not a male. But, she is not sure what she *is*. As it is, self-awareness is not easy to acquire; it is more difficult in the case of someone whose identity is (wilfully or helplessly) challenged. Being born and growing up in Indian culture where phallus worship is an important element in religious life, it is not easy for Sharda (or for that matter, for most of us) to isolate self-concept from sexual organs. That fundamental, philosophical question, 'Who am I?' starts with some obvious biological and social roles, and gradually gets convoluted with numerous cultural connotations. Persona literally covers our shadow. If we don't know what is it that we are trying to mask (that is, what is our shadow), it is not easy to develop a mask (persona) for it. Sharda's dilemma is not to mask or not to but rather, what is it that needs to be masked? If my dark side is under too much scrutiny, I would need to mask it really well. On the other hand, if my dark side is not at all under scrutiny, there is no pressure to mask it. In either of these situations, shadow is a free-floating entity. Most of us are in between these extremes. Sharda is a *hijra*. People around her *know* that she was not born a woman, and is a *simulated* woman. Sharda *knows* that others know this. She has less pressure to mask her primal identity in and around her neighborhood than if she were to immigrate to a foreign land. And, since her social role (namely, *hijra*) is transparent insofar as others see her as a man in the 'guise' of a woman, the boundary between her shadow and persona is, in a way, more conceptual that real. She is kind of an 'intervening variable' between male on the one hand and female on the other.

Let us now review her responses to illustrate our comments.

Response 2: 'There is no place for uterus . . .'. This is as if Sharda is saying, my persona is woman but my shadow is an incomplete woman: I can't have a baby. A woman who can't have a baby is often seen as a cursed person. Archetype of infertility. An infertile woman *baanjh aurat* is an unfortunate woman.

Response 5: 'If a *hijra* sleeps with a man . . . [inquiry], well, actually, a *hijra* does not need a man'. In Response 2, Sharda feels that without a uterus, she is like an incomplete woman. A further elaboration occurs in Response 5, where she is making a statement: I may be an incomplete woman but so what, I don't need a man.

An additional denial is seen in Response 7, where she sees a woman but it is a wanton woman (as if saying, I don't feel bad about being a semi-woman, after all the women out there are not morally too strong either).

Anima and Animus:

The archetype of femininity and masculinity is much more strongly evident than of persona and shadow. It is, however, important to emphasize that there is a lot of overlap between archetypes. It is the predominance of one theme rather than another that differentiates archetypes. The same response may imply influence of more than one archetype. Also, as mentioned earlier, many responses on the other hand may illustrate the impact of only a single archetype.

All the 10 responses of Sharda illustrate her inability to reconcile the conflicting experiences of femininity and masculinity. This is not surprising. Her whole life experience revolves around the issue of 'he' versus 'she'. 'She' wants to be a she. 'She' also knows that she was initially a 'he'. Then, begin complicated cognitions. 'She' is not a full woman. 'She' is also not a full man. In fact, her being half-man was the driving force underlying her need to be a woman. But then, she cannot conceive a child. No uterus and, therefore, even artificial insemination is not possible. No vagina and, therefore, natural, male–female intercourse is also not possible. She reconciles with the idea of anal sex (Response 6). However, it is not accepted as normal (Response 4, Response 5). The natural (vaginal sex) is not possible. The possible (anal sex) is not natural. The outcome? Anger (Response 8) and disgust (Response 9, Response 10).

In summary, Sharda is in an unenviable position. She is caught between the merger–separation conflict. Fortunately, culturally she has some relief insofar as she is able to reduce her hurt by living amongst other *hijras*—peer support.

SUMMARY

We started this chapter with a quotation from Jung—'the mirror does not flatter'—and a similar theme in an Indian film *Gaman*. Couched against the context of the Jungian way of understanding the world through the collective unconscious (archetypes), we described McCully's approach of looking at the Rorschach responses, namely, (*a*) pragmatic schema (persona–shadow, anima–animus), (*b*) Rorschach process analysis in terms of quadrants (horizontal axis A–B, vertical axis C–D), and (*c*) identifying archetypal influences in the responses based on the potential of each Rorschach card to arouse archetypal images.

Following this overview, we then illustrated McCully's approach through two protocols: Anu, a twenty-three year old Indian female, and Sharda, a thirty year old Indian *hijra*.

McCully's approach is based on the assumption that the Rorschach experience is capable of arousing images in our collective unconscious. Looking at the responses from this perspective provides a phenomenologically meaningful way of understanding human personality in a cultural context.

From McCully's (Jungian) Archetypal Approach, based on the Jungian collective unconscious, we now move on to describing an approach based on the Freudian individual unconscious—Roy Schafer's Psychoanalytic Ego Psychology Approach.

7 SCHAFER'S PSYCHOANALYTIC EGO PSYCHOLOGY APPROACH

Sigmund Freud (1856–1939)—the Austrian physician–neurologist—founded a city: Psychoanalysisville, Freudpur. Like any new, developing town, it had one main street—Unconscious Avenue. There were two side streets: Impulse Street and Oedipus Complex Road. There was a big mansion on Impulse Street, Sex *Mahal* ('Palace'). And then, there were a few *kutchee sarkayen* ('dirt roads') here and there: repression, resistance, etc.

Freudpur was more like a big suburb of a metropolitan town. Everyone knew about the big city. Not many were aware of this suburb. It did exist though. When big-town folks got tired or stressed-out, they traveled to this suburb for a brief reprieve. Some stayed there longer than others. Well, everyone knew that all of them visited this place, but it was kept a secret: publicly confidential.

Like any other town, over the years this town also grew and kept growing. There were many developers who took interest and realized its potential for growth. New colonies emerged—Jung's Collective Unconscious Nagar, Adler's Individual Psychology Nagar, Karen Horney's Culture Street, Rado's Adaptational Dynamics Bazaar, Hartmann's Ego Psychology Highway, Fairbairn's Object Relations Superhighway, and so on. The original, small rural town Freudpur has, over the past 100 years or so, developed into a megalopolis.

Hermann Rorschach (1975) used basic psychoanalytic concepts in analyzing the responses of Dr. Oberholzer's patient. Robert McCully developed a way of looking at the Rorschach responses from Jung's collective unconscious point of view. Roy Schafer conceptualized Rorschach protocols from the Psychoanalytic Ego Psychology Approach. And Paul Lerner developed the Psychoanalytic Object Relations Theory for understanding human personality as reflected through the Rorschach responses.

Since both Schafer's and Lerner's theories are contextualized in psychoanalytic concepts, we feel it would be helpful to present a brief overview of psychoanalytic concepts as a background for Schafer's and Lerner's systems. Section I outlines psychoanalysis. Section II presents Schafer's approach. Finally, Section III presents two protocols illustrating Schafer's system.

SECTION I: PSYCHOANALYSIS

Understanding human behavior essentially means explaining behavior (both verbal and non-verbal). What causes us to *think, say* or *do* anything. Freud observed a great variety of behaviors in his patients. He attempted to explain them by suggesting various factors that may be causing these behaviors. He was a physician, specializing in neurology, as well as a scientist. He reasoned from data to theory. He kept examining the link between data and theory. If an initially formed theory did not explain the data, he did not question data. He questioned theory.

We have organized the brief overview of psychoanalysis in two ways here: (*a*) seven points, and (*b*) narrative description. We must caution the readers that it is impossible to present a comprehensive picture of psychoanalysis here due to space constraints. The writings of Freud contain rich clinical material and are presented with interesting case histories. Readers are encouraged to consult the original works (Freud, 1900, 1923, 1933). What we are presenting here is only a brief sketch.

Seven Points

1. Like physical events, mental events also have a cause—*psychic determinism*.
2. The nature of psychic determinism may be understood in terms of a dimension of awareness (unconscious, preconscious, conscious, conscience).

   One end of the dimension of awareness is *primary process*. The other end is called *secondary process*. Primary process is all fantasy. As one moves along this dimension toward the secondary process end, behavior comes increasingly under control of reality limitations. This dimension of awareness is reflected in the various levels of *psychic functioning* and represents different degrees of fantasy or reality orientation.

Psychosis is essentially a primary process determined behavior. On the other hand, neurosis is essentially a secondary process determined behavior. Then, there are behaviors in between these two; borderline conditions in which we see a person alternating between fantasy and reality. No behavior is exclusively fantasy (primary process) or reality (secondary process) determined. It is usually a little of one and more of the other.

3. The foundation of a person's personality, said Freud, is laid down in the first five years of his/her life. He conceptualized this development on the basis of physical functions that are focused as a means of seeking gratification: eating, biting, swallowing (oral stage); urinating, defecating (anal); playing with, including feeling a loss of penis (phallic). To concretize this pleasure-seeking process, he gave it a Latin name libido (meaning pleasure). In other words, when he said that during the oral stage libido is centered in the mouth, what he meant was that during this stage, the mouth was the main organ of the body for seeking pleasure and satisfaction.

4. Id, ego, superego are collective nouns referring to the unconscious, conscious and conscience respectively. They represent different levels of primary process and secondary process effects. Most of the times, a behavior reflects the effects of all three, though the relative amounts/proportions vary.

5. Objects (that is, people, events, things, experiences) have two components: ideational and emotional. Since often it is the emotional component that causes discomfort, emotions tend to get separated from objects and get attached to other objects (displacement). You get angry at your boss; you come home and take it out on your spouse: *dhobee say jeet nahin paayey, gadahay kay kaan umaythayen* ('you lost the fight with the washerman, so you hurt his donkey').

6. Noticing that often his patients showed high amounts of attachment as children with the parent of the opposite sex, Freud borrowed the story of the Greek myth of Oedipus and called this the Oedipus complex. The idea of Oedipus complex is very helpful in understanding many abnormal (perhaps also normal)

forms of behavior. He found that unresolved Oedipal complex issues caused many behavioral problems in his patients (for example, the cases of Little Hans and the Rat Man).

In view of the fact that the Oedipus complex plays an important role in psychopathology, we will digress here and narrate the story of Oedipus from Greek mythology. The narrative here is based on the story as described in Bulfinch (1981).

Literally, Oedipus means swollen-foot (*Oidein* = to swell, *pous* = foot). Oedipus was the son of Laius and Jocasta, king and queen of the ancient city of Thebes in South Egypt on the River Nile (the modern sites of Luxor and Karnak). When he was born, astrologers told Laius that this child would end up killing him. Laius thus ordered that the child be killed. The shepherds took him away to the forest to kill him. They, however, felt sorry for him and decided not to kill him. Instead, they tied his feet and hung him from the branch of a tree (perhaps hoping that this way they would not have to kill him, and yet, indirectly, would have obeyed Laius's orders because eventually the child would die). Well, as destiny (law of karma) would have it, the feet-tied, hanging child was discovered by a farmer passing by on the road. He untied the child and took him to his master. The master and his wife adopted the child. And, since his feet were swollen from being tied for so long, they named the child Oedipus (swollen-foot).

Many years passed. Oedipus grew up to be a strong young man. Once, on one of his travels, Laius and Oedipus ran into each other coming from opposite directions in their *raths* ('chariots'). It was a narrow road. One of them had to step aside to let the other pass. Laius was the king, so his servant expected Oedipus to step aside. Oedipus was strong. He expected the king's chariot to step aside. Both refused to give in. Laius's servant killed one of the horses of Oedipus's *rath*. Fuming with anger, Oedipus then killed both the king (who was actually his father) and the servant. Thus, Oedipus (unknowingly) killed his father.

A few years later, a monster by the name of Sphinx started terrorizing the citizens of Thebes. Now, this monster had the lower part of its body like a lion and the upper part like a woman. He used to hide at the top of a mountain on the outskirts of Thebes. He would stop people traveling along that road. His deal was that if they could not solve his *paheli* ('riddle'), they would lose their lives. The riddle was: What is it that walks on four feet as a child, on two feet as an adult, and on three feet when it gets old?

No one could solve this *paheli*. Sphinx would then kill these people. The city of Thebes was understandably terrified. Then, Oedipus decided to do something about it. When he reached the spot, Sphinx stopped him as he had many others before him. 'Unless you solve my riddle, I'm going to kill you' said Sphinx and recited the riddle. Oedipus solved it.

'Man', he said, 'man is that animal who walks on four feet as a child, on two feet as an adult, and with the help of a *laathee* ["walking stick"], on three feet, when old'. Sphinx had finally found someone to match him. He (It?) could not take this shock. He jumped off the top of the mountain and committed suicide.

The news of Sphinx's death and the bravery of Oedipus reached the citizens of Thebes. Everyone was ecstatic and relieved. They decided to reward Oedipus for freeing them from the wrath of Sphinx. So, they made Oedipus their king. And, since the queen's husband (Laius) was dead, the citizens married Oedipus to the queen (who was actually his mother). Thus, Oedipus married his mother.

Years passed by. Thebes was hit by famine. People started dying of hunger. Astrologers explained that the famine was God's way of punishing the citizens of Thebes for having committed the sin of marrying Oedipus to his mother. When Queen Jocasta learnt about this horrible fact, she committed suicide. Oedipus blinded his eyes and left the city to wander in the forests. Everyone in Thebes abandoned him. Everyone, that is, except his daughters. They remained loyal to their father. After suffering a miserable life, Oedipus finally died. Thus ended the life of a miserable man called Oedipus who unknowingly killed his father and married his mother.

Freud in his clinical work noticed that often sons were closer to their mothers than their fathers. He used this myth of Oedipus to dramatize this observation. Often, emotional problems in adulthood may be traced back to this metaphorical Oedipus complex. And, it seems the archetype of mother-in-law (where the mother perceives that the daughter-in-law has separated her from her son, or when the wife feels\the husband 'listens' to his mother rather than to her) has beneath it a touch of this Oedipus complex.

Having digressed to describe the Oedipus complex and its critical role in psychoanalytic theory, we now go to the last of the seven points in summarizing psychoanalysis.

7. Using the early developmental stages of seeking pleasure (libido) through oral and anal behaviors, Freud identified character types (basic and core personalities) based on this tendency. Thus, there are oral characters and anal characters.

Narrative Description

Freud's basic theory may be described in one word—psychic determinism. Everything that happens, happens *because* of something. There is always a cause. And, as events in the physical world are caused, so are things in the mental world. Corresponding to the concept of physical determinism, he said, there was psychic determinism. Most of Freudian theory follows from this basic concept of psychic determinism. For instance, if we do not know the cause of a behavior, it is because it was caused by something we were not aware of. Things that we may not be aware of exist in our unconscious. Awareness is a matter of degree. We are more aware of some things than others. To account for this semi-awareness, he suggested that perhaps between conscious and unconscious there was another level of awareness—preconscious. Just like there is evening between day, on the one hand, and night on the other— the twilight zone.

When we are infants, we want to satisfy our basic needs of food, water, urination, defecation, etc. We want to satisfy them as soon as they arise—no delay, instantly, impulsively. With realities of life (mother is in the bathroom or feeding the other baby and cannot rush to respond to the first child's need to eat, urinate or defecate), we realize that we have to learn to wait, tolerate delay. But deep down we still do not give up our need for instant gratification. We just control it. Freud pointed out that these impulses (expecting/demanding instant satisfaction) are pushed back *somewhere*. He gave a name to this *somewhere*—the unconscious. That's *it*. And because of his vast knowledge of languages, cultures and religions, Freud used the Latin word for 'it'—id. If someone asked where is your need (impulse) to grab food from your friend's *thaalee* ('plate'), you may answer, 'it' (id) (unconscious) had got it. Id is the unconscious. Since it is always fun to have your needs gratified immediately, id (a kind of collective noun for the impulses in the unconscious) keeps struggling to come out for satisfaction. So, after the 'shock' (primal shock maybe) that we have got to learn to wait for things, we start building up our house of awareness—*possibles* and *impossibles*. We (are forced to) learn that it is just impossible to eat as soon as we feel hungry or to urinate as soon as we need to. The part of the personality that contains this 'knowledge' of what is possible and what is not Freud called the conscious. Again, he used the Latin word ego (self) to describe the contents of the conscious. In between the unconscious (id) and the conscious (ego), there exists preconscious, indicating that sometimes we may do things while we may not be fully aware of doing them; like doodling while talking to someone on the telephone or humming a tune while taking a bath.

As part of our growing up, the distinction of awareness in terms of possibles versus impossibles is further differentiated in terms of desirables versus undesirables. Everything that is possible, may not be desirable. We are not only expected to engage in possible behaviors, but also in behaviors that are appropriate and desirable. It is possible, for instance, to sprinkle colored water on people around us, but it is not desirable except on the day Holi is celebrated. On that day, it is possible and desirable to smear colored powder (*abeer-gulaal*) on the faces of our friends. Festivals give us outlets, also excuses. *Eed kaa din hai, aaj toe galay mil lay zaalim! Rasmayduniyaa bhee hai, mausam bhee hai, dastoor bhee hai* ('Oh, ruthless! today is *Eed* [a holy day of joyous celebration]. At least today, you may let me hug you. Not only is that a tradition [to celebrate by hugging], but the setting too is romantic, and then, it is also a custom').

The part of our personality that deals with desirability/appropriateness of behaviors is called superego. It is still ego because it is related with reality. But it 'fine-tunes' reality not only in terms of possibles/impossibles but also in terms of appropriates/inappropriates. Hence, the prefix 'super' in ego.

Thus, id, ego and superego correspond to unconscious, conscious and conscience, and constitute basic units of our personality.

Human beings avoid lots of things; thinking, saying, doing many things. We avoid them because it is not considered right or appropriate to think, say or do certain things. It is not right or appropriate because people around us say so. For instance, it is not right to have a death wish for someone you love: father, mother, wife, child. It is not right to say, for instance, 'May you die' or 'May you be struck by lightning!' to anyone, and definitely not to those you care about. Cursing, using profanities, is an absolute 'no, no'. And, it is not right to steal, rob or rape.

While we are aware of not thinking, saying or doing many things, we often *wish* we did have that freedom. However, if wishes were horses, beggars would fly. Well, it seems wishes indeed are horses and we do ride on them—in our fantasy though.

We avoid things only insofar as we do not express them to ourselves and to others. However, we do not get rid of them. They exist. Within us. Freud called that container of wishes the unconscious. Undesirable, painful, inappropriate wishes are pushed back into our unconscious. 'Pushing them back' he called repression. We repress them because we do not want to feel bad about ourselves. Most of the time, we all have good self-images. We all believe we are great, God created us. Usually, our parents make us feel that way ('our prince/queen/sunshine/apple of our eyes'). In order to maintain our good self-image, we do not want to admit that we have 'bad' wishes.

The process by which we learn what is good and bad or appropriate and inappropriate (reality orientation) is called ego. Ego (self) maintains our contact with our environment by keeping a watch on the desirability/appropriateness of our thoughts, words and actions.

A good self-image is sought and maintained by using many techniques, e.g., (*a*) by refusing to admit bad wishes (denial), (*b*) by seeing these 'bad' things in others (projection), (*c*) by justifying that what we think as bad is really not bad (rationalization), and (*d*) by thinking, saying or doing just the opposite of what we really want to think, say or do (reaction-formation).

This is how ego protects its status. Freud called them defense mechanisms. These are ego's defenses. Some defense mechanisms do not allow expression of the 'bad' wishes. Repression, denial and projection are a few examples. Others allow expression in socially/culturally approved ways, e.g., sublimation (creative writing, art, festivals). Sublimation is a dressed-up, camouflaged expression of our wishes and fantasies. You cannot express your love for someone because of social/cultural pressures, so you write a play about that person. Or, when you are hurting, instead of thinking of suicide, you compose a poem.

In the Hindi film *Teesri Kasam*, traveling on a bullock-cart in rural Bihar with the *gaaree-wan* Heeraaman (Raj Kapoor) on her way to perform in a village *nautankee* ('theater'), Heeraa Baai (Waheeda Rahman) notices that people looked happy. They were singing folk-songs, looked relaxed and were just enjoying life. *Yehaan kaa hur aadmi geet gaataa hai, aur yehaan kee bhaashaa mayn toe geet aur bhee achchaa lugtaa hai* ('Everyone around here looks so happy; singing; and songs in their dialect sound all the more sweet') she says.

Aray, geet naheen gaaye gaa toe aur karaygaa kyaa, responds Heeraman, adding, *kahtay hain, phatay kalejaa gaao geet, dukh sahnay kaa yahee reet* ('What else would he do if not sing? We have a saying, "the only way to cope with grief and hurt is to sing songs"').

Repression, projection, denial, reaction-formation, rationalization and sublimation—all are ways for the ego to defend itself against the attack/pressure of undesirable/inappropriate wishes or impulses. Impulses keep struggling for expression. They want satisfaction. If we don't provide them with outlets, they seek creative ways of expressing themselves.

One such outlet is dreams. Dreams, said Freud, are the royal road to the unconscious. In dreams, impulses come out in raw form (e.g., you are setting fire to your home) or in symbolic form (that is, you are chopping the branch of the tree you are sitting on).

Another outlet is slips of the tongue and the pen. *Kuttay kay saath cinema jaa ruhay hain* ('I am going to the movies with the dog'). You have a 'friend' whose last name is Gupte. You feel he is a pest. Still, being a courteous and polite person, you don't want to refuse when he invites you to see a movie. Someone asks you, where you are going. And you want to say you are going to see a movie with Gupte. But, instead, *kuttay* (rhyming with Gupte) slips out. The wish for expressing your dislike of him comes out in a slip of the tongue.

Slips of the pen serve the same purpose, namely, providing an outlet for the repressed wish/impulse. A few interesting examples appeared in the October 1995 issue of the US edition of *Reader's Digest*. The signs in three hotels in the Far East, Europe and Asia read as follows (MacNeil, 1995, p. 151):

1. You are invited to take advantage of the chambermaid.
2. Because of the impropriety of entertaining guests of the opposite sex in the bedrooms, it is suggested that the lobby be used for this purpose.
3. Please leave your values at the front desk.

To recapitulate, the unconscious, the most important concept in psychoanalysis, is not easy to understand. It conceals things that a person wants to do, say or think. By its very nature, however, it is inaccessible. But then, the force of the things repressed is often quite strong and does not let them lie dormant. They come out in many forms and shapes. And since facing them would be uncomfortable for the ego, it defends itself against them by avoiding direct confrontation. It uses the subtle techniques of denial, projection, reaction-formation, etc., to let them come out without causing too much trouble.

Developmentally, a child is essentially a bundle of impulses out of sheer biological necessity (a child cannot control the time or place for defecating or urinating); in fact, he/she cannot even eat by him/herself. Care-givers (parents, daycare workers) realize this helplessness and provide care and support to the child and do not mind if he/she defecates or urinates at odd times/places.

Gradually the child is expected to tolerate delays in getting food; still later, he/she is expected to tolerate delays in excretory functions and to learn to hold defecating/urinating until a *proper place* is available. (The concept of proper place is relative to physical and cultural settings. It could be a nice, fancy, marble-floored bathroom in a royal palace, or on the other extreme, it could be an arhar khet [*arhar* = a kind of lentil, *khet* = field] in an Indian village; and in between these two extremes we may have the back alley of a house or behind a tree on a country road.) The child gradually progresses in his/her ability to control physiological urges.

Starting with biological behavior, the child moves on and is taught to control his social behavior, e.g., not to call people names. A child on seeing his uncle may say 'I hate you' or 'You have bad breath'. An adult 'disciplines' the child to control these negative comments. 'It is alright if you feel a certain way; but please do not express these feelings'. Impulses to steal, to call people names, to urinate/defecate in your clothes are slowly 'tamed' as a result of the socialization process.

When we are emotional (in love, anger or fear), we do not care much about what is appropriate or inappropriate and express our impulses with little or no inhibition. We have heard people say, 'I don't know what happened, I was so mad, I just didn't care about anything and called him names/beat him up/tore his shirt/threw my food away', and so on.

In describing ego's defense mechanisms, Freud talks about regression as one of the ways in which we handle stressors. Since id is the initial component in the development of the psychic structures (comprising of the substructures of id, ego and superego), when ego (which evolves out of id) is not able to handle crisis, it regresses. The regression is intended to protect ego from disintegrating. Id represents untamed impulses. Regressing to an earlier level 'saves' ego from being punished by superego. Hence, 'regression is in the service of the ego', said Kris (cited in Schafer, 1954, p. 80).

Extending this concept of regression, Schafer (1954) suggested that parallel to the less effective way of dealing with stressful situations, namely regression, ego also acquires more effective ways of modulating impulses within the framework of social controls and values. This he called 'progression in the service of the ego' (ibid., p. 81).

Under pressure we regress. Ego defends itself by regressing. We regress to an earlier effective method of dealing with pressure and stress. Id regresses, ego progresses. Both protect us from defying norms of behavior.

How far and for how long we regress depends on our frustration tolerance and also on the response of the people around us. We feel depressed, we feel like crying, but wait until we get home and meet our loved ones. This is an example of a situation when we could 'control' regression. There may, however, be situations when we are not able to control ourselves: *dar kay maaray tatee nikel gayee* ('I was so afraid, I just could not control myself and defecated').

The extent of regression could go back to the developmental stages of oral, anal, phallic, latency (pre-genital) and genital levels of psychosexual development. Freud talked about four stages of psychosexual growth based on the body organs involved in seeking gratification of the impulses of eating, defecating, urinating and using genitals for functions other than defecating/urinating. Enjoying eating, drinking and talking involve the mouth. Freud called this the oral stage. The first need of an infant is food. After eating, the next step is to eliminate the waste from the body. In this process our anus is involved. This is the second stage in psychosexual development. Freud called it the anal stage. In the third stage, we start paying attention to the organs involved in urinating and defecating—our genitals. Focusing on the phallus, Freud called this the phallic stage of psychosexual development. All these stages follow each other closely in the first five years of our life. Then, noticed Freud, there is a period when apparently no interest is shown in genitalia. This indifference from around age five to puberty (around age ten) Freud called latency period. Interest in sexual functions becomes visible around puberty, when there are noticeable bodily changes. This stage was labeled the genital stage.

Relationship between Unconscious/Conscious; Id, Ego, Superego; and Psychosexual Stages

Id refers to that part of the personality which enjoys, just loves to be able to do whatever it wants. It does not care about anything. It thus has close connection with the unconscious, because usually the undesirable impulses are pushed back into the unconscious. Id is like a gatekeeper to the house of unconscious. And, extending that analogy a bit further, id is a pretty liberal gatekeeper. Since it wants fun, it does not care about what comes out from inside the house of unconscious. In fact, id would want everything to come out. It is like a police officer on traffic duty at a busy crossing who is tempted to sit on a bench under a tree by a roadside tea shop enjoying a hot cup of tea while traffic from all directions comes and goes at the same time causing a traffic jam, accidents and hot tempers. Everything comes to a halt. Id does not care. It fantasizes.

Because of this pressure, a part of the id separates itself and realizes that this commotion (chaos) cannot go on forever. Something has got to be done. This part is more in touch with reality. This is ego.

Ego recognizes that everything cannot be done in a 'free-for-all' fashion. We have got to respect the rights of others. So, this traffic police officer goes back to his/her small circular raised platform in the middle of the crossing and starts directing traffic. Gradually and slowly, traffic starts to move again. Thus, while id *believes* that everything is possible (all traffic can go any which way), ego *realizes* that everything is not possible. Id believes. Ego realizes.

Beliefs are more powerful. Realizations are weak. Beliefs are based on faith. Faith does not care about anything. Realizations do. They are based on reality. Reality recognizes what is possible and what is not. Beliefs do not.

For example, when we hear a clinician commenting about a patient, 'his/her reality orientation is poor', we take it to mean that this patient has little regard for the limitations involved in meeting his/her needs. Customarily, we notice a statement in mental status examination (MSE) notes that the 'patient was oriented × 3', indicating that the patient *knew* the three things that are important in judging whether he/she was in touch with reality. These three things are: (a) oriented to person (patient is able to correctly answer the questions 'Who are you? What is your name?'), (b) oriented to place (he/she is able to correctly answer the questions 'Do you know where you are? What is this place?'), and (c) oriented to time (patient correctly gives the date, month and year at the time of the interview: 'Do you know what is today's date? What month is this? What year?'). Ego orients.

Then there is the issue of appropriateness or desirability. Everything that is possible may not be appropriate. It is possible, for example, to eat human feces. It is not appropriate though. Why? Because (a) our culture and society prohibits eating feces, and (b) one may get sick. Whatever is possible is not desirable. So, what? What if we did what was not desirable? We would have to pay the price (consequences). It is possible to rob a bank. It is not desirable. One may still do it and end up in jail. It is possible to eve tease (e.g., making lewd remarks at a girl or pinching her) but one may also get beat up by the people around. There is a part of our personality, said Freud, that helps us not to do everything that is possible to be done. He called it superego. 'Super' ego is better than ego, just like a super-deluxe bus is better than the regular bus.

Superego guides us into doing appropriate things. It also guides us into not doing inappropriate things. What happens if we defy the superego? We experience guilt, fear of punishment, depression, self-hate, and so on.

Id is all fun. Ego controls id by limiting fun to what is possible. Superego controls ego by limiting fun to what is desirable.

Most of the stuff of the unconscious is governed by id. Ego covers the things in the conscious. Superego deals with things that constitute our conscience. Under stress and pressure, superego may lose control. Under more pressure, it becomes ego's turn to lose control. And then? Then id takes control. With id in charge, we deny reality and take refuge in fantasy. We relish fantasy. We regress. Depending on the intensity of the stress or pressure, we may regress to our earliest stages of development: oral, anal, phallic, latency (pre-genital) or genital.

The relationship between (*a*) unconscious/conscious, (*b*) id, ego, and superego and (*c*) psychosexual stages may then be summarized as follows:

1. The unconscious holds impulses and is controlled by id.
2. The conscious contains limitations imposed by reality; ego controls it.
3. The conscious also contains limitations imposed by religion, culture and society in the form of values (right/wrong, consequences of right/wrong behavior). It is controlled by the superego.
4. When faced with stressful situations (e.g., death of a parent, immigration from rural to urban areas or from one country to another), ego defends itself in different ways like regression, projection, denial, reaction-formation and/or rationalization.
5. Of the various defenses, regression is used more often than other techniques. We may even say all stressors make us regress. Essentially, regression means going down our developmental scale. It seems as if we reduce our level of maturity and start behaving like we are younger than what we are. The advantage of this is that it rationalizes our age-inappropriate behavior.

Also, the more intense the shock, deeper is the regression. We notice that under a traumatic experience, a person loses his/her voice. He/she is so much in shock that he/she cannot talk. Inability to talk is the earliest stage in our growth. Learning to talk precedes learning to walk. Depending on the shock, a person may regress to the genital level (e.g., masturbating in public), or to the anal level (smearing feces), or to the oral level (eating feces).

In this section, we have attempted a very brief sketch of Freudian psychoanalytic theory. As we said in the beginning, Freudpur started as a small country town around the 1880s. Over the past 100 years, this small town has evolved into a *mahanagar* (megalopolis). We just cannot even try to summarize the growth and development of this monolithic theoretical system and its numerous extensions and modifications. We have, therefore, just managed to give a glimpse of psychoanalysis here. It was somewhat necessary to do this with a view to providing a context for Schafer's approach to Rorschach data. Our description of psychoanalysis was done at two levels: (*a*) seven points, and (*b*) narrative description.

With this background, we now move on to a description of Schafer's system of interpreting Rorschach responses.

SECTION II: PSYCHOANALYTIC EGO PSYCHOLOGY

'*From the point of view of psychoanalytic ego psychology . . .which is the point of view of this theoretical approach . . .*', explains Schafer, '*all thought and behavior must be understood in part as expression of a particular balance of ego dynamics and id dynamics, that is, of progressive, adaptive trends and regressive, autistic trends*' (Schafer, 1954, p. 81, emphasis in original).

This is a pretty pregnant statement to Schafer's approach. The key terms are: (*a*) all thought and behavior, and (*b*) balance of ego dynamics and id dynamics.

Any behavior (e.g., crying, attempting suicide, writing a letter to one's beloved expressing love, beginning or breaking a relationship) or any thought (e.g., what should one wear for the job interview, how should one greet the divorced wife of one's best friend, how would one deal with one's mother's death, what gift or present should be bought for a casual friend's wedding), reflects a balance of ego dynamics and id dynamics.

Before we discuss the issue of balance, we need to elaborate on the issue of ego dynamics and id dynamics. And, we may have to go one step back and describe the concept of the levels of psychic functioning.

Psychic functioning is governed by what Freud called primary and secondary processes. Primary process functioning is characterized by fantasy. Secondary process, on the other hand, is marked by reality. At one end of psychic functioning is primary process determined behavior and thought; at the other end is secondary process determined behavior and thought. We all tend to fluctuate between these two ends. A child is more at the primary process end; an adult is more at the secondary process end.

Primary process reflects unmodulated impulsive behavior and thought. Secondary process features reality-oriented behavior and thought. An important point to note is that reality-oriented behavior and thought may be characterized by either a defensive effort or an adaptive effort. Impulses may thus be defended or adapted. In defensive efforts, expression of impulses is denied, protected. In adaptive efforts, on the other hand, impulses are acknowledged and then regulated within the demands of the id, ego and superego. Adaptive efforts usually involve manipulating environmental demands.

Let us look at a few examples. Impulse to choke someone to death—id. Reality orientation would suggest that it is just not possible to do that because of the consequences—ego. A defensive effort may involve using different techniques to protect (defend) the ego from this impossible thought. Ego may use the techniques of denial (it is just not true), projection (he wants to choke me) or reaction-formation (I actually care for him, how could I think of hurting him?). All these are defensive efforts. In addition, ego may also use adaptive efforts (that is, expressing impulses in consideration with internal and external environmental, social and cultural expectations). Adaptation is a less painful form of defense. It is, relatively, a higher level of psychic functioning than defense.

Based on the discussion so far, it may be stated that:

1. infantile impulses need expression. It may be done defensively or adaptively, and
2. each behavior or thought has three components:
   (*i*) impulse (e.g., drinking tea with loud slurping sounds),
   (*ii*) defense (e.g., making a comment, 'I hate people when they don't drink but slurp tea'), and
   (*iii*) adaptation (e.g., making a comment, 'I had this friend of mine who just couldn't drink tea without making loud slurps like this . . .' and then demonstrating how his friend drank tea).

Schafer points out that each level of psychic functioning (that is, the degree of primary and/or secondary process), is marked by specific relations between id, ego and superego. In other words, there is this impulse—defense—adaptation unit comprising each episode of behavior or thought. Depending on the location of this behavior/thought along the continuum of psychic functioning, one may expect a different configuration of this unit (of impulse, defense and adaptation). These are configured differently at the id, ego and superego levels. This is what constitutes id dynamics and ego dynamics.

To repeat, when Schafer describes the Psychoanalytic Ego Psychology Approach as understanding behavior/thought as a balance between id dynamics and ego dynamics, he means that when we isolate a behavior episode or a thought, we should try to figure out what kind of balance is being shown in this behavior or thought between id dynamics and ego dynamics.

The key concept in psychoanalytic ego psychology is defense. Ego processes aim at protecting and maintaining the ego's integrity. Defenses play an important role in this process. We would, therefore, spend some time looking at ego defenses.

Ego's Defense Mechanisms

There are two main features of defenses that need our attention: (*a*) defenses are direct attempts to prevent expression of impulses, and (*b*) defenses do not occur in isolation.

Defenses as Direct Attempts

By their nature, defenses *fight* discharge of impulses prohibited due to cultural and social values, and standards. This impulse fighting is done at the unconscious level. We would not fight if we were aware of it. In that case, we would adapt. In fact, defense is an unhealthy adaptation. Adaptation involves a mature compromise between what we would love to do, on the one hand, and what we should do, on the other. For instance, repression, denial, projection and, what Schafer calls, the obsessive–compulsive defense syndrome (namely, regression, isolation, intellectualization, reaction-formation and undoing), are defenses to protect the ego from undesirable impulsive urges.

Not only abnormal but also normal behaviors reflect a combination of

1. impulsive urges (e.g., urge to kill someone),
2. defensive attempts (e.g., diverting your mind by praying to God to prevent you from such 'bad' thoughts), and
3. adaptive attempts (e.g., writing an essay describing your intended target with choice epithets, reading it to your close friends and

then throwing it away; or going to a *Tantric* and having a spell cast on your enemy).

Defenses do Not Occur in Isolation

The second important feature of defenses is that they do not occur in isolation from each other. Any defensive effort often does include more than one defense. A defensive effort, for example, could include a little of denial, some projection, and a bit of regression and undoing. Creative writings often illustrate a combination of impulse, defense and adaptation, and a multiplicity of the defenses in behaviors and thoughts.

We will present two examples here: (*a*) Devdas' letter to Parvati breaking their relationship in Sarat Chandra's (1990) immortal love story *Devdas*, and (*b*) Lady Macbeth's concern over blood spots following Banquo's murder in Shakespeare's *Macbeth* (1944).

Devdas' Letter: Devdas, son of a rich, upper caste, zamindar, and Parvati, daughter of a poor, lower caste, commoner, lived in a village near Calcutta. They grew up together, went to the same school, played after school. They cared a lot for each other. As adults, they wanted to marry each other. This was not possible according to Devdas' father. How could a girl from a lower caste family where accepting, rather than giving, dowry was the custom, marry a boy from an upper caste, rich family? said Deva's father. A hurt and humiliated Paro loved Deva. She could not even think of having any man other than Deva as her husband. Staking her reputation, she made a last minute desperate attempt to see if Deva would marry her against his parents' wishes. Late one night, she went to Deva's place, into his bedroom, and pleaded with him to marry her. Deva wanted to, but was hesitant to defy his parents. However, he did promise that as long as he lived he would never ever forget her. Hurt and embarrassed, Paro went back home.

The next day, Deva left home for Calcutta. After a couple of days, he wrote a letter to Paro (Chandra, 1990, pp. 51–52).

Parvati,
   I've been here in Calcutta now for two days. All this time, I have been thinking about you and how you expressed your feelings for me that night when you visited me. Both my parents don't want us to get married. It would hurt them if I married you. I cannot do that. Also, I cannot defy them.

Would I ever write to you again? I don't think so. In fact, that is why I am trying to be honest and writing you this letter. You know, your family belongs to a caste lower than ours. My mother would never like the idea of having a girl as her daughter-in-law from a family where they accept, rather than give, dowry. She would also not like the idea of having her son's in-laws live next door to her. And, you already know how my father feels about it.

I am sorry. I really am. I think about you visiting me that night in my room. I can well appreciate the amount of guilt and embarrassment it must have caused to your pride and self-respect. It must have caused you a lot of pain and hurt.

And, one more thing. The thought of me loving you never ever did cross my mind. In fact, even now as I am writing this, I don't feel too bad about it. I do realize and feel sorry that you'd be hurting a lot for me. Well, try to forget me.

I sincerely wish and pray that you be successful in your efforts to forget me.

—Devdas

Let us look at this letter as a Rorschach response of Devdas to the 'inkblot' of Parvati in terms of the configuration of impulse, defense and adaptation at different levels of psychic functioning (fluctuating between primary process and secondary process). As we mentioned earlier, each episode of behavior (or thought) reflects a balance between id dynamics and ego dynamics. The dynamics of id and ego include interactions between impulse, defense and adaptation. Let us see what kind of balance between id dynamics and ego dynamics is reflected in this behavior, that is, Deva's letter.

Id Dynamics: The impulse—defense—adaptation configuration in id dynamics is governed more by the primary process end of the dimension of psychic functioning. The impulse of breaking off all contact with Paro (e.g., 'Would I ever write to you again? I don't think so')—defense (e.g., 'The thought of me loving you, never, ever crossed my mind' [denial])—adaptation (e.g., 'I cannot defy them') configuration at the level of id is close to the primary process end of psychic functioning.

Ego Dynamics: The same configuration (namely, impulse—defense—adaptation) at the ego level is close to the secondary process end. For example, the impulse of wishing that Paro would forget him is defended by combining projection ('try to forget me') with intellectualization ('the thought of me loving you never, ever crossed my mind'), and adapted by dressing it up in social courtesy ('I sincerely wish and pray, that you be successful in your efforts to forget me').

Balance Between Id Dynamics and Ego Dynamics: The balance between id dynamics and ego dynamics in this letter is around the mid-point along the scale of psychic level functioning. It keeps fluctuating between primary process (e.g., 'Would I ever write to you again? I don't think so'; 'The thought of me loving you never, ever crossed my mind') and secondary process (e.g., 'I would have to hurt them [parents] if I married you'; 'I cannot defy them'; '. . .try to forget me').

Obviously, Devdas' anger and disappointment towards his parents is displaced onto Parvati. The comment 'I cannot defy them' is actually a reaction-formation: he does indeed want to defy them but wants to repress it and intellectualizes it by dressing it up as socially approved behavior of not disappointing his parents. The guilt of hurting Paro is covered by denial of love for her.

Lady Macbeth's Concern: Lady Macbeth is rubbing her hands. She is obsessed with the blood spots. She continues washing her hands. She has no success in getting rid of the spots.

Yet, here's a spot . . . . Out, damned spot? I say! One; two; way then? 'tis time to do't: Hell is murky! Fie, my lord fie! a soldier, and afraid? What need we fear who knows it. When none can call our power to account? Yet, who would have thought the old man to have so much blood in him? . . . . Here's the smell of the blood still: all the perfume in Arabia will not sweeten this little hand. Oh, Oh, Oh! . . . . Wash your hands, put on your nightgown; look not so pale: I tell you yet again, Banquo's buried; he cannot come out on's grave (Macbeth, Act V, Scene I).

My hands are of your color; but I shame
To wear a heart so white . . . .
A little water clears us of this deed:
How easy is it then! . . . . (Act II, Scene I)

Id Dynamics: The impulse (e.g., fighting fear of discovery)—defense (undoing, e.g., washing hands, mentioning Arabian perfume)—adaptation (e.g., 'wash your hands, put on your nightgown, look not so pale') configuration is fairly close to the primary process end of the continuum of psychic functioning; much closer than was the id dynamics in Devdas' letter. There are two reasons for it. One, Devdas had the luxury of organizing his thoughts; he had more time. Lady Macbeth, on the other hand, is dealing with a here-and-now live situation. Two, both Devdas and Lady Macbeth are coping with similar emotions: guilt. However, the similarity ends here. Accompanying guilt in the case of Devdas is a sense of embarrassment, shame. For Lady Macbeth, accompanying guilt is anxiety, fear. The actual stressors facing them are also very different. Deva is coping with a 'how-to-tell' situation (how to 'reject' Paro). Lady Macbeth is dealing with a 'how-to-hide' situation. Telling something is usually easier than hiding something from others. Deva has 'decided' to tell Paro. Lady Macbeth knows she cannot tell; not only can she not tell, she has got to make sure that no one finds out either. That is not easy. When we are in such a situation, anxiety and fear take control. The focus is more on defense than on adaptation.

Id dynamics is individualized, unique to each one of us. So is ego dynamics. The uniqueness lies in the configuration of impulse—defense—adaptation.

Ego Dynamics: The impulse (e.g., anger over non-washable blood spots) is defended (moderated) by focusing on purity of heart ('My hands are of your color; but I shame to wear a heart so white') and adapted by trying to emphasize (*a*) the need to appear normal, and (*b*) the ease with which blood may be washed away with a little water (' . . . put on your nightgown; look not so pale; . . .a little water clears us of this deed').

Balance Between Id Dynamics and Ego Dynamics: Unlike Devdas' letter in which ego dynamics was slightly more dominant than id dynamics, here, in case of Lady Macbeth, both id and ego appear to be in competition with each other. There is a tug-of-war going on between the two. There is an intense need to undo the fear of being related to Banquo's murder and, at the same time, there is anxiety that the efforts to do this may not succeed ('Here's the smell of the blood still: all the perfumes of Arabia will not sweeten this little hand [note the focus on "little hand" implying its innocence: how could a little hand like this commit a horrifying act of killing someone; yet, rationalizing the helplessness in removing blood spots] . . . . Yet, who would have thought the old man to have so much blood in him?'). A need to 'wash blood' (symbolizing washing guilt) counter-balanced by a fear that all the perfumes in Arabia would not be able to sweeten the little hand, is again counter-counter-balanced by the thought that there is nothing to it: a little water would wash it off; not only that, a creative compromise is sought by saying that she does not mind the smell of blood (because no amount of perfume would take that smell away because it is less of an evidence than visual blood spots), but she certainly does need to clean the spots, and a little water should do that.

Lady Macbeth is frantically engaged in playing the 'yo-yo' game of alternating between anxiety—fear—guilt, now defended with id dynamics (perfumes of Arabia, who thought the old man would have so much blood in him, a little water would wash it) and now with ego dynamics (put on your nightgown, look not so pale, Banquo is dead and buried and cannot come out [to testify that you killed him]).

Compared with Devdas' situation, Lady Macbeth is seeking and maintaining a precarious and fragile balance between id dynamics and ego dynamics.

Summary

We may now briefly summarize the main points in Schafer's Psychoanalytic Ego Psychology Approach to Rorschach data before presenting two Rorschach protocols to illustrate this approach.

1. Rorschach test responses may be seen as a product of the creative process in the subject.
2. Creative products indicate varying levels of psychic functioning.
   (*i*) Psychic functioning operates at different levels.
   (*ii*) Levels of psychic functioning are based on the extent to which one sees the effects of primary and/or secondary processes.
      (*A*) Primary process is characterized by no regard for reality; it is all fantasy, like childish, infantile thinking.
      (*B*) Secondary process indicates awareness of reality.
   (*iii*) Behaviors/thoughts may be understood in terms of
      (*A*) the degree to which behaviors/thoughts manifest the influence of primary process or secondary process, that is, *fluctuation in the levels of psychic functioning.*

(*B*) The range within which behaviors/thoughts fluctuate, that is, *the spread of psychic functioning.*

3. The concept of psychic functioning is related to the psychoanalytic divisions of the psyche in terms of id, ego and superego. Id manifests primary process thinking, while ego and superego reflect secondary process thinking.

4. Ego functions include (*a*) reality orientation (what is possible and what is not possible; also, what it appropriate and what is not), (*b*) defending itself from engaging in unreal/undesirable behaviors/thoughts, and (*c*) adapting ('taming') unreal, infantile impulses to the demands of social, cultural values.

5. Each behavior or thought has three elements in it: impulse, defense and adaptation. Impulse is defended and then expressed adaptatively.

6. Ego plays a critical role in recognizing impulses, in defending them and in adapting them to the socially–culturally approved outlets for expressing them. This is the psychology of ego— ego psychology.

7. Psychoanalytic ego psychology means that we attempt to understand how these ego processes (namely, impulse recognition, impulse defense and impulse adaptation) are carried out, in individuals in general and in any one person in particular.

8. The Psychoanalytic Ego Psychology Approach to the Rorschach test means looking at the Rorschach responses in order to understand how the subject's ego is performing its functions.

9. Since impulses may be felt either at the id level or at the ego level, both id and ego manifest an interaction between impulses, defenses and adaptation. Since the relative influences of these three are in a constantly fluctuating state, we have the units of id dynamics and ego dynamics.

10. Thus, to elaborate on the statement made earlier (No. 5), each behavior/thought has in it id dynamics and ego dynamics, and most importantly, the balance between these two dynamic forces.

11. Finally, looking at the Rorschach responses from the Psychoanalytic Ego Psychology Approach involves developing a personality picture of the subject in terms of his/her ego processes, that is, the interplay between id dynamics and ego dynamics.

We now describe this approach as per the categories listed in Chapter 4, and then the protocols of (*a*) Ramu, a twenty-two year old Indian male, and (*b*) Janet, a seventeen year old bi-racial American female (Caucasian mother, African–American father) to illustrate Schafer's Psychoanalytic Ego Psychology Approach.

Context
Schafer points out the context of the testing is extremely important. He draws attention specially to the tester–subject interactive relationship.

Rapport
In view of the important role of the examiner–subject unit's effect on test performance, it is very important to be sensitive to the nature and extent of a trusting relationship. Covering the tester–testee relationship issues under 'Interpersonal Dynamics in the Test Situation', Schafer (1954) devotes over 67 pages to the various clinical factors that may affect the test performance. Essentially, the fears and expectations, personal needs to impress each other, inability/unwillingness for mutual trust, and the way both tester and testee defend themselves against real/imaginary fears, need to be attended to for making the test performance worth its while.

Seating Arrangement
Face-to-face.

Instructions
'What could this be? What might it look like?'

Free Association Phase
If the testee gives only one response to Card I, he/she should be encouraged to give more (at least one more) response. A minimum of two responses is expected; the subject should be encouraged to try for one or two minutes.

Inquiry Phase

Inquiry is done after the subject has given the response to each card. It is *not* done at the end when all the 10 cards have been responded to.

Recording Responses

Verbatim.

Coding Responses

Same as in Rapaport's system. (Note: Lerner's system also uses the same coding system with slight modifications.)

Placing Responses in a Format

The structural summary is prepared in the same way as recommended by Rapaport; it looks similar to the ones developed by Hermann Rorschach and Samuel Beck.

In addition to a quantitative summary, Schafer also recommends an in-depth qualitative analysis. If fact, he cautions against too much reliance on quantitative scores. 'Rorschach technique has tended to restrict attention to scores and their sequences to the point where scores often become barriers between the tester and the patient . . . . Rapaport's emphasis on analysis of verbalization represents an important break with the score-oriented tradition . . .' (Schafer, 1954, p. 186).

Furthermore, emphasizing the need to attend to in-depth clinical issues instead of doing a superficial quantitative anlaysis, Schafer observes,

. . . it is the researcher's obligation to recognize and respect the structural and dynamic complexity of human psychic functioning and its expression in the test responses . . . comparing Rorschach scores and score averages even with the help of Cronbach's 'pattern tabulation' . . . or of multiple regression equations . . . can never do justice to the processes shaping the individual Rorschach record. Score analysis is *minimal* analysis (1954, p. 427, emphasis in original).

Schafer suggests formatting responses in terms of the range and spread of psychic functioning, impulse—defense—adaptation interactions at the id level and ego level, analyzing contents for themes of oral, anal, phallic and genital images.

Interpreting Responses

As a logical corollary to the psychoanalytic ego psychology frame, responses are interpreted in terms of the ego processes as exhibited in the id dynamics and ego dynamics relative to psychic functioning, and the thematic analysis of the contents.

Psychic functioning focuses on the range of and the shifts in primary and secondary processes. Essentially, this is examined in reference to id dynamics and ego dynamics and how they balance with each other.

For thematic analysis, one needs to look at the content of the responses in much the same way as one examines the content in Thematic Apperception Tests (TAT), dreams or free association. Thematic analysis is done for (*a*) the sequence in quantitative scores of location, determinants and content, (*b*) test attitudes and behaviors, and (*c*) dynamic themes in content. For example, in the thematic analysis of the sequence of quantitative scores, observes Schafer, one would ask, 'How is this sequence an expression of the same problems and means of coping with problems as are expressed in the dynamic themes in the content and in test attitudes and behavior?' (1954, p. 119).

Writing the Test Report

The format of the test report is in terms of the ego processes and in the way these processes are reflected in the integrative efforts on the part of the subject. Of course, the issues of diagnostic assessment and treatment are addressed within this context.

Following this description of Schafer's approach in terms of the Rorschach procedure categories, we now present the illustrative protocols.

SECTION III: ILLUSTRATIVE PROTOCOLS

Protocol 1: Ramu

Card I, Response 1: A mask that the actors use.

The external shape is like that of a mask. It has eyes, and nose cavities, side protruding flaps to tie in the head.

Card I, Response 2: Looks like a structural monument.

The structure and external periphery resembles like some monument.

Card II, Response 3: Two tribal dancers.

The external shape is like that of dancing tribal; it has eyes, horns.

Card II, Response 4: Some animal in charging position.

The shape is like that of an animal.

Card III, Response 5: Looks like a bow.

The shape resembles like a bow.

Card III, Response 6: Looks like a garden with trees, road.

The black structures look like trees and white space as road.

Card III, Response 7: Two pieces of log.

The shape and the cut portions look like piece of log.

Card III, Response 8: Two supernatural beings.

They have nose, mouth, but are not normal human beings because of special shape.

Card IV, Response 9: A supernatural being in walking position.

It has legs; upper portion is like mouth; the shape is not like that of a normal being.

Card IV, Response 10: Looks like 'shahnaai', an Indian flute.

It looks like a 'shahnaai' because of the shape tapering at one end; conical in shape.

Card V, Response 11: A bat.

It has spread wings; body looks like that of a bat.

Card V, Response 12: An arch.

The shape is like that of an arch found in religious places.

Card VI, Response 13: A toy gun.

Its shape is like that of a toy gun; it has nozzle, handle and trigger.

Card VI, Response 14: Skin of an animal, spread out flat.

On joining the skin, it will take the shape of an animal.

Card VI, Response 15: Two beastly figures.

The shape is like that of an animal; they have mouth, nose, hands and tail.

Card VII, Response 16: Two animals.

These have ears, mouth; they resemble some animal.

Card VIII, Response 17: A fur jacket.

It looks like a jacket because of color, shading and its shape.

Card VIII, Response 18: A volcano.

RAMU

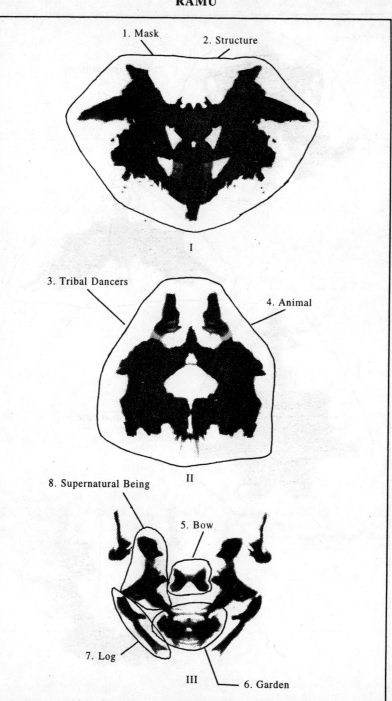

1. Mask   2. Structure

I

3. Tribal Dancers   4. Animal

II

8. Supernatural Being   5. Bow

7. Log

III   6. Garden

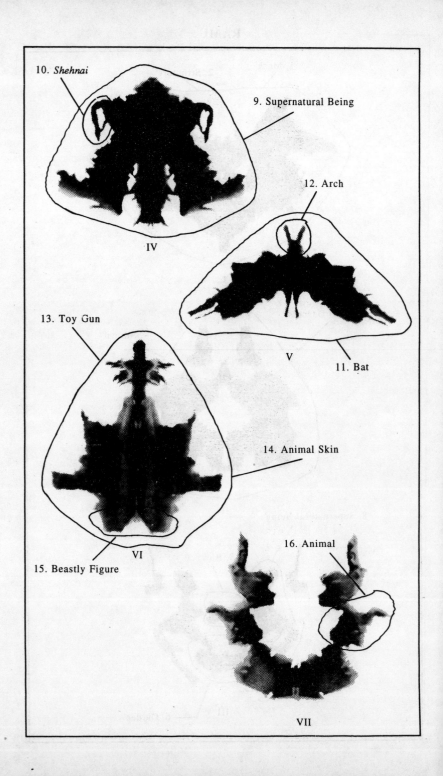

10. *Shehnai*

9. Supernatural Being

12. Arch

IV

13. Toy Gun

V

11. Bat

14. Animal Skin

16. Animal

VI

15. Beastly Figure

VII

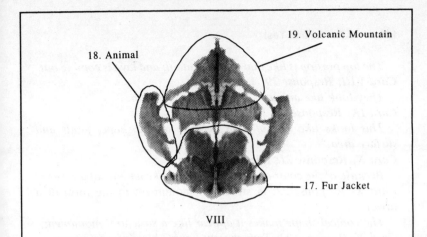

18. Animal

19. Volcanic Mountain

17. Fur Jacket

VIII

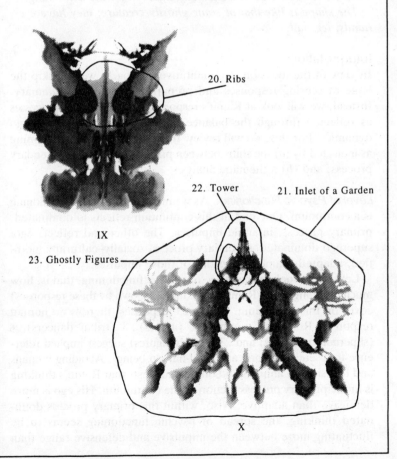

20. Ribs

IX

22. Tower

21. Inlet of a Garden

23. Ghostly Figures

X

The top portion is like that of a mountain; and lava is coming out.
Card VIII, Response 19: Two animals.

They look like animals; they have legs, mouth.
Card IX, Response 20: Ribs of man.

This looks like ribs of man because of the shape, joints and surface area.
Card X, Response 21: Inlet of a garden.

Because of the color and shape, it looks like an inlet of a garden.
Card X, Response 22: A structural monument in the form of a tower.

The conical shape makes it appear like a structural monument.
Card X, Response 23: Two ghostly figures blowing something.

The shape is like that of some ghostly creature; they have eyes, hands, leg, tail.

Interpretation

In view of the focus on the qualitative approach, we will skip the issue of scoring responses and preparing a structural summary. Instead, we will look at Ramu's responses in terms of ego processes as reflected through the balance between id dynamics and ego dynamics. For this, we will review the level of psychic functioning as indicated by (*a*) the shifts between primary process and secondary process, and (*b*) a thematic analysis.

Level of Psychic Functioning: As we may recall, psychic functioning is a continuum. One end of this continuum reflects id dominated, primary process, infantile impulses. The other end reflects ego/superego dominated, secondary process, socially–culturally modified, adapted ('tamed') versions of those impulses.

Let us first look at the range of psychic functioning, that is, how much of a range does Ramu's thinking (as shown by these responses) cover on this continuum. Of the 23 responses, there is no human response. Response numbers 1 (actors), 3 (tribal dancers), 8 (supernatural beings) and 23 (beastly figures) suggest implied reference to 'pseudo' (actors) and semi-human beings. Avoiding humans and focusing on animals and objects suggests that Ramu's thinking is in the primary process section of the continuum. His ego is more defensive than adaptive. Also, within this primary process dominated thinking, the spread of psychic functioning seems to be fluctuating more between the impulsive and defensive range than in the impulsive–adaptive range. A review of the sequence of responses would illustrate these observations.

Starting with a defensive posture in Response 1 (mask), he withdraws more toward the primary process in Response 2 (monument). In Response 3 (tribal dancers) there is again a shift in psychic functioning toward the secondary process (from inanimate monument to animate tribal dancers). The next shift is again back toward the primary process end of the continuum (Response 4: 'animal'); the shift continues in the primary process direction (Response 5: 'bow': impulse of aggression is dealt with defensively [attack]). Response 6 (garden with trees, road) shifts toward the secondary process and ego uses an adaptive approach. The next response (7) switches back to a defensive, passive posture ('two pieces of log'). Looking for some excitement in a kind of magical way, the level of psychic functioning shifts towards the secondary process (humans, rather than animals); however, the normal, earthly beings are perhaps difficult to relate to because that would require adaptive techniques; this perceived pressure is defended by seeing these persons as 'supernatural beings'; feeling a little bit relaxed, in the next response (9), the supernatural being is in a walking position. Perhaps that is enough of a normal, humanoid environment. Response 10 is 'shahnaai'; a benign, phallic, oral, incorporative, representation in a card (Card IV) that often evokes a masculine, authoritative, empowering image (often called 'the Father card'). Putting Responses 9 and 10 together, one may suspect Oedipal conflicts in Ramu. A shift back to the primary process is implied in Responses 11 (bat) and 12 (arch). Impulse (anger, sarcasm around male sexuality) is evident in Response 13 (a toy gun). It is both a defensive and adaptive response. It is a gun, but it is a harmless toy gun. One would look for evidence of inadequacy around masculinity (ego identity as well as ego ideal). The passive–aggressive tone in 'toy gun' is adapted and intellectualized in the next response (14): 'skin of an animal, spread out'. In Response 15, the movement is back toward the primary process end ('two beastly figures'); impulse (anger) is defended, and then adapted in Response 16 ('two animals'); and is expressed adaptatively in the next response (17: 'fur jacket'), as if saying, 'O.K. Enough of niceties; let me get real'. The next response (18: 'volcano') pushes psychic functioning pretty close to the level of the primary process. Response 19 again shows adaptation by diluting the intensity of the previous response and 'volcano' is 'replaced' with 'two animals'. He wants to humanize his response but can only get as close as a raw, undressed, person—Response 20 is 'ribs of man'. The next response again softens impulsivity (from 'volcano' to 'ribs of man' to 'inlet of a garden'). Feeling somewhat threatened with too much emotion, he shifts back to the adaptive level (inanimates) and Response 22 brings back a structural monument. Shifting again toward the secondary process (humans) but in a cautious manner, Response 23 is 'two ghostly figures, blowing something'. They are not killing or casting spells, but blowing.

In terms of levels of psychic functioning, Ramu shows a relatively small range (volcano, building, logs, garden, musical instrument, animals, humanoids). Although the range is not wide, the shifts are frequent.

Based on these observations, the balance between id dynamics and ego dynamics is tilted more toward id than ego. Coping mechanisms feature more defenses than adaptations.

Having commented on the range and shift in the levels of psychic functioning, we will now look at the thematic content in Ramu's responses.

Thematic Content: The ego processes are also seen at work in the content of the responses. The content needs to be examined in terms of what Schafer calls thematic analysis. Categorizing contents in terms of, for example, human, animal, household and architecture is, according to Schafer, a *static* way of looking at content. This does not tell us much about the ego processes as when we examine content for *dynamic* significance.

An illustration of thematic analysis is presented here. We are, however, focusing only on the dynamic content. Under ideal conditions, this needs to be supplemented by a thematic analysis of scores as well as test attitudes and behaviors.

Most of the content in Ramu's responses reflects a controlled, emotional tone—'mask', 'monument', 'animal', 'logs'. There is a slight indication of sadistic tendencies in 'bow', and a strong engulfing fear/anger in 'volcano'. One-word, somewhat muffled, responses suggest caution: a defensive rather than adaptive style of coping with problems. A tinge of benign softness is evident in 'trees', 'road' and 'inlet to garden'. Withdrawal and isolation: some indication of withdrawal is also seen in his avoidance of human responses.

Some of the comments about Ramu's level of psychic functioning as reflected in his response sequence and thematic analysis contrast sharply with the ones regarding the next protocol.

Protocol 2: Janet

Card I, Response 1: Pretty much I see a bunch of—, I don't see nothing—it looks like, it seems like—I see bats; a bat right here and a bat right here; and, they are just bats; I see two bats.

One is here; one is here; they ain't doing nothing or something; just chilling out; you know, chilling out; cooling in the breeze.
Card II, Response 2: It looks like, somebody—like somebody in trouble, you know; like in pool of blood—; well, it look like, they are inside a house, like, in dining room or something.

Like, they are shot or something; and laying in a pool of blood; seem like, a lot of people; like, in a street or something; like, someone ran and called an ambulance or something.
Card III, Response 3: I see two people—arguing—like, fighting or something—like—.

Two people here—; red stuff here, looks like blood.
Card IV, Response 4: I thought, I saw a big, old monster—; guess, he is in a forest or something.

He is big;—looks like, he is big—; looks like, he is watching out—for his prey or something to eat; this part is forest; forest is behind him.
Card V, Response 5: I see,—just a bat—looks like a bat.

It looks like a bat.
Card VI, Response 6: I don't know about that one;—like, something in a forest or something; like an animal or something—like, top of a tree or something.

This is forest here; and this is the animal on top of tree;—he is watching out—see nothing would go wrong; he could be watching for himself and his family.
Card VII, Response 7: I see—two people or something—like, they are talking;—peacefully—no argument or nothing; no fighting.

It is peaceful because I see no hands or weapons or nothing—it's quiet here—you don't see anything going on here—they could be talking about world.

JANET

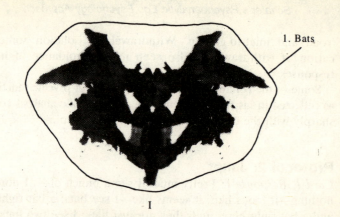

1. Bats

I

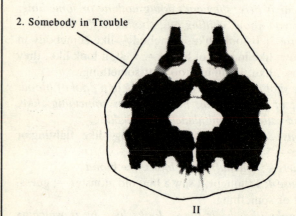

2. Somebody in Trouble

II

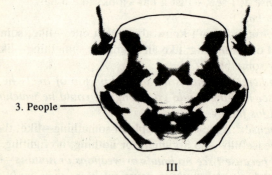

3. People

III

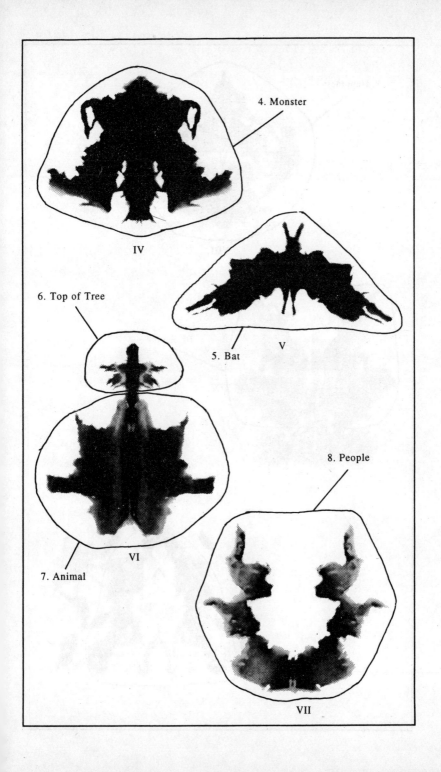

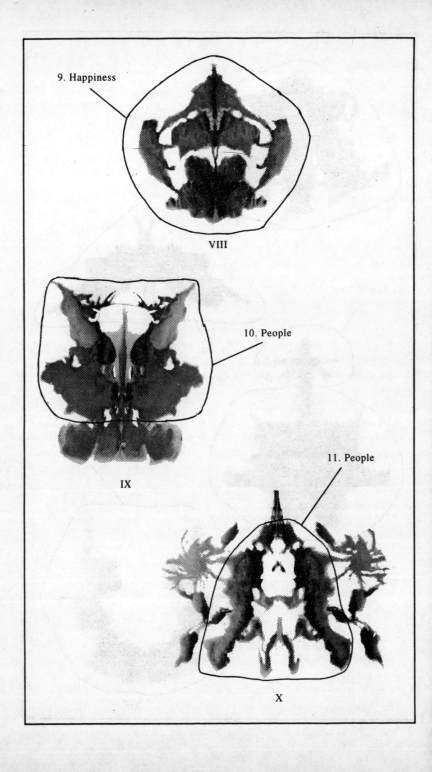

9. Happiness

VIII

10. People

IX

11. People

X

Card VIII, Response 8: I see happiness; um—I see people or something or whatever—like, they're having fun—could be a party or something at park or anywhere.

These are people here—like, they're playing basketball or something—they're having fun; it's like, colorful.

Card IX, Response 9: I see peoples fighting—I see a lot of people— like, a gang fight or something.

It just seems like, it—this is a line here in the middle between these two groups of people—looks like, they are trying to get across this line; like, a crowd of them are going here; it could be [named an area high school]—*high school*—.

Card X, Response 10: Um! I see two people having fun and enjoying whatever they are at;—I see other people out here, you know;—other people trying to make problems.

These two here are having fun, you know; like, when I go out with my boyfriend—people trying to make trouble—; he gets mad and gets into fight.

Interpretation

As in the case of Ramu, we will first comment on the level of psychic functioning and then follow it up by a thematic analysis.

Level of Psychic Functioning: Compared with Ramu, Janet's level of psychic functioning is influenced more by primary process thinking. Emotions and impulses are not only more intense but are also expressed more openly.

Janet seems to be seeing nothing else and is telling us something else. In Response 1, she starts by saying, 'Pretty much I see a bunch of—', and then clams up ('I don't see nothing'). A fear of letting something inappropriate out is repressed and then dressed up as something routine: 'bats'. In the inquiry, however, one sees that initially it was not bats that she saw because these are not just bats but the ones that are 'chilling in the breeze', as if they have had a hectic run of things and are now chilling in the breeze. 'Chilling' is often used as an antidote for anger and excitement. The impulse of hostility has been diluted by ego's defenses and is presented as something socially desirable. A more direct, in fact raw, manifestation of this repressed hostility is seen in Response 2, where aftermath of violence is seen: people are shot and are lying in a pool of blood; an ambulance has been called. Apparently, the hostility repressed was too strong for the ego to be contained. It broke lose. The indication of the intensity of the sadistic theme is too strong to exhaust in Response 2, and it continues in Response 3, where two people are fighting and there is blood. Card IV provides a calming relief, although violence is still an over-powering theme: 'He is big . . . watching out for his prey . . . forest is behind him'. Having fought and bled, there is time now for a little reprieve; although, one still has to be vigilant. Defense of naked violence (fighting, pool of blood) is now adapted (becoming cautious and alert). The hostility is adapted later by reaction-formation in Response 7: '. . . two people . . . like they are talking peacefully, no argument or nothing, no fighting'. With an intermittent tone of happiness in Response 8 ('happiness', 'party'), the theme of violence comes back in Response 9: 'I see peoples fighting . . . like a gang fight or something'. Finally, in Response 10, there is an attempt to defend aggression by adaptation: 'I see two people having fun . . . [but] other people trying to make problems'.

Thematic Analysis: Essentially, sadistic themes (violence, blood) dominate Janet's responses (Responses 2, 3, 9 and 10). She also uses projection (Response 10), undoing (Response 10) and reaction-formation (Response 7). Janet's responses are marked by sadistic images. Violent aggressiveness seems to be her preferred mode of handling problems and conflicts.

Compared with the responses of Ramu, Janet's psychic functioning reflects more defensive and adaptive dynamics. The balance between id dynamics and ego dynamics is disproportionately leaning toward the former than the latter.

Before closing this chapter, we must mention Schafer's cautions while doing a thematic analysis of the Rorschach responses. He stresses that (*a*) biographical information, (*b*) looking at the total protocol while examining the individual responses, and (*c*) reviewing the data from other tests should be taken into consideration for thematic analysis. He strongly advises against taking a mechanical approach for doing this. Specifically, he outlines a set of six criteria to ensure a reasonable amount of link between the data and the inferences. These are called 'Criteria for Judging the Adequacy of Interpretation'.

Criteria for Judging Adequacy of Interpretation

There are six criteria to be considered:

1. *Sufficient Evidence*: No data, no inference. Limited data limit our ability to interpret them. Looking at the demographic variables of the subject (age, sex, education, economic status, social and cultural background, etc.), examining the total protocol, reviewing the data from all the tests administered to the subject—all these need to be reviewed before interpreting the responses.

2. *Depth*: The dimension of depth varies along the continuum of primary process–secondary process. One needs to examine responses for evidence of primitive, naked impulses reflected in the responses on the primary process end (e.g., 'penis', 'vagina', 'breasts', 'buttocks') and the 'dressed up', ego/superego controlled expressions on the secondary process end (e.g., 'genitals', 'upper body') to estimate the depth of percepts.

3. *Manifest Form*: The criterion of manifest form involves identifying the impulses and conflicts underlying the responses (the form in which the psychological world appears). Material from life history, other tests, clinical interviews and behavioral observations are all necessary to address this criterion.

4. *Intensity*: Intensity involves assessing the strength of the trends observed. How strongly, for instance, do the oral tendencies affect the subject's behavior? Are they limited to the area of Oedipal conflicts? Are they reflected in interpersonal relations?

5. *Hierarchic Position*: This criterion is essentially based on the earlier mentioned criteria of depth, manifest form and intensity. You do not want to wander too far away from the data. At what level of intensity does a drive manifest itself? Is the anal retentive feature indicated at the primary process impulsive level reflected in most of the subject's behaviors? Is it limited to the ego ideal? Do we suspect that this drive has been sufficiently moderated by social–cultural values and is seen only in an adaptive way?

6. *Adaptive and Pathological Aspects*: This criterion focuses on identifying the balance between the adaptive and pathological aspects in a subject's personality. The final test report should not (as it frequently does) look like an inventory of the disabilities and limitations in the subject's personality. It is as important to identify the strengths of the subject as it is to point out his/her

limitations. For this, looking again at the total picture and all the data (specially the social–cultural context) is extremely important.

A Comment on the Criteria: Schafer points out that it is almost impossible to meet all of the above criteria. However, the goal should be to meet as many of them as possible. The larger the number of criteria met, more valid will be the report and its usefulness in clinical work.

SUMMARY

Schafer's approach is based on psychoanalytic theory, specially ego psychology. We started this chapter by providing an overview of Freudian psychoanalytic theory in Section I. In Section II, we presented Schafer's approach for looking at the Rorschach responses from the ego psychology orientation of psychoanalytic theory. Section III then provided two illustrative protocols.

A caution is in order. 'More than a solid grounding in Rorschach principles and technique is required for an adequate reading of this book', says Schafer in the Preface to his monumental work, 'The reader should also have had a general introduction to psychoanalytic theory and to the data of psychoanalytic observation' (1954, p. xiii).

What we have been able to do in this chapter is provide a glimpse of the complex approach. Readers are encouraged to consult the original work (Schafer, 1954) for a comprehensive understanding of this important approach for appreciating the theoretical value of the Rorschach test from a psychoanalytic perspective.

The next chapter, Paul Lerner's Psychoanalytic Object Relations Approach, provides yet another testimony to the rich potential of psychoanalytic theory for understanding human behavior.

8   LERNER'S PSYCHOANALYTIC OBJECT RELATIONS APPROACH

Schafer's (1954) Psychoanalytic Ego Psychology Approach to the Rorschach looks at the responses in terms of ego processes (namely, reality orientation, defense mechanisms and integrative efforts). Lerner's (1991) work, *Psychoanalytic Theory and the Rorschach*, integrates classical psychoanalytic concepts with the recent advances in the field, specifically the object relations approach for understanding human personality. He, like Schafer, draws heavily upon the original contributions of David Rapaport and enriches them with the current developments in the field of psychoanalysis.

In summary, Lerner reiterates the significance of the (*a*) tester–subject relationship, (*b*) dimensions of the Rorschach, (*c*) analysis of content, and (*d*) analysis of sequence within a psychoanalytic diagnostic scheme for developing an integrated personality picture of the subject.

In view of this object relations orientation, we will briefly outline the basic concepts of object relations theory in Section I. The next, Section II, will then describe Lerner's approach. Finally, Section III will present two illustrative protocols.

SECTION I: OBJECT RELATIONS THEORY

Object relations theory has evolved out of the classical psychoanalytic theory of personality development and psychopathology. Freudian theory states that:

1. the pleasure seeking tendency (conceptualized through the term libido) seeks satisfaction developmentally first through food (oral stage), next through excretory functions (anal stage) and then through physiological interest in genitals (genital stage),

2. the obstructions in seeking oral, anal or genital satisfaction cause frustration (anxiety, anger),
3. the inability to choose between various outlets for seeking satisfaction of the basic needs cause conflict,
4. psychopathology results when we insist on (*a*) only a certain way of seeking satisfaction of the needs (e.g., demanding to eat only say, *makkay de roti aur sarsoen daa saag* [corn-bread and mustard greens]), and/or (*b*) a rigid sequence of meeting these needs (e.g., no matter what, Bhola Babu has to have a cup of fresh cow-milk for his *poojaa* before having his breakfast), and
5. treatment of psychopathology involves 'back-tracking' the origins of such fixed/rigid behaviors to early childhood experiences (often traumatic experiences) related to oral, anal and genital stages.

In contrast to the Freudian theory, the development of personality and psychopathological behavior according to the object relations theory may be stated as follows:

1. The basic need of an infant is *not* seeking satisfaction of physiological needs but rather satisfaction of *relationship needs*.
2. The child seeks pleasure/satisfaction through *human contacts*, not through a milk-bottle or a clean, dry diaper; the object sought is *not* the bottle of milk, but the mother who provides warmth, comfort and security; the focus is on the mother and not on the milk-bottle ('I need my mother, not a milk-bottle; I know, she will of course, give me milk but she will give me a lot more than that: comfort, security'). Mother is everything. The child probably already has the archetype of mother in his/her collective unconscious. Goes a Hindi film song: *Uskoe nahin dekhaa humnay magur per uskee zaroorat kyaa hogee, aiy Maa, tayri soorat say alag Bhagwaan kee soorat kyaa hogee* (I haven't seen Him, but I don't need to, O! Mother! How could God's face be different from yours?).
3. For Freud, the term 'object' meant persons, events, places, animate objects and inanimate objects. In object relations theory, the term 'object' means only human beings.
4. The child sees and experiences human beings ('objects') around him/her; gradually, these human beings acquire a place in the mental world (psyche) of the child. In other words, they are *internalized* by him/her.

5. Thus, there exists two sets of worlds for the child (in fact, for all of us). There is the *external world of objects* (mother, father, siblings, *naanee* [maternal grandma]) and then there is the *internal world of objects* (mother feeds me, father changes my diaper, brother plays with me, *naanee* tells me stories).

6. There is yet another very important object in this world of objects—*self*. There is, for instance, mother-object, father-object and *naanee*-object. Well, there is also the self-object. A very important object relations theorist (Otto Kernberg) places a hyphen between self and object: *self-object*). For Kernberg (1984), self-object is representation of the parents in the child's mind.

   Another important object relations theorist, Heinz Kohut (1971, 1977), emphasizes the concept of self and also includes significant persons (parents, siblings, grandparents) in the child's life as part of his/her self. In Kohut's theory self consists of real people, not people in the outside world who are represented in the child's mind. And, because of this difference in conceptualization, Kohut gets rid of the hyphen (that we find in Kernberg's concept). For Kohut, it is *selfobject*—'I am me *and* my significant others'.

7. Object relations theorists hold that personality development takes place not in terms of moving from oral to anal to genital stages, but rather in terms of changes in structures/patterns/units of object relations.

   For example, according to Margaret Mahler (1952; Mahler, Pine and Bergman, 1975), personality develops in three phases of object relations:
   (*i*) *autistic phase*: birth to four weeks, child is not aware of others around him/her, breast-sucking is like reflex action,
   (*ii*) *symbiotic phase*: four to five weeks to five months, the world still is without objects, mother has yet to be experienced as a separate entity, and
   (*iii*) *separation–individuation phase*:
      (*A*) *differentiation sub-phase*: five to six months to about 10 months, child tends to separate mother perceptually, beginnings of 'separation anxiety',
      (*B*) *practicing sub-phase*: 10 months to about 16 months, 'hatching' phase, child crawls, wandering around but

periodically comes back and checks out the mother is available, a kind of tasting, experiencing independence, and
(*C*) *rappoachement sub-phase*: 16 months to about 30 months, child starts enjoying independence, yet, also wants/needs reassurance from mother.

According to another very influential object relations theorist, Melanie Klein (1975), the development in terms of object relations takes place in that the infant moves from what she calls one position to another position.

A fear of losing the mother makes him/her suspicious and guarded. This is the first position from birth until about four months of age; Klein calls this the *paranoid–schizoid position*: fear of losing mother and, therefore, settling down to being alone. During this phase, the infant encounters the first object—the breast of the mother (actually, this is 'part-object' because, he/she has not yet formed a whole picture of the mother). The child enjoys sucking (it provides nourishment) and also like to 'destroy' it (Klein did subscribe to Freud's theory of life instinct and death instinct). This is the beginning of splitting of 'good' and 'bad': good breast versus bad breast. We may note here that Kernberg has identified splitting as an important coping mechanism in adults. It is used pathologically by persons suffering from borderline personality disorder (also characterized by disturbances in impulse control, ego identity and self-mutilating behaviors).

The second position, says Klein, is the *depressive position*, beginning from six months to about 12 months. At this stage (rather, in this position), mother evolves from the 'part-object' to a 'whole-object'. Most importantly, unlike the first paranoid–schizoid position when splitting is 'either good *or* bad', in the second position, splitting is compromised: splitting is 'good *and* bad'.

8. In classical psychoanalytic theory, psychopathology resulted from the fact that libido (that is, the process of seeking need satisfaction) shifted from appropriate objects (both human and non-human objects) to inappropriate objects (again, both human and non-human).

In the object relations theory, psychopathology results from lack of separation and/or integration in patterns of object relations, that is, in the lack of differentiation between self and objects (only humans, not non-humans). The boundaries between self and non-self (human beings) are fuzzy, blurred, foggy. For example, one person may over-incorporate others around him/her. Another may over-exclude him/herself from people around him/her.

In summary then, object relations theory is an advancement over psychoanalytic drive theory and ego psychology. It has expanded the unit of study from the individual in isolation to individuals in relationships. The prototypal unit is the mother–child relationship. Some of the key concepts in object relations theory are:

1. Fairbairn's (1992) three stages of growth: (*a*) infantile dependence (early oral stage: breast of the mother [part-object], late oral stage: mother with breast [whole-object] treated as a part-object), (*b*) transitional stage (whole-object treated as contents), and (*c*) mature dependence (whole-object along with genitals),
2. Melanie Klein's (1952) paranoid–schizoid position and depressive position,
3. Margaret Mahler's (Mahler, Pine and Bergman, 1975) pre-objectal experiences, and growth in terms of autistic, symbiotic and separation–individuation,
4. Otto Kernberg's (1984) internalized object relations, introjection and ego-splitting, and
5. Heinz Kohut's (1971) selfobject.

We have provided here only a brief capsule-view of the object relations theory mainly to contexualize Lerner's approach. Readers interested in a detailed discussion of the object relations (O–R) theories may want to consult Frank Summers (1994). For an appreciation of the theoretical foundations of the object relations theory, an excellent source is Kernberg (1984).

SECTION II: PSYCHOANALYTIC OBJECT RELATIONS APPROACH

Lerner's (1991) theoretical orientation to the Rorschach represents a robust blend of classical psychoanalytic theory, and its recent developments in the fields of object relations theory, psychodynamic developmental theory and self psychology. It recognizes but does not stress formal scores. It is patient-centered, not psychometric data-centered. Like Schafer, Lerner stresses the significance of the patient-examiner relationship. Lerner's approach may be described in terms of:

1. elements in the psychological test report,
2. diagnostic system,
3. dimensions of the Rorschach test,
4. analysis of content, and
5. analysis of sequence.

Elements in the Psychological Test Report

A psychological test report should describe the subject in terms of (*a*) *character structure* (e.g., hysterical, depressed, obsessive–compulsive, narcissistic, masochistic, paranoid, infantile, schizoid), (*b*) *organization of thought* (e.g., rigid thinking characterizing an obsessive–compulsive character, emotional thinking of the hysterical character, the way the subject approaches problem-solving situations), (*c*) *organization of emotions* (e.g., how does the subject experience emotions phenomenologically, his/her 'affect capacity', affect management), (*d*) *core dynamics* (e.g., significant motives, urges featuring the subject's behaviors and thoughts, sexuality, disturbances in object relations, problems in developing/maintaining self-cohesion), and lastly (*e*) suggestions for *treatment planning*.

In order to prepare the psychological test report addressing these areas, a tester has to conceptualize not only a diagnostic system for core character features, but also a system to examine specific Rorschach dimensions and a process for drawing inferences from these dimensions. Lerner proposes a psychoanalytic diagnostic system, identifies specific Rorschach dimensions and the specific steps for analyzing content and sequence, and finally, develops inference statements integrating the total personality picture of the subject.

Diagnostic System

Based on psychoanalytic concepts, Lerner identifies eight core character types and six levels of personality organizations. The eight core characters are (*a*) hysterical, (*b*) obsessive–compulsive, (*c*) depressive, (*d*) masochistic, (*e*) infantile, (*f*) narcissistic, (*g*) schizoid, and (*h*) paranoid.

The six levels of personality organization are: (*a*) level of instinctual development, (*b*) manifestations of ego weaknesses, (*c*) level of defensive organization, (*d*) level of internalized object relations, (*e*) level of superego development, and (*f*) level of ego identity. A brief description of each of these follows.

Core Characters

Hysterical Character: Emotional, exhibitionistic and lively, and hysterical personalities portray their self in emotional terms. They *feel* rather than *think*. '. . .central to the hysteric's presentation is a sense of self as part child and part adult' (Lerner, 1991, p. 31).

Obsessive–Compulsive Character: Fixated at the anal level in terms of psychosexual development, obsessive–compulsives show rigidity, obsession with details and come across as perfectionistic. 'For these individuals, preoccupied with issues of control, activity has a marked driven quality' (Lerner, 1991, p. 31).

Depressive Character: Unable to manage aggression, depressive characters also indicate fear of losing love, and are overly critical of self and others. 'To bolster their defenses against the expression and experience of anger, depressive characters are often ingratiating, subservient, and deferential' (Lerner, 1991, p. 32).

Masochistic Character: Masochists enjoy suffering. They feel it is their *bhaagya* ('destiny') to be punished. If you praise them, they suspect your motives. 'Masochists tend to provoke those whom they feel disappointed by; that is, behind the provocation is a disappointment in love' (Lerner, 1991, p. 32).

Infantile Character: Infantiles are in many ways like the hystericals; only more childish and theatrical. 'The infantile patient begins relationships with great hopes and unrealistic expectations and feels bitter when the relationship fails and the expectations of rescue, nurturance, and unlimited care are not fulfilled' (Lerner, 1991, p. 33).

Narcissistic Character: 'If there is God/Goddess on this earth, it is me' is the theme of a narcissistic person. Excessive need for love and recognition and never ever able to get what he/she rightfully deserves keeps him/her resentful towards the world at large. Narcissists are 'hypervigilant, hypersensitive, thin-skinned, and painfully vulnerable' (Lerner, 1991, p. 34).

Schizoid Character: 'I love you so much that I want to stay away from you lest I smother you to death.' That's the theme song in schizoids. 'Out of a refusal to invest in objects in the outer world, the schizoid individual radically invests in his or her inner world' (Lerner, 1991, p. 34).

Paranoid Character: Paranoids are highly suspicious and guarded. No one does things without an ulterior motive they believe. They 'see' connections in remote events and justify their mistrust of others. '. . . such individuals are rigid, malignantly distrustful, highly suspicious, and continually embattled with persecutory objects' (Lerner, 1991, p. 35).

Levels of Personality Organization
In addition to understanding personalities in terms of descriptive features as described earlier, following Kernberg (1970), Lerner recommends that the descriptive categories be supplemented by also looking at the different levels at which these core characters are organized. Each of these levels may indicate three degrees of intensity in different core personality characters: low, intermediate and high.

Level of Instinctual Development: Instinctual development describes growth in terms of oral, anal, phallic, latency and genital stages of psychosexual development, specially in terms of genital and pre-genital stages. A lower level indicates organization at the pre-genital aggression. An intermediate level reflects pre-genital, oral regressive features. At the higher level, impulses are organized at the genital stage.

Level of Manifestations of Ego Weaknesses: At the lower level, one sees poor impulse control. At the intermediate level, impulses are relatively structured. And, at the higher level, ego functions are relatively intact. The primary process seems to have been replaced by the secondary process.

Level of Defensive Organization: The lower level manifests splitting as a predominant defense. Reaction-formation is more evident at the intermediate level, and repression appears to be the preferred mode of defense at the higher level.

Level of Internalized Object Relations: The lower level internalized object relations lack constancy and center around instant satisfaction. The intermediate level internalized object relations are somewhat non-pathological; but one does notice conflictual patterns in external object relations. At the higher level, internalized object relations are normal, indicating constancy and whole-objects.

Level of Superego Development: There is hardly any superego evidence at the lower level. One sees paranoia and sadistic tendencies. At the intermediate level, ego–superego boundaries are fuzzy. At the higher level, however, superego comes across as hyper-critical and demanding.

Level of Ego Identity: At the lower level, ego is not integrated. 'Bad' and 'good' elements of self are split. There is some integration at the intermediate level; however, there is evidence of contradictory tendencies because of a flexible value-system. The higher level ego identity reflects integration along with a stable self-percept.

In Lerner's system the diagnostic system in terms of the eight core characters and the six levels of personality organization is interfaced with the six Rorschach test dimensions, namely, (*a*) human movement, (*b*) form, (*c*) form level, (*d*) color, (*e*) shading, and (*f*) blackness. Having mentioned the core characters and levels of personality organization, we will now describe these six dimensions.

Dimensions of the Rorschach Test

Lerner lists here the major test scores that need to be reviewed for understanding how the subject reflects the relative evidence for the eight core characters and at the various levels of personality organization.

Human Movement Response

Human movement response on the Rorschach test provides extremely rich information for understanding personality. Lerner draws upon the contributions of Mayman (1977) in emphasizing the value of this dimension. Lerner reiterates the importance of Mayman's five variables that affect experience of movement on the test:

1. *Perceptual Determinants*: The subject feels uncomfortable with the phenomenologically experienced 'imbalance' in the inkblots and 'introduces' movement to create what the Gestalts call a 'good figure' (law of *Pragnanz*).
2. *Fantasy*: Capacity to fantasize is important for experiencing movement.
3. *Kinesthetic Experience*: The way movement is felt (as shown in the content of the responses), indicates how the subject is experiencing his/her 'self-hood'.
4. *Object Representation*: Movement responses also reflect object representation. This is shown in the objects seen in movement.
5. *Empathy*: One may be able to infer the capacity for empathy in the subject through the nature and extent of his/her movement responses.

Form Response

The second Rorschach test dimension, says Lerner, is the use of form as a determinant by the subject. Incorporating the contributions of Schachtel (1966), Lerner points out that the form responses indicate (*a*) the *attitude* of the subject ('active attitude'—a detailed processing to 'fit' the inkblot to the memory images and a 'typical attitude' in which form is used in a cut-and-dry routine manner), and (*b*) the *perceptual hold* (how strongly or feebly does the subject grasp the image aroused by the blots).

Form Level

In addition to the use of form as a determinant, there is also the 'sub-issue' of the quality of the form seen: good form (F+), ordinarily seen forms (Fo), weak but acceptable forms (Fw+), unacceptable forms (Fw−), arbitrarily seen forms (F−), etc. The range in levels of forms may vary from one end of the scale where a form appears to be creative within the reality of the blot features, to the other end where there is no evidence of respecting reality and, as a result, form level is arbitrary and defies reality.

Color

Supporting the findings and observations of Schachtel (1966), Lerner points out that color on the Rorschach is a *phenomenological, affective experience* indicating a *perceptual style* and helps us understand the close relationship between color and emotions.

('Come on, let's throw colors at each other, it's the colorful day!') *Khaloe rung humaaray sung, aaj din rung-rungeelaa ayaa* goes a film song celebrating the Indian festival of Holi when it is permissible to sprinkle colored water on each other and rub colored powder (*gulaal, abeer*) on each other's face!

Color makes things look better (color TV is considered better than black-and-white TV). Color implies fun and excitement. When CocaCola was the in-thing in India, a commercial jingle used to be, *Rung jamaataa hai CocaCola* ('CocaCola makes things colorful').

Shading

The way color relates to emotions, shading relates to anxiety. Use of shading as a determinant (including rejection of the black-and-white cards, e.g., I, IV, V and VI) may indicate the possibility of intolerance of ambiguity. Lerner lists a number of problems involved in anxiety assessment like different forms of anxiety (e.g., bounded, free-floating, panic), not evident as distinctly as say, emotions, etc. He suggests that it is important for the tester to understand how the subject *experiences* and *expresses* anxiety, specially in terms of defensive organization, and the impairment caused by anxiety in the subject's functioning.

Blackness

The last Rorschach dimension discussed by Lerner is perception and the experience of blackness. Lerner's (1988) research has identified blackness as a critical variable to look out for while examining Rorschach protocols. He points out that blackness indicates a developmentally earlier form of depression. It brings out the phenomenological experience of depression characterized by feelings of emptiness. According to him, there are three indications of this experience of depression on the Rorschach, namely, (*a*) little or no use of determinants of movement, color and shading, (*b*) themes of hollowness and emptiness, and (*c*) contents indicating a quality of injury.

The six Rorschach test dimensions constitute the nucleus of data in Lerner's system. In addition, he also suggests examining two other important areas—content and sequence.

Analysis of Content

Lerner considers content analysis as an important area to be examined in the test. It provides 'an experiential perspective' (Lerner, 1991, p. 108). While pointing out that content analysis is a step removed from the response, he also advises against not looking at content to develop an integrated personality picture. 'To exclude content altogether', says Lerner, 'is to ignore an immensely rich and valuable source of information' (ibid., p. 107).

In analyzing content, Lerner recommends looking at (*a*) the whole verbalization of the subject (both during free association as well as inquiry phases), (*b*) embellishments, (*c*) specific links between the data and the inferences drawn, and (*d*) conceptualizing content as a way of accessing the subject's internal object relations.

He suggests using three out of Mayman's (1977) five criteria in connection with human movement responses, namely, the role of fantasy in shaping content, kinesthesia as indicative of self-experience, and actual figures involved in movement indicating the subject's object representation.

Analysis of Sequence

Finally, it is also important to examine the sequence in which responses are given to assess the nature and extent of fluctuations in the primary process and secondary process thinking in the subject. We may recall this is also an important element in Schafer's system. The focus in Lerner's system, however, is on looking at (*a*) the sequence in the form level of the responses, and (*b*) the sequence in responses involving deviant verbalizations (e.g., fabulized, confabulized, contaminations, etc.).

Having done the Rorschach protocol analysis in terms of the earlier mentioned five areas (namely, human movement responses, form responses, form level, content and sequence), Lerner specifies a sequence for drawing inferences from the data for developing a personality profile of the subject. Here he brings back the basic elements in the psychological test reports, namely, character structure, organization of thought, organization of emotions, core dynamics and treatment planning.

Having outlined the basics in Lerner's system, we will now present his system within the framework of the areas listed in Chapter 4, on the Rorschach procedure, that is, context, rapport, seating arrangement, instructions, free association phase, inquiry phase, recording responses, coding responses, placing responses in a format, interpreting responses and writing the test report.

Context and Rapport

In addition to the purpose of testing, physical setting, demographics, etc., an important issue addressed by Lerner that includes both context and rapport is the unit of the tester–subject, or what he calls patient–examiner, relationship.

In classical psychoanalytic literature, the issue of the tester–subject relationship was examined in terms of defenses. Lerner (1988) re-frames this relationship with reference to advances in psychoanalysis in the areas of object relations and self psychology. Sensitivity to these factors not only enhances the richness of the context and rapport but also provides additional data for interpreting test data.

Lerner draws our attention to the fact of transference and counter-transference in the patient–examiner relationship. He recommends looking at it at three levels: (*a*) externalization of internal object relations, (*b*) empathy, and (*c*) *mirroring* and *idealizing* transference.

Lerner points out that the subject may attribute either the role of internal object (from the self-object relation) or the role of self onto the examiner. Counter-transference on the examiner's part involves identifying with the internal object or with the self respectively. In either case, it is based on the mechanism of projective identification.

The tester–subject relationship can be used by the examiner to review the extent to which he/she has been able to empathize with the subject. Such information could be important data for other indicators of empathy in the Rorschach test (e.g., human movement response).

Finally, Lerner (1991) draws attention to the specific transferences of *mirroring* and *idealizing* in conceptualizing the patient–examiner relationship. In the case of mirroring transference, the subject expects special, privileged treatment by the tester. In idealizing transference, on the other hand, the expectation is to be 'mothered' by the examiner. In both situations, counter-transference of the examiner could result in influencing the test responses.

Seating Arrangement
Face-to-face.

Instructions
'Tell me please, what do you see? What might this be?'

Free Association Phase
In case of rejections, the subject is to be encouraged to try for about two minutes.

Inquiry
Inquiry is done *after* each card, *not* at the end when all 10 cards have been responded to.

Recording Responses
Verbatim. Notes are also made of behaviors/attitudes.

Coding Responses
Responses are coded for location, determinants, form level, content, deviant verbalizations and special scores. We present the details of each of these.

1. LOCATION
W   Whole blot or almost whole blot, e.g., bat (Card I), two bears dancing (Card II), monster (Card IV).

D   Commonly used area is selected, e.g., monkey, upside down (Card III, top red area), big feet (Card IV, lower sides), peacock (Card X, lower, middle, green part).

Dd   Less commonly used part of the blot is used, e.g., belt buckle (Card I, center, small whitish part), statue of God (Card II, middle white, top part), gateway to island (Card VII, bottom, center).

Dr Rare detail, arbitrarily selected, perceptually imbalanced, often shading is a determinant, e.g., pieces of flesh (Card I, sides, below the wing-like area), dinosaur (Card IV, top, sides), angry pig (Card VII, middle, sides).

S White space, e.g., temple (Card II, middle, white part), *gharaa* (baked clay-pot) (Card VII, middle white area), fog (Card IX, top middle, whitish area).

De Detail edge, using contours of an area, e.g., damaged temple dome (Card II, middle white part, lower edges), melted edge of a burnt out candle (Card IV, center, bottom part), torn leaf (Card VI, lower, sides, end parts).

Do Oligophrenic detail, responding to an area by isolating it from the whole blot or from a commonly used area, e.g., heads (Card III, top parts of human-like figures), open mouth (Card VII, top parts of human-like faces), tail (Card VIII, part of the rodent-like side figures).

2. DETERMINANTS

F Form, e.g., bat (Card I), temple dome (Card II, middle, top), rats (Card VIII, side figures).

M Human movement, e.g., two boxers fighting (Card II), two men bent down, picking up something (Card III), monster, walking away from you (Card IV).

FM Animal movement, e.g., baby elephants, standing with their trunks together (Card II), bat, flying (Card V), two peacocks, dancing (Card X, lower, center, green part).

FC Form and color—however, form is primary, dominant, e.g., torn, bluish grey flag (Card VIII, middle part), rodents, pink (Card VIII, side figures), crabs, blue (Card X, top, side area).

CF Color and form—however, color is primary, dominant, e.g., pretty, red butterfly (Card VIII, lower middle part), strawberry icecream (Card IX, lower area), green peacock (Card X, lower, center).

C Pure color, e.g., blood (Card II, lower part), *Holi* colors (Card X), pretty colors (Card X).

FC arb Form and color—however, color is used arbitrarily, e.g., red monkey (Card III, top, sides), bone marrow, looks pinkish (Card IX, lower area), yellow tigers (Card X, lower, middle area).

FCc, CFc, Cc Texture or nuances of shading are used, e.g., cottonball candy (Card IX, lower pink part), blob of cow-dung (Card IV, middle area).

FCh Light–dark shadings (chiaroscuro) are used with as much significance as form, e.g., stormy clouds (Card IV), sky, after rain (Card IX, middle white part).

FC' Form and blackness—however, form is dominant, e.g., black vampire (Card V), black monster (Card IV).

C' Blackness only, e.g., gloom (Card IV), darkness (Card I).

C'F Blackness and form—however, blackness is dominant, e.g., black river (Card IV, middle part), Mother Kaali's face (Card III, lower, middle part).

Fc Form and shading nuances to describe the boundaries of the percept, e.g., face of devil, eyes, mouth (Card IX, middle part), islands, under sun (Card VII).

3. FORM LEVEL

F+ Convincing, articulate, e.g., two persons, trying to pick up something (Card III), giant monster, sitting on a tree-trunk (Card IV).

Fo Percepts seen with little effort, e.g., bat (Card I), butterfly (Card V).

Fw+ Not convincing, although, acceptable, e.g., top of mountain, with snow on it (Card IV), persons doing gymnastics (Card I).

Fw− Percepts hardly matching with blot areas, e.g., mountain God (Card I, lower, middle part), river, surrounded by mountains (Card II).

F− Percepts seen do not match at all with the blot areas, e.g., people sitting under a tree (Card X, whole), woolen dress (Card VII, lower, middle part).

Fv Objects seen have a vague form, e.g., rocks facing each other (Card II), explosion (Card IX).

Fs Spoiled form, incongruent details, e.g., snake with the head of a chicken (Card IV), turtle with four legs and a beard (Card VI).

4. CONTENT

H Whole human, e.g., monster (Card IV), two women (Card III).

Hd Part human, e.g., face of a clown (Card II), big feet (Card IV).

A   Whole animal, e.g., bat (Card V), rats (Card VIII).

Ad   Part animal, e.g., pig's face Card VII), peacock wings (Card X).

Obj   Inanimate objects, e.g., open book (Card VII), round table (Card III).

Pl   Plants, flowers, trees, leaves, e.g., tree trunk (Card IV), autumn leaves (Card IX).

Ant   Anatomy, e.g., spinal cord (Card VI), cerebellum (Card VIII).

Geog   Geography, e.g., map of Asia (Card I), mountains (Card VII).

Arch   Architecture, e.g., castle (Card II), entrance to cave (Card VII).

Cl   Clouds

Bl   Blood

Sex   Sexual, e.g., breasts, vagina, penis.

5. DEVIANT VERBALIZATION

Fab   Fabulized responses: excessive emotions/specificity, e.g., Bramha, Vishnu, Mahesh (Card X), looks like someone in trouble, you know, like in a pool of blood (Card II).

Fab-Comb   Fabulized combinations, e.g., bear shaking hands with a lizard (Card VIII), two hens playing, 'sailor went to sea, sea, sea' (Card II).

Confab   Confabulized: excessive embellishment, e.g., two monkeys poking the paws of this bear, both monkeys want to eat the reddish part (Card III), two rocks, linked with peace, and peace has built this temple (Card II).

Contam   Contaminated: two separate percepts seen as one, e.g., I wanted to say, butterfly, but it is a butterfly mixed with bat, like, Spielberger's thing (Card V), two snakes with the neck of a chicken or turkey (Card II).

Aut   Autistic logic, usually based on position of the blot area, e.g., this is the woman's, you know, that's where it is, you know (Card VII, bottom, center), there is no uterus here, and unless there is a uterus, a baby can't be conceived, the breasts, however, can develop (Card II).

Pec   Peculiar, out of context, e.g., two chickens wanting to wash their feet before entering this temple (Card II).

Queer   Unusual, unconventional verbalizations, e.g., I see blood, yesterday, I cut my finger when I was lifting, there was blood, you know (Card II).

Vague   Percepts with an 'almost-looks-like' statements, e.g., almost looks like a spider, without legs (Card II).

Conf   Confusion, unsure about the percept, e.g., I don't know about that one; like, something in a forest or something, like, an animal or something, like top of tree or something, I don't know (Card VI), what's that cartoon character? Snaggletooth? That looks like, Snaggletooth; looks like a female organ too; is that what it is? (Card VI).

Incoh   Incoherence, verbalizing irrelevant material, e.g., when girls press their breasts against the chest of boys, their breasts sag down (Card X).

6. ADDITIONAL SCORES

m   Inanimate movement, e.g., floating clouds (Card VII), fire rising up in the jungle (Card IX).

C denial,   Color, blackness, shading are used in a negative
C' denial,   manner, e.g., a leaf, without lots of colors (Card
Ch denial   VI), if you exclude the lighter portion, it appears very magnificent chandlier (Card IV).

C ref,   Color, blackness, shading are mentioned but are not
C' ref,   integrated with the percept, e.g., these are red
Ch ref   jackals (Card VIII), pretty combination of lightness and darkness, very pretty (Card VII).

C avoid,   Color, blackness, shading is implied, but not expli-
C' avoid,   citly mentioned, e.g., this looks like something you
Ch avoid   see on New Year's eve, after you have had a couple [of drinks] (Card X).

C impot,   Inability (impotence) to utilize color, blackness,
C' impot,   shading, is expressed, e.g., face of a monkey, like
Ch impot   langoors, you know (Card VII), I don't know what this blue thing in the middle is (Card X).

C symbolism Color is mentioned symbolically, e.g., green
symbolizes worship (Card X), pink is heat, green
is harmony (Card IX).

Once the responses have been coded (scored), they are placed in a
format for drawing inferences about the subject's personality. It
needs to be noted that Lerner recommends not restricting oneself
with an overemphasis on quantitative scores.

Placing Responses in a Format
The format for analyzing responses is essentially (*a*) the whole
protocol, and (*b*) a simple listing of the form level frequencies of
the responses, the actual content of kinesthesia and of human
figures in the responses. One does not need to prepare a comprehensive structural summary.

Interpreting Responses
The interpretation process in Lerner's system consists of two phases:
(*a*) first order inferences, and (*b*) transformations.

First order inferences involve examining the form level of the
responses, kinesthesia and human figures in the responses. In the
transformations stage, one goes through each response, both during
the free association as well as inquiry phases, one by one and
transforms their clinical significance within the theoretical system
(as developed by Lerner), namely, core character structure (e.g.,
hysterical, depressed, infantile, schizoid, etc.), organization of
thought (e.g., reality testing, boundaries between self and object,
etc.), organization of emotions (e.g., emotional control, impulsivity,
defenses, etc.), core dynamics (e.g., motives, conflicts in sexuality,
object relations, cohesion in self, etc.) and diagnostic/treatment
issues (e.g., differential diagnosis, danger to self/other, treatment
focus, etc.).

Writing the Test Report
Finally, the statements in these two sections (first order inferences,
and transformations) are synthesized into a test report, providing
an integrated personality picture of the subject in terms of character
structure, thought organization, affect organization and core
dynamics, addressing the specific issues and concerns for which
testing was done.

Having briefly described Lerner's psychoanalytic object relations
system for analyzing, tabulating and interpreting the Rorschach

test, we will next illustrate his system by reviewing two protocols: (*a*) Anil, a twenty-three year old, Indian male, and (*b*) JoAnn, a thirty-four year old, African–American female.

SECTION III: ILLUSTRATIVE PROTOCOLS

Protocol 1: Anil
Card I, Response 1: Flying moth.
   Midway; there are two tentacles; and a tail; this moth is grey; not absolutely, absolutely black.
   Score: W, Fo, A, C denial.
Card I, Response 2: Crown of a king.
   This is conical in structure; similar to crowns in old fables.
   Score: W, F+, Obj.
Card II, Response 3: Bears, clapping hands; head looks very different.
   The colors are like the colors of a bear; the animal is stocky, and conical; two appendages-like legs; they are clapping hands; the red smears are something typical.
   Score: W, FMo, C', A, C avoidance.
Card III, Response 4: Two apes involved in some activity: churning or some manual task.
   Black figures look like apes; specially the face; limbs stretched out as if they are doing some manual task.
   Score: W, FMo, C', A.
Card IV, Response 5: Frog, hung upside down for dissection.
   Frog stretched out, on a tray, for dissection, trunk is very bulky; the color midway is red, which is the position of the heart; limbs are pinned down on the dissecting tray.
   Score: D, Fw+, C, A.
Card IV, Response 6: Two big boots of ancient days.
   Boots; heel; jack boots; color is a big thing as the boots are black in color.
   Score: D, Fo, C', Obj.
Card IV, Response 7: Lichen which forms on the bark of trees.
   A big formation; no particular or specific border or outline; it is zig-zag and curling up; the color is usually black and white.
   Score: D, Fv, C', Pl, m.

Card V, Response 8: Flying bat.
Wings are stretched out; limbs protruding.
Score: W, Fo, A.
Card V, Response 9: Butterfly.
Stretched wings; appendages as you find in butterflies.
Score: W, Fo, A.
Card VI, Response 10: Looks like the stretched hide of a hunted animal.
Whiskers stretched out; limbs protruding.
Score: W, Fo, A.
Card VII, Response 11: Looks like small angels; picture.
Instead of ears they have wings; very small boys dressed as angels; this is a stereotypical identification of the sex of the child; the whole picture is not depicted.
Score: D, F+, Hd, Pec verbalization.
Card VII, Response 12: Entrance into a small den.
This here, looks like entrance; small; into this den.
Score: Dd, Fo, Arch.
Card VIII, Response 13: These two look like leopards.
These are four legs; tail missing; maybe, (it is) curled up the other way.
Score: D, Fo, A, vague.
Card VIII, Response 14: The rest of the card is analogous.
Bony structure of the brain; as studied in Class XII.
Score: D, Fv, Ant.
Card IX, Response 15: Looks like a prawn dish.
Color is similar; tentacles are present.
Score: W, FC--, Prawns.
Card X, Response 16: Only two things make sense; green ones look like peacocks.
Long tails like a peacock; similar to color of a peacock as peacock is not completely green.
Score: D, FCo, A.
Card X, Response 17: Yellow stains look like lions.
In old shields and badges lions are depicted in this manner and the color is somewhat yellow.
Score: D, FCo, A.
Card X, Response 18: Blue ones look like crabs with lots of tentacles.

ANIL

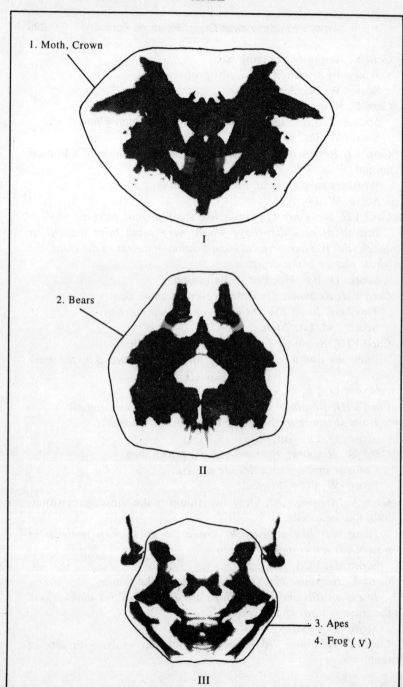

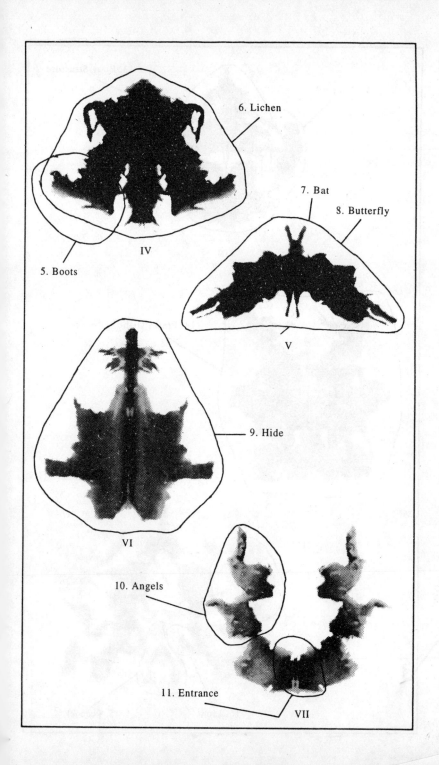

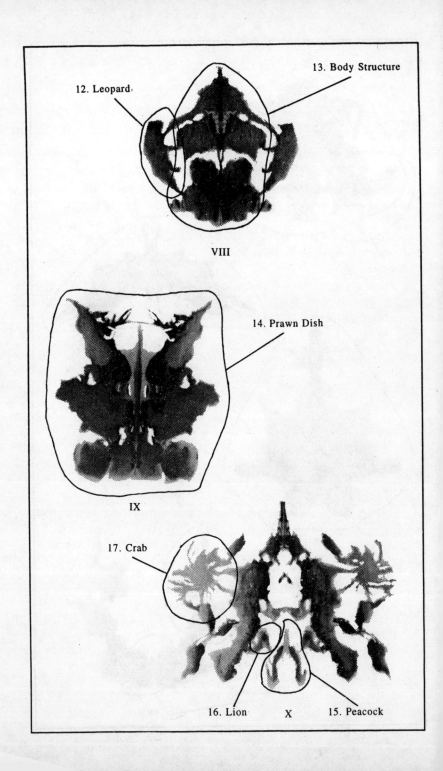

12. Leopard

13. Body Structure

VIII

14. Prawn Dish

IX

17. Crab

16. Lion

X

15. Peacock

Tentacles; eight legs; and the structure is the same as that of crabs;
the color is also somewhat dark; though crabs are not blue.
Score: D, FCo, A, C denial.

Analyzing and Interpreting a Protocol

We might recall, in Lerner's Psychoanalytic Object Relations
Approach, a protocol is examined in terms of,

1. Human movement responses (M), focusing on,
   (*i*) perceptual determinants, e.g., sensitivity to imbalance,
   (*ii*) fantasy,
   (*iii*) self-expression,
   (*iv*) object representation, and
   (*v*) empathy.
2. Responses in which Form (F) was a determinant (e.g., nature
   of hold on reality).
3. Level of the form in form-determined responses (e.g., extent of
   hold on reality, F+, Fo, F−, etc.).
4. Color-determined responses (e.g., 'affect capacity').
5. Shading-determined responses (e.g., experience of anxiety).
6. Blackness-determined responses (e.g., feelings of emptiness).
7. Analysis of content (e.g., fantasy, self-experience, object
   representation).
8. Analysis of sequence (e.g., progressive and regressive shifts in
   personality organization).

Once these areas have been analyzed, an attempt is made to
articulate the analyses and develop with as much adherence as
possible to Schafer's (1954) six criteria of interpretation (that is,
sufficiency, depth, manifest expression, intensity, hierarchy and
adaptive/pathological aspects of tendencies inferred) an internally
consistent and integrated personality profile of the subject in terms
of

1. character structure (e.g., hysterical, depressed, infantile, etc.),
2. thought organization (e.g., rigid, nonspecific, systematic, etc.),
3. affect organization (e.g., how emotions are experienced, expressed and managed), and
4. core dynamics (e.g., conflicts in areas of sexuality, object relations, self-cohesion, etc.).

In order to develop the above personality picture, Lerner (1991) recommends going through three specific steps.

Steps in the Inference Process

Avoiding an excessive (and unnecessary) emphasis on quantitative scores, ratios and percentages, Lerner suggests listing only (*a*) number of responses with form level of F− (incorrect match between percept and the blot area) or Fs (form spoiled)—an acceptable percept like F+ or Fo is spoiled by introducing an inappropriate feature (e.g., Card V: 'bat, but it has a green beak'), and (*b*) number of responses with the form levels F+, Fo, F−, Fw and Fv.

The second step is first order inferences. Here, interpretive comments are developed based on (*a*) form level, (*b*) kinesthesias, (*c*) responses with human content, (*d*) analysis of content, and (*e*) analysis of sequence. These comments may be written against each individual response.

The third and final step is transformation. This is the most important part of interpretation. At this stage, individual response comments are transformed into the headings of (*a*) character structure, (*b*) thought organization, (*c*) affect organization, and (*d*) core dynamics.

The information thus generated constitutes the psychological test report which also includes the referral questions like diagnosis and treatment planning.

With this recapitulation of Lerner's approach, we would now take a look first at Anil's, and then, JoAnn's protocol.

Analyzing and Interpreting Anil's Protocol

Quantitative Analysis:

1. There are no spoiled form (Fs) responses. There is one response (Card IX, Response 15) indicating an inappropriate match between percept ('prawn dish') and the blot area (whole blot).
2. The form levels of responses are as follows:

F+	2 (Responses 2 and 11)
Fo	12 (Responses 1, 3, 4, 6, 8, 9, 10, 12, 13, 16, 17 and 18)
Fw+	1 (Response 5)
Fv	2 (Responses 7 and 14)

3. *Kinesthesias*—here, all movements irrespective of the content (human, animal) are noted. The kinesthesias in Anil's protocol are:

   clapping hands (Response 3)
   churning (Response 4)
   curling up (Response 7)

4. Next in the quantitative tabulation are noted human figure responses. There are no human figure responses in Anil's protocol.

5. *Analysis of Content*—In analyzing content, Lerner (1991) recommends applying Mayman's (1977) three (embellishment, self-experience and object representation) out of the five (the other two being perceptual imbalance and empathy) criteria that he suggests for examining movement responses.

   Let us now look at Anil's response contents based on these criteria.

   (*i*) *Embellishments*: Responses 2, 3, 5, 6, 7 and 11 indicate more embellishment than a few others, e.g., Responses 13 and 14.

   (*ii*) *Self-experience*: Phenomenologically, Anil seems to be experiencing himself and his world at a regressive, primary process level—'clapping', 'churning', 'curling'. A relatively blurred sense of happiness ('clapping'), combined with trying to extract some sense of the world at large ('churning') and feeling a need to protect himself by regressing to a fetal position ('curling') indicates a yet-to-be-firmed-up kind of self-experience.

   (*iii*) *Object Representation*: Lerner (1991) observes that, '. . . object representations are thought of as unconscious images of others that are rooted in early object relations and provide a substratum for all subsequent relationships' (p. 71).

   For Anil, self-representation images seem to comprise— 'crown of king' (Response 2), 'frog, hung upside down' (Response 5), 'lichen which forms on the bark of trees' (Response 7), 'stretched hide of a hunted animal' (Response 10) and 'prawn dish' (Response 15).

   Lerner suggests that the percepts referring to self should be further examined for whether they reflect what the subject experiences about him/herself, or whether these images indicate what he/she idealizes and would wish to be.

In Anil's case, it appears that the images reflect what his experiential self is: great and powerful ('crown') on the one hand, and a victim ('frog', 'stretched hide') on the other. The image of a direction-less, insignificant growth ('lichen') is accompanied with a wish for being incorporated ('prawn dish').

6. *Analysis of Sequence*—As mentioned earlier, sequence analysis tends to show the shifts in primary process–secondary process thinking (we might recall Schafer [1954] calls it shifts and fluctuations in levels of psychic functioning).

A regressive shift from living form ('moth') to inanimate object ('crown') moves up the scale towards the secondary process end in the next response ('bears'); goes still up in the next one ('apes'), and then reverts back to an about-to-die state ('frog, hung upside down for dissection'). There is again further regression to inanimate objects ('boots') and still another regression ('ancient days'). The next percept is living, yet a kind of dependent, symbiotic thing ('lichen'). This is followed by an entry into a higher level (from plant to animal) of psychic functioning. Again, there is a regressive move: animal hide. An additional regressive, benign shift occurs in the next response ('angels'). However, the embellishment provides a 'twist' implying that although the small boys are dressed as angels it still is a 'stereotypical identification of sex'. The next response goes further deep down into fantasy: a wish to go back to the mother's womb where it was safe and secure. And, the second time that I come into this world, he seems to be saying to himself, I am going to come out as a leopard, maybe, as two leopards, but the tail (symbiotic link) would be missing, or rather, would not be visible to others ('curled up the other way') so that they would not be able to see that I am Mommy's baby (or, alternatively perhaps, I would be able to hide my dependency more effectively). A desire to be cognitive (literally, to be brainy) comes to the surface in the next response: 'bony structure of the brain'. The overpowering theme of wishing to re-start life is reiterated in 'prawn dish'. The (cooked) prawns, however, have tentacles, so do crabs in the last response. Evident in this is Anil's need to be alert and vigilant. After food ('prawn dish'), there is again a move toward secondary process thinking ('peacocks'), then, back to inanimates ('yellow stains') which actually look like lions.

With this overview, we are now ready to move on to the next very important step in Lerner's system, namely, developing first order inferences. This is where, says Lerner (1991), the actual interpretive work begins. 'This step constitutes a convergence of all sources of information, that is, the formal scores, analysis of content, sequence analysis, and indications of the patient–examiner relationship' (ibid., p. 132).

First Order Inferences: In this step, an attempt will be made to draw inferences about Anil's personality in terms of self-object, thought processes, emotions and motives, conflicts underlying his emotions including outlets for sexuality, object relations distur-bances, impairments in developing a cohesive self, etc.

For drawing first order inferences, we will look at the total picture, e.g., scores, sequence and content, and not at any one of these in isolation from each other.

Absence of humans in the protocol is significant. It indicates Anil's inability to establish object relations. His internalized object relations are at the infra-human (Response 3: 'apes') and supra-human (Response 11: 'picture of small angels') levels. Kinesthesias ('clapping', 'churning', 'curling') reflects efforts to seek a cohesive self. The sequence in movements signifies a trend from being just happy to be somebody ('clapping') to a search for the core of this 'somebody' ('churning'), to a realization of being somebody who is still nobody away from its roots ('curling')—a symbiotic bond with a mother figure. This 'dependent' link is reiterated in Response 11 to Card VII (which often arouses an experience of nurturance, security, space). First, it is a 'picture' of angels; not real, live, angels. Second, these angels have 'wings, instead of ears', indicating a flight away from reality (may also imply a reaction formation: denial of need to know what is going on around him). Third, another denial of self-identity is seen in the comment that these are 'very small boys' who are 'dressed as angels'. The underlying implication is, 'I am a very small boy; helpless; dependent; but I want to appear as an angel (with magical powers) to fly away from whatever I don't like, or whenever I want to'. Fourth, the comment that dressing up 'very small boys as angels' is 'a stereotypical identification of the sex of the child' suggests a wish to appear as an average Ram Pershad (or John Doe as they say in the US) and not as anyone unique or special. And fifth, the last comment in this response climaxes the *aadhaa-adhooraa* ('incomplete-half') sense of self: 'the whole picture is not depicted'. This response (free association and inquiry) is a graphic illustration of the blurred boundaries between self and non-self. The next response (Response 12) tends to validate this observation—'entrance into a small den'. A sense of lacking cohesiveness in self is sought to be compensated by merging with what Kohut would call selfobject.

A recurring theme of 'tentacles' (Responses 1, 15 and 18), and 'appendages' (Responses 3 and 9), and 'protruding limbs' (Responses 4, 8 and 10) signify a need to be vigilant about surroundings as well as a desire to reach out and mark self-boundaries. However, an inability to be able to do that is manifested in a sense of helplessness (Responses 5, 7 and 13). Intensity of helplessness is reflected in Response 5: a frog is hung upside down, limbs pinned down, on a dissecting tray. It is continued in Response 7—lichen with a big formation, 'no specific border or outline; it is zig-zag and curling up'—and again in Response 13, where the leopards are without a tail but maybe, the tail is curled up the other way. Responses 7 and 13 portray a sense of lack of boundaries between self and non-self.

In terms of thought process, most of the responses match blot areas. His hold on reality is reasonably intact. Embellishments reflect creativity as well as a need to 'dress-up' reality to make it interesting and tolerable.

Associated with this somewhat fuzzy and blurry self-representation and non-human object representation are strong emotions. Emotions, however, seem to be experienced with a sense of hesitation and denial. Feelings of depression are experienced more readily than excitement, although hesitancy is common to both—Response 1: 'moth is grey, not absolutely, absolutely black', Response 7: the color of lichen is 'usually black and white', Response 16: 'peacock is not completely green', Response 17: color of lions is 'somewhat yellow', and in Response 18: structure is of crabs but not color, it is 'somewhat dark, though crabs are not blue'.

In core dynamics there are indications of conflicts in self and object representation as pointed out earlier. A need to be 'somebody' conflicts with wish to be 'not somebody'—assertion by negation.

Aggressiveness is reflected in Responses 5 and 10. The pervasive emotion, however, appears to be depression marked by a feeling of emptiness and what Lerner (1991) calls 'a quality of injury' (p. 92). Examples: Response 5 ('frog hung upside down for dissection'), Response 10 ('stretched hide of a hunted animal'), Response

13 ('tail missing'), Response 11 ('the whole picture is not depicted') and Response 12 ('entrance to a den').

Having gone through the first two steps, namely, quantitative analysis and first order inferences, we now move on to the third and final step (before writing the psychological test report) in interpreting Anil's protocol, namely, transformation. At this stage, the goal is to develop an integrated personality profile in terms of character structure, thought process, affective process and core dynamics.

Transformation: So, then, what kind of person is Anil? What is the main character structure of his personality? Is he a hysterical character? An obsessive–compulsive character? Depressed character? Masochistic character? What are the sub-character structures in his personality? How are these characters organized in terms of say, instinctual development, manifestations of ego weaknesses, defensive organization, internalized object relations, etc? How does he think? How does he feel? What are the contents of his thinking and feeling? While we have commented on each of these earlier, we need an overall integrated picture. It is described briefly here.

Based on his Rorschach test responses, Anil seems to reflect the main character of a depressed personality with sub-features of masochistic, infantile and schizoid character structures. His personality organization appears to be at an intermediate level in the areas of instinctual development, ego weakness and superego development. In the areas of defenses, internalized object relations and ego identity, his personality suggests a lower level of organization. A relatively intact thought process keeps him effective and functional in relation to reality. Emotions are intense; congruent with cognition, though. A major concern (conflict) centers around self versus non-self differentiation. Apparently, internalized object relations are at the Melanie Klein's (1952) paranoid–schizoid position, or Margaret Mahler's (1952; Mahler, Pine and Bergman, 1975) practicing sub-phase of the separation–individuation stage in the development of object relations.

So, that's what Anil looks like on the Rorschach test—phenomenologically and experientially. It is important to emphasize that here we have described and not evaluated Anil.

We will now illustrate Lerner's Psychoanalytic Object Relations Approach to the Rorschach through another protocol.

Protocol 2: JoAnn

Card I, Response 1: To me, it looks like, a man is chasing a woman; she is in a car being followed by a man.

The darkness and the spaces; there is only a limited amount of space.

Score: W S, MC', Car, Blackness, Confab.

Card II, Response 2: To me, that looks like, somebody is beating a woman up in the bus shelter and no one is helping her.

Blood stains and the darkness.

Score: W, MCC', H, Bl, Arch, Blackness, Confab.

Card III, Response 3: In a mental hospital; it looks like, someone in a mental hospital and they are afraid.

This is the ward; and these are the mentally insane people.

Score: W, F−, Arch, H, Confab.

Card IV, Response 4: A lady is having a miscarriage; and she is afraid to go to hospital because afraid, they'll kill her baby.

It looks like a pelvis and this looks like the child coming.

Score: W, M−, H, Birth, Confab.

Card V, Response 5: Let me see—children left abandoned in a house with no food, no heat and no parents.

The darkness and I see people gathered in this darkness.

Score: W, M−C', H, Blackness, Confab.

Card VI, Response 6: A child being molested.

The darkness, the closed-in.

Score: W, MC', H, Blackness, Confab.

Card VII, Response 7: Um!—um, drug dealers dealing out of their homes.

It is dark and gloomy.

Score: W, M−C', H, Blackness, Confab.

Card VIII, Response 8: A girl on a swing and for the first time she's meeting a girl supposed to be her sister out of wedlock.

Swing set; girl, and girl out of wedlock.

Score: W, Mo, H, Confab.

Card IX, Response 9: Somebody following me.

The closed-in part.

Score: W, M−, H, Confab.

Card X, Response 10: Abandoned, condemned house.

The different colors and the spaces in between.

Score: W, FC−, Arch, Confab.

JOANN

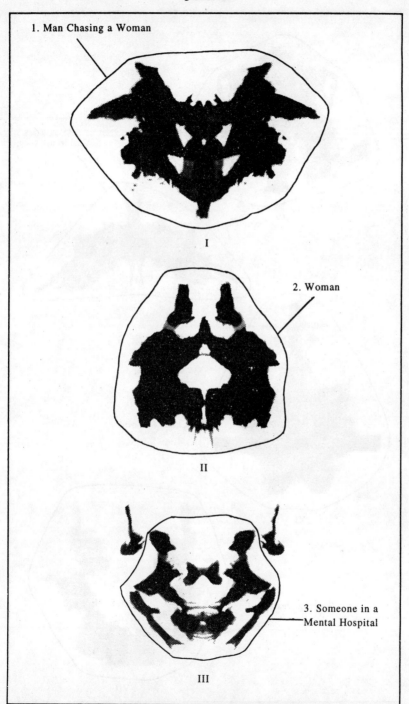

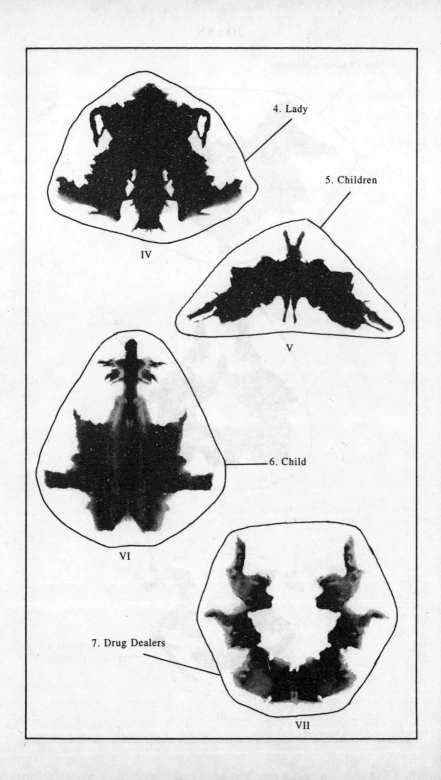

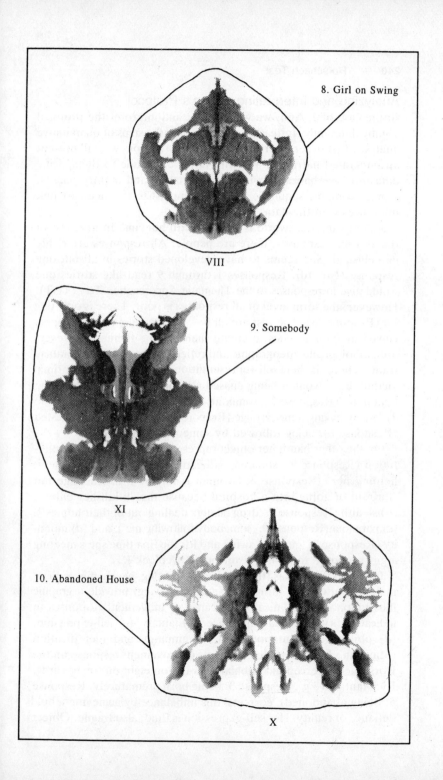

8. Girl on Swing

VIII

9. Somebody

XI

10. Abandoned House

X

Analyzing and Interpreting JoAnn's Protocol

In the case of J.·Ann, we will analyze and interpret the protocol slightly differently. Instead of going through the steps of quantitative analysis, first order inferences and transformation, we will present an integrated narrative. We will, however, allude to the specific data (e.g., verbalizations in free association and inquiry phases, scores, content, sequence, etc.) to emphasize the need to link inferences with the data.

JoAnn's internal world is flooded with humans. In nine out of the 10 total responses, there are people. All responses are richly embellished. She seems to have developed stories in all but one response (No. 10). Responses 1 through 9 read like stories one would give in responses to the Thematic Apperception Test (TAT). However, the form level of all responses is poor. There is only one Fo (Response 8). The rest are all F−. She appears to have apperceived inkblots as cues to create themes. The themes, however, are pathologically ideographic and reflect a 'free-ride' on a fantasy train. There is her self-representation in the form of 'primal victim', e.g., woman being chased (Response 1), a woman being beaten up (Response 2), someone in a mental hospital (Response 3), a lady having a miscarriage (Response 4), a child being molested (Response 6), being followed by someone (Response 9).

On the other hand, her object representation reflects (*a*) exploitation (Response 2: 'someone is beating a woman and no one is helping her', Response 4: 'woman is having a miscarriage but is afraid of going into a hospital because they'll kill her baby'), (*b*) stealth (Response 7: 'drug dealers dealing out of their homes'), (*c*) paranoia (Response 9: 'somebody following me'), and (*d*) morality (Response 8: 'girl on a swing and for the first time she's meeting a girl supposed to be her sister out of wedlock').

JoAnn's kinesthesias (that is, chasing, beating, having miscarriage, molestation, dealing [drugs], meeting, following) provide a graphic illustration of the clinical significance of movement responses in indicating (*a*) perceptual imbalance, (*b*) fantasy, (*c*) self-expression, (*d*) object representation, and (*e*) empathy and identification (Mayman's [1977] five determinants of movement response on the Rorschach). Perceptual imbalance is felt on eight out of 10 cards. Rich fantasy (e.g., Response 3: being born prematurely, Response 5: being abandoned) 'corrects' this imbalance by achieving a bold defiance of reality. Her self-expression is fluid; also fragile. Object representation focuses on her inner life: people who are aggressively sadist (Responses 2, 4 and 6) as well as domineering and controlling (Responses 1 and 9).

It is a fluid, fragile self-representation that is struggling to relate to a cold, hostile object representation. As a result, JoAnn's thought organization is leaning more towards what Mayman calls 'reality abrogation' rather than toward 'reality adherence'.

Interfacing this fantasy-rich thinking is the organization of her affects. She is experiencing emotions intensely; kind of wallowing in a swamp of emotions! Phenomenologically, she is actively engaged in activities that are cognitively flexible and emotionally chaotic. Color-related aggressiveness in Response 2 is intense. But much more intense is her blackness-related depression in Responses 2, 3, 4, 5 and 10.

The sequence of her responses tends to dramatize her struggle to free herself from objects, on the one hand (Responses 1, 5, 9 and 10), and a need to re-connect with them, on the other (Responses 4 and 8). There are sharp shifts between regressive and progressive levels of psychic functioning. However, she does tend to stay most of the time at the primary process level.

A strong passive–aggressive object relational mode stands out in JoAnn's response content. Flooded with primary process libidinal urges, now she wants to be tied to objects (e.g., Responses 5 and 6), and now she wants to be left alone (e.g., Responses 1, 2 and 9).

In summary then, what kind of person do we make out of JoAnn based on this overview of her Rorschach response patterns? JoAnn reflects a masochistic character and a depressive character (almost competing with each other) in her personality. Sub-features of her core character also include hysterical, infantile and narcissistic characteristics, in that order. The level of her personality organization is apparently at the lower level in all areas, that is, instinctual development, ego weakness, defensive organization, internalized object relations, superego development and ego identity. She is as keen on separating–individuating as on blurring and merging.

SUMMARY

In this chapter, we have described and illustrated Paul Lerner's (1991) psychoanalytic object relations theory of analyzing and interpreting the Rorschach test data. Section I presented an overview of the object relations theory. Section II comprised a description of Lerner's system. Finally, Section III illustrated Lerner's system by analyzing and interpreting two protocols—Anil, a twenty-three year old, Indian male, and JoAnn, a thirty-four year old, African–American female.

9 SUMMARY

Living and working in an atmosphere featuring important events in the fields of science, arts and literature, Hermann Rorschach developed a method of looking into the psyche of people, specially mental patients. 'What might it be?' they were asked when shown a set of 10 symmetrical inkblots. These inkblots were clear enough to be seen as objects, yet ambiguous enough to be interpreted differently by different persons. The things the patients saw (e.g., humans or animals) and *how* they saw them (e.g., with/without movement, color, shade, blackness) provided meaningful insights into their mental processes. Comparing the *phenomenological experiences* of these patients with the so-called normals helped diagnose and treat mental patients.

Rorschach found, for example, that the persons suffering from thinking disorder (e.g., schizophrenia) saw things that had little or no resemblance to the shapes of the blots. For example, we found schizophrenics seeing 'a bad dream' (Card X) or 'two owls shaking hands' (Card VIII). On the other hand, those who suffered from emotional disorders (e.g., manic–depressive psychosis), would often see color where there was none ('green scum'—Card IV) or did not see any color where there was ('leg'—top red parts in Card III).

During Rorschach's times (end of the 19th and beginning of the 20th centuries) there was a lot happening: psychoanalysis, phenomenology, research on schizophrenia, surrealism in art and existentialism in literature. Rorschach's method of using colored and black-and-white inkblots for exploring the psyche fitted right into the *zeitgeist* of his social and cultural climate.

In spite of Rorschach's sudden and premature death at the age of 37, his creative method of understanding mental processes has consistently continued to generate theoretical and clinical research all over the world among psychologists and cultural anthropologists. Literally, hundreds of books and thousands of research papers have appeared using this method. As is often the case, some names and some works have attracted more attention than others.

In this book, we have presented the significant contributions of four major Rorschachers: John Exner (1991, 1993), Robert McCully (1971), Roy Schafer (1954) and Paul Lerner (1991). Selecting these four approaches does not in any way minimize the seminal contributions of many others, e.g., Beck (1952, 1976), Piotrowski (1957), Bohm (1958), Weiner (1966), Rickers-Ovsiankina (1977), Boyer et al. (1988) and Aronow, Reznikoff and Moreland (1994). It is just that we felt a beginner student of the Rorschach method should be introduced to the systems of Exner (1991, 1993), McCully (1971), Schafer (1954) and Lerner (1991) because:

1. Exner's Comprehensive System incorporates many features from the systems of major Rorschachers: Beck, Hertz, Klopfer, Piotrowski and Rapaport,
2. McCully's system looks at the Rorschach responses from the Jungian archetypal system and blends well with the Eastern philosophy and Indian culture,
3. Schafer's approach, based on psychoanalytic ego psychology, focuses on the dynamic significance of the Rorschach test from the perspective of impulsive—defensive—adaptive functions of the ego, and
4. Paul Lerner's Psychoanalytic Object Relations Approach represents an excellent, integrated synthesis of classical psychoanalysis, ego psychology and object relations theories for understanding personality on the basis of the Rorschach test.

Starting with the *zeitgeist* of Rorschach's times in Chapter 1, we tried to contextualize the test against the backdrop of psychoanalysis, schizophrenia, the Gestalt school, the phenomenological movment, Cubism, Dadaism, Expressionism, Fauvism and Existentialism.

Demonstrating the test's links with literature insofar as the subject responding to the Rorschach cards reflects the same creative process as a writer's, artist's, poet's or playwright's to narrate a story, draw a painting, compose a poem or write a play, in Chapter 2 we interfaced three authors (*a*) Amritlal Nagar (*Yeh Kotheywaalian* ['These dancing girls']), (*b*) Franz Kafka (*Metamorphosis*), and (c) R.K. Narayan (*Swami and Friends*) with three Rorschach protocols: Shakher, Ibrahim and Mary.

An overview of the work on the Rorschach test in India was provided in Chapter 3. Hermann Ebbinghaus (1850–1909), the experimental psychologist who invented nonsense syllable for understanding memory, said, 'psychology has a long past but only a short history' (cited in Boring, 1950, p. ix). The Rorschach test too in India has a long past but a short history. The first Rorschach study, Prasad and Asthana's (1947), appeared around the same time when many fundamental contributions were published in the field (e.g., Klopfer and Kelly, 1942; Beck, 1945; Rapaport, Schafer, and Gill, 1945, 1946). However, a *PsycINFO* search generated only 41 studies between 1966 and 1990 on the test in Indian journals. And, if we count the studies from 1947 to date in which the Rorschach test was used, the number goes up to over 120 (Prabhu, 1984).

Although there appears to be a lull between 1990 and 1994 (Asthana, 1994), we did start conducting regular workshops/ seminars on the Rorschach in 1990, training interested students and workers. The interest and enthusiasm shown in these work-shops and the absence of a Rorschach text in the Indian context prompted us to do this book.

In Chapter 4, we described the specifics of the Rorschach test— the Rorschach procedure—by listing 11 elements: context, rapport, seating arrangement, instructions, free association phase, inquiry phase, recording responses, coding responses, placing responses in a format, interpreting responses and writing the test report.

Chapters 5, 6, 7 and 8 described the systems of Exner, McCully, Schafer and Lerner respectively.

Exner's (1991, 1993) system (Chapter 5) consists of over 300 variables organized into 11 key variables and seven clusters. The 11 key variables are: schizophrenia index, depression index, adjusted difference between experience actual (EA) and adjusted experience stimulation (Adj es), coping deficit index, adjusted difference (Adj D) negative, Lambda, reflection responses, experience balance: introversive, experience balance: extratensive, passive movement responses and hypervigilance index. The seven clusters are: affect, controls, ideation, interpersonal perception, mediation, processing and self-perception.

An integrated personality picture is developed based on the subject's response patterns in terms of the key variables and clusters.

McCully (1971) (Chapter 6) approach frames the Rorschach responses in three areas.

1. *Pragmatic Schema*: *Erlebinstypus* (experience balance) is analogous to the concept of *karm-siddhaant* in Indian philosophy. One's phenomenological experience of the world is predetermined by an infinite system of cause-effect relationships. The unconscious

   . . . does not represent a simple repository for rejected material or unwelcome debris . . . . Like the sea, the unconscious is a vast container and repository of collective human experience. It is the little sleep that surrounds our little lives of consciousness . . . its ebb and flow across the ego make up our Karma, our *Erlebinstypus* (McCully, 1971, p. 12, emphasis in the original).

   The archetypes, he observes, are the 'great connectors' of our present with the past.

2. *The Rorschach Experience*: According to McCully, a person taking the Rorschach test experiences (*a*) intra-psychic confrontation insofar as the cards arouse various archetypes, and (*b*) he/she experiences the same creative processes as that of a poet or author; the Rorschach response is the end result of this creative process.

3. *The Rorschach Process Analysis*: Understanding the Rorschach experience involves looking at the responses for the archetypal material and also placing them along the axes of withdrawal from and expansion toward the environment (Axis A–B) and conscious-unconscious (Axis C–D).

The next chapter, Chapter 7, presents Schafer's (1954) Psychoanalytic Ego Psychology Approach to the Rorschach. Emphasizing the critical role of situational dynamics (tester–testee relationship, purpose of testing, etc.) and interfacing the Rorschach experience with dream images, he draws attention to the shifts and range in the levels of psychic functioning along the continuum of the primary process and secondary process in the Rorschach responses. His system involves looking at the responses as reflecting varying levels of psychic functioning in terms of the key ego processes of reality orientation, namely, (*a*) awareness of impulses, (*b*) defending impulses by repression, and (*c*) adapting need-satisfaction through socially–culturally approved modes. Each Rorschach response could (should) be analyzed for this impulse × defense × adaptation relationship. Understanding these relationships in terms of (*a*) what is it that is seeking satisfaction (impulse), (*b*) how is the subject controlling this impulse (defense), and (*c*) how is he/she modifying this impulse to suit the social–cultural demands related to the satisfaction of this particular impulse (adaptation), would help us profile the personality of the subject from the Rorschach responses within a psychoanalytic ego psychology framework. An extremely important contribution of Schafer in this context is the listing of the six specific criteria that need to be addressed while drawing inferences about the subject's personality from the Rorschach data, namely, sufficiency, depth, manifest form, intensity, hierarchic level and adaptive/pathological coping strategies.

Finally, in Chapter 8, we looked at Lerner's (1991) Psychoanalytic Object Relations Approach. Incorporating the recent advances in object relations theory (namely, it is the individual–object [human] relationship unit and not the person as an isolated individual that needs to be focused on for understanding personality) and self psychology (namely, self incorporates ego, we need to grasp the bigger unit of self instead of ego to comprehend personality growth and development), Lerner recommends reviewing Rorschach responses to identify (*a*) core character (e.g., hysterical, depressive, schizoid, infantile), and (*b*) levels of personality organization (e.g., level of instinctual development, level of manifestations of ego weaknesses, level of internalized object relations, level of superego development and level of ego identity). In order for us to be able to do that, he identifies five major dimensions of Rorschach responses (that is, human movement responses, form responses, form level, color and blackness).

Most importantly, Lerner cautions against putting excessive emphasis on the quantitative analysis of Rorschach responses. Instead of looking at each individual score, he examines the dynamics of dimensions underlying the scores (the five major dimensions).

A FEW GENERAL COMMENTS

The Rorschach test simulates our world of objects. Looking at the cards is like making a short movie out of your experiences. During those 30 to 40 minutes, you are the actor, producer and director. It is the subject's story; his/her narrative. The bricks and mortar of archetypal roots take him/her all the way back to thousands of years when we felt 'connected' with the gods and goddesses; we asked for and were granted food, water, peace and happiness. The Rorschach experience also re-activates the period of birth and infancy when the subject felt one with 'someone' and the big, buzzing, booming confusion (to borrow William James' description of consciousness) started with the nipple and gradually evolved into breast, two breasts, face, trunk, feet, and finally, mother, the figure/object who conceived and carried an object inside her body for nine months and experienced the agony of pregnancy and the ecstasy of creating a human being—the subject.

Each Rorschach card arouses these experiences: *individual* as well as *collective*. It is not a cold, 'scientific' experience. It is an experience that is unique to the subject, personal. The responses the subject provides tend to articulate these individual and collective experiences. It is a creative process. The end-product is a story—the subject's story.

The story thus created is as unique as Firaaq's poem *Aadhee Raat Koe* ('In the middle of the night') when he sees trees as steeples and spires connecting earth with sky; the stories of Lulu's mother or Badray Muneer in Nagar's *Yeh Kothey-waaliaan* ('These dancing girls'), or Swaminathan's story in Narayan's *Swami and Friends*, or the story of Gregor Samsa in Kafka's *Metamorphosis*.

Like any other story, the Rorschach story too has a main plot, a few sub-plots, a main character, a villain, a supportive cast and conflicts, emotions and suspense. Some elements may be like the (a) stereotyped 'boy-meets-girl' kind, Bollywood (Bombay's Holly-wood) stuff, or (b) the family relations theme in many Tamil movies, or (c) the subliminally subtle emotionality of Satyajit Ray's films against the backdrop of Calcutta. Yet, there is a lot that is never ever to be found elsewhere. It is unique. It is this uniqueness, in the context of the mundane, that makes a protocol fascinating.

The Rorschach has come a long way from Hermann Rorschach's *Psychodiagnostics* (published in 1921) to recent publications, e.g.,

Aronow, Reznikoff and Moreland (1994, 1995), Weiner (1994), Acklin (1995), Ritzler (1995). Contributions have addressed controversies and debates.

Often, it feels like the test has had a little more than its share of controversies. Partly, it may be because of the premature death of Rorschach and partly because of the test's naive appearance (a bunch of 'dumb-looking' inkblots claiming to understand the most puzzling animal on this planet: humans). Some of the recent debates involving the Rorschach include:

1. How comprehensive is the Comprehensive System? Some feel it is (e.g., Exner, 1974, 1991, 1993). Others don't (e.g., Aronow, Reznikoff and Moreland, 1994, 1995), because it emphasizes quantification and neglects projection.
2. Is the Rorschach a projective or a psychometric tool? For Exner (1989, 1991) it is a psychometric tool addressing problem-solving situations. It is not a projective tool (e.g., Exner, 1989). For others, e.g., Schafer (1954), Miale (1977), Philips (1992), it is very much projective.

    Schafer (1954) states that depriving a person of control over choices (as happens in the Rorschach situation) tends to reduce the strength of defenses. 'From the psychoanalytic point of view, this *defense* aspect of the "projective hypothesis"—the active structuring of the world according to inner requirements and outer demands—is of crucial significance' (Schafer, 1954, p. 37, emphasis in original).

    Miale (1977) presents a convincing argument favoring treating Rorschach symbols as illustrating, what she calls, *the self-referent hypothesis*, that is, (*a*) 'self-expression in projective material is not different in kind from that which occurs in life situations . . .' (ibid., p. 422), and (*b*) '. . .projective material need not involve "breakthrough" of unconscious contents for it to be diagnostically valuable . . .' (ibid., p. 423).

    Philips (1992) cautions against overstressing the objectivity of the Rorschach. 'I'm unhappy with the recent "Americanization" of the Rorschach test and its reconstruction as simply an objective, formal test of perceptual and personality functioning . . .' (ibid., p. 9)
3. Is the Rorschach a test? Or is it a method? Weiner (1994) says it is a method and recommends that we call it the Rorschach

Inkblot Method (RIM). Acklin (1995) argues it is a test. 'Perhaps the most compelling reason to continue to call the Rorschach a test, despite the valid reasons presented elsewhere for ceasing to do so, is the importance of *data* as the basis of inference' (Acklin, 1995, p. 237, emphasis in original).

Debates and controversies are healthy and necessary. Interfacing theory and research, searching for easy answers to difficult questions and then doubting them is how knowledge grows. The Rorschach is no exception.

IN CLOSING

Exner's (1974, 1991, 1993) system is comprehensive insofar as it includes some of the important contributions of many major Rorschachers (e.g., Beck, 1944; Rapaport, Schafer and Gill, 1945, 1946; Klopfer et al.,1954; Piotrowski, 1957; Hertz, 1970). It is also *not comprehensive* in that it appears to have ignored some important contributions of many other major Rorschachers (e.g., Bohm, 1958; Schachtel, 1966; Lerner, 1975; Beck, 1976; Rickers-Ovsiankina, 1977; Boyer et al., 1988; Lerner and Lerner, 1988; Lerner, 1991).

Beck's (1976) analysis of translating literary writings into Rorschach language is quite a phenomenological way of understanding the potential of the test. He calls this process 'reverse Rorschach'.

All great literature projects psychological experience. 'Here I am reversing the usual method of teaching the test. I am mirroring the personalities in the Rorschach glass . . . [the] selfless loyalty of Lear's Kent; the tumultuous emotions in Dostoievski's Dmitri; the narcissism in Ibsen's beautiful Hedda . . . . These are the men and women through whom I have, in part been teaching my classes for some thirty years or more. The students have found it an interesting and rewarding exercise' (Beck, 1976, p. vii).

Bohm's (1958) work not only represents a systematic text for beginners and advanced students of the Rorschach but also focuses on important non-quantitative aspects of the test. The fact that it was translated from German into English by Samuel Beck and Anne Beck bears additional testimony to its value.

We cannot get too far in understanding protocols by limiting ourselves to the formal aspects of the test, says Bohm. 'The fact is that the Rorschach test, besides, contains a great number of factors which cannot be counted or weighed quantitatively. These are called, the "imponderables"' (Bohm, 1958, p. 86). These imponderables are designated as the test's *special phenomena*. Bohm lists 67 such special phenomena, e.g., overcompensated color shock, overcompensated dark shock, pseudo-color responses, suppressed movement, perseveration: ruminating type, perseveration of the perceived area, illusion of similarity, disavowal, fusion of figure and ground, censorship: initial and final, and sexual symbol stupor.

Boyer et al. (1988) provide a system for scoring affectivity in the Rorschach responses. 'Psychoanalysis provides the basis for this system, in particular: theory of affects and capacity to symbolize, psychosexual development, and the vicissitudes of defensive structure' (ibid., pp. 4–5). Responses are scored in eight categories: anxiety, dependency, depression, hostility, neutral, positive, sexuality and somatization.

Paul Lerner (1975) reviews various Rorschach scales for assessing cognitive and perceptual functioning, pathological thinking, levels of self-experience, affective and motivational states, interpersonal relations, intrafamilial interactions, suicide and homosexuality.

Lerner and Lerner (1988) view Rorschach responses from the perspective of primitive mental states. Ranging from the concepts of pre-genitality, psychology of self, through internalization of depression, cognitive regression, to trans-sexualism and representation of object relations in feminine boys, this work sharpens the experiential frame for understanding the Rorschach.

Rickers-Ovsiankina's (1977) volume reinforces the value of having a theoretical perspective for understanding the test. 'Any systematically thinking psychologist has no difficulty in recognizing how the interpretive significance that is assigned to the various perceptual–cognitive components of his test is implicitly rooted in a well thought-out, broadly integrated personality theory' (ibid., p. v). Refreshingly, this work also has a chapter by Robert McCully 'Jung's Depth Psychology and Rorschach Patterning' (McCully, 1977).

A much overdue avenue of Rorschach theorizing grows out of the profound affinity between Rorschach's conceptions of personality patterning and those of Carl G. Jung . . . . By following the course of image formation during a Rorschach experience [McCully] endeavors to demonstrate how such an approach can extend our grasp of the range and nature of psychic processes, of the Self as it is 'becoming' (Rickers-Ovsiankina, 1977, p. vii).

Schachtel's (1966) contribution focuses on experiential aspects of the test.

The experiential significance of the inkblots lies in the fact that their phantastic and unknown quality presents a powerful appeal to encounter them, to experience them freshly because the ready label of routine 'recognition' is not offered by them and therefore the possibility to dispose of them by transforming them into cliches is made more difficult (ibid., p. 22).

The lack of structure arouses anxiety. Schachtel compares this feeling with Kierkegaard's idea of dizziness of freedom. Possibilities cause anxiety and trigger a search for meaning.

Our intent in mentioning Bohm (1958), Schachtel (1966), Lerner (1975), Beck (1976), Rickers-Ovsiankina (1977), Lerner and Lerner (1988) and Boyer et al. (1988) is to stress the importance of looking at the Rorschach not as a statistical mosaic but rather as a kaleidoscope of slowly, yet constantly, changing landscapes of personality.

The Rorschach illustrates Salvador Dali's paranoic–critical perspective, a 'spontaneous method of irrational knowledge based on the critical and systematic objectivity of the associations and interpretations of delirious phenomena' (Descharnes, 1985, pp. 30–31) for *experiencing* personality; personality as it is happening.

The test captures an interpersonal situation in which the subject interacts with (*a*) the tester, and (*b*) a set of carefully constructed inkblots. What emerges out of this interaction is a sample of the world of objects surrounding the subject. It may not be structured or coherent like a scientific chart; but it is real, personal. It is like the worlds of people around us. Like the worlds of Apu (in Satyajit Ray's film *Apur Sansar* ['The world of Apu']), Gregor Samsa (in Kafka's *Metamorphosis*), Swami (in Narayan's *Swami and Friends*), Lulu's mother and Badray Muneer (in Nagar's *Yeh Kothey-waaliaan*) and 'Firaaq' (in which dark trees turn into their own shadows, looking like tall towers connecting earth with the sky, in which reflects a village [an exotic dream of romantic scenes] in a mirror of moonlight).

APPENDIX

An illustrative sample of Good Form (F+) and Poor Form (F−). (The location numbers of blot areas are per Beck's system.)

Responses on Indian subjects (N = 500).

Compiled by H.S. Asthana (1976–77). Published here with author's permission.

We would like to thank Dr. Asthana for permission to publish these responses.

CARD I

DESCRIPTION: Black-and-white. Two winged figures on sides. A human-like figure in the middle.

Card I. Whole.
F+.

 Animal or human face
 Acrobatic gymnastic show
 Bat
 Beetle
 Bird
 Butterfly
 Bones, of pelvic girdle
 Cross-section of body, human
 Cross-section of bone
 Crown
 Door (of wooden carving)
 Cloudy sky
 Eagle
 Fairy
 Gate, decorated
 Hip-bone
 Hill
 Historical decoration
 Insect
 Map
 Messenger, of God, with stretched wings
 Mountain
 Pelvis
 Scenery
 Shield
 Smudgeography
 X-ray plate

Card I. Whole.
F−.

 Cage
 Chest
 Inside of stomach
 Leaf
 Spider
 Tortoise

Card I. D1. The middle human-like figure.
F+.

 Anatomical something
 Dress

Coat
Hip
Fossil
Human figure
Oriental temple
Person: double
Policeman, with raised hands
Sculpture work
Stony structure
Card I. D1.
F−.
Animals
Bat
Bird
Bottle
Fly
Skeleton of breast
Tortoise
Tree
Wasp
Water animal
Card I. D2. The winged figures on sides.
F+.
Animal, with wings
Bird
Bird-like beast
Man
Mountain
Person
Soldier
Card I. D2.
F−.
Horse, flying
Leaf
Card I. D3. Lower part of the human-like figure in the middle.
F+.
Baby's head
Bud of lotus
Human head
Human faces
Skulls, wearing goggles
Card I. D3.
F−.
Calf's head
Card I. D4. Middle human-like figure
F+.
Crab
Horns of deer

Insect (V)
Human hands
Lantern
Card I. D4.
F−.

Animal, wild
Sword
Card I. D5. Part protruding on top of the side winged figures.
F+.

Head, of bat
Head, bird's
Edge of mountain
Card I. Dd 22. Top head-like portion of the middle human figure.
F+.

Animal heads
Insect
Pillar heads
Card I. Dd 23. Small dots, below the winged figures on sides.
F+.

Bones of animal
Crab
Card I. Dd 23.
F−.

Animal
Pelvis
Card I. Dd 24. Lower half of the middle human-like figure.
F+.

Skeleton of breast
X-ray picture of chest
Card I. Dd 25. Protruding portion on sides just below the wings.
F+.

Bat
Butterfly
Like earth
Card I. Dds 26. Four white spaces in the middle.
F+.

Bell
Crown, royal
Card I. Dds 26.
F−.

Lungs
Card I. Dd 27. Small, buckle-like circular portion in between four white spaces.
F+.

Belt buckle
Band of belt
Card I. Dds 29. White spaces in the middle, lower two spaces.
F+.

Head, child's
Head, human

Card I. Dds 30. White spaces in the middle, upper two spaces.
F+.
   Wings of butterfly
F−.
   Human skeleton.

CARD II

DESCRIPTION: Black-and-white and red. Two bear-like black figures. Red spots at bottom and on top. White space in middle.
Card II. Whole.
F+.
   Human form
   Animal
   Anatomical something
   Butterfly
   Bears, two, with caps on
   Cross-section of bone
   Demons, with crowns on
   Humans, two
   Men, of polar regions
   Old men, with caps on
   Santa Claus
F−.
   Anandam showering *sukham* ('Bliss showering happiness')
   Chicken, two
Card II. D1. One of the black bear-like figures.
F+.
   Ape
   Animal
   Dog
   Bear(s)
   Bull
   Cow
   Elephant(s)
   Eskimos
   Face of animal
   Field
   Hare
   Human(s)
   Human body
   Mountain cave
F−.
   Bird
   Lungs
   Money
   Tiger
   Tortoise
   Wolf

Card II. D6. Both black figures in center.
F+.

    Crater of volcano
    Crack
    Fan
    Lake
    Lamp shade
    Globe
    Monument
    Pillar
    Pitcher
    Reflector
    Soul
    Temple
    Waterfall
    Water jug
    Waterway

F−.

    Bird
    Butterfly
    Inside of body
    Opening, lower part
    Stomach
    Uterus
    Wound caused by bullet

Card II. D3. Red part, lower bottom.
F+.

    Ancient building
    Bird
    Blood
    Butterfly
    Cloud
    Eruption of volcano
    House
    Evil
    Female organ
    Flame
    Light
    Mountain, through which light cannot emit
    Sun
    Sunlight
    Sunrise (V)

Card II. D3.
F−.

    Animal
    Bones
    Brain, dissected, human
    Breast's outer part
    Cat

Cocks (chicken, male), pair
Fly
Flower plant
Grasshopper
Human
Human body
Lobster's head
Lungs
Mosquito
Pelvis
Map
Skin
Stomach

Card II. D4. Top part in center, above the white space.
F+.

Fort
Folded hands
Gate
Peal of temple
Trunk, elephant

Card II. D4.
F−.

Boar
Earthworm
Island

Card II. DS 5. White space in center.
F+.

Bowl
Cane
Funnel
Gate
Hole
Lamp shade
Pond

Card II. DS 5.
F−.

Cat
Dancer
Moth

Card II. D7. Top, side part of the central black figures.
F+.

Dog's head
Elephant's head
Head of polar bear

Card II. D7.
F−.

Bird
Mask
Mountain

Card II. Dd 23. Small protruding part, bottom of black figure, adjacent to bottom red area.
F−.

Crab
Face of animal
Mahadev (Lord Shiva)

Card II. Dd 24. Middle, vertical small space in between bottom, red area.
F+.

Light
Streak of water
F−.

Face of an animal, with long beak

Card II. Dd 25. Two protruding parts of the bottom, red area.
F−.

Claws of bat
Lion

Card II. Dd 26. Small red area on top, side of black figure just below top red part.
F−.

Lower portion of a human
Scorpion

Card II. Dd 27. Middle white area, top part.
F+.

Light-rays

Card II. Dd 27.
F−.

Pelvis

CARD III

DESCRIPTION: Black-and-white; red. Two black, human-like figures in center; a round, bowl-like area at bottom in between the black figures; red butterfly-like part above the bowl-like area in center, in between the figures; two red parts on top, sides.

Card III. Whole.
F+.

Fountain in a garden
Mountain, with flower plants

Card III. Whole.
F−.

Face

Card III. D1. Two black figures along with the bowl-like part.
F+.

A pose in dance
Caricature
Cocks (male, hen)
Dragon
Europeans
Football [soccer] players
Ghost(s)

Hip-bone
Human beast
Human form
Man (any variety)
Man, of symbolic art
Mountain
Shadow of a man
Skeleton (human)
Two-legged pre-historic creature
Women-folk
Card III. D1.
F−.

Animal
Clouds
Elephants
Frog
Map
Monkey
Sky
Tree
View of roadside
Card III. D2. Top red parts on sides.
F+.

Animal
Bird
Dog
Flower plant
Heart (human)
Insect
Monkey
Red bird
Squirrel
Card III. D2.
F−.

Arm
Flesh
New born baby
Card III. D3. Middle, butterfly-like, red part.
F+.

Butterfly
Bow-tie
Hair-clip
Kidney
Lungs
Spinal cord
Card III. D3.
F−.

Blood
Stained object

Flower plant
Palate
Ribs

Card III. D7. Bowl-like, black part at the bottom.
F+.

Abdomen
Bus
Flower pot
Football
Flower vase
Hat
Hip
Pertaining to water
Pitcher
Skeleton
Something heavy
Tree amidst shadow

Card III. D7.
F−.

Beak
Bones of crab
Backbone
Foot
Heart
Male organ
Pillar
Water animal
X-ray plate

Card III. D8. Middle part in the bowl-like area.
F+.

Dried up tree
Human
Human beast
Lower side of human
Old-fashioned architecture

Card III. D8.
F−.

Mountain

CARD IV

DESCRIPTION: Black-and-white. A giant-like figure; a tree-trunk-like area in the middle; big feet-like parts on sides; a flower-like, light part on top.

Card IV. Whole.
F+.

Animal skin
Animal, large
Animal, hilly
Animal, of a pre-historic age

Ape-man
Architecture
Bat
Bird
Bone structure
Cloud
Earth, heap of [dirt]
Flower
Gorilla
Grasshopper
Insect, aquatic
Jelly-fish moth
Mountain
Person
Skeleton
Scenery
Swan
Tiger's skin
Tree-bush amidst shadow on hill top

Card IV. Whole.
F−.

Fly
Frog
Hole in the tree-trunk
Owl
Peacock
Rib

Card IV. Tree-trunk-like part down in the middle.
F+.

Animal
Branch of tree
Candle
Hand
Long-necked bird
Neck of crane
Root of tree
Swan
Trunk of elephant

Card IV. D1.
F−.

Bat
Beak of crow
Crane
Fallopian[tubes]
Flower
Tube
Peacock

Card IV. D2. Big feet-like parts, lower, sides.
F+.

    Foot
    Giant's leg
Card IV. D2.
F−.

    Flesh
    Hare
    Garment
Card IV. D3. Flower-like part on top.
F+.

    Enlarged insect
    Flower
    Head of crocodile
    Head of fish
    Ice slab
    Lion's head
    Tiny head
Card IV. D3.
F−.

    Animal's head
    Bone
    Cauliflower
    Spinal cord
    Tree-trunk

CARD V

DESCRIPTION: Black-and-white, bird-like figure.
Card V. Whole.
F+.

    Aeroplane
    Animal (V)
    Ape-man
    Bat
    Beetle
    Bird
    Butterfly
    Bone
    Cloud
    Deer, two, running
    Flying bird
    Flying fox
    Grasshopper
    God on hill top
    Hills, around statues
    Humans, two

Insect
Necklace
Peacock, with feathers spread out (V)
Water-animal
Card V. Whole.
F−.

Backbone
Bee
Crane
Owl
Vulture
Card V. D1. Upper part of the wing ends, on sides.
F+.

Foot, animal's, human's
Ghost-like
Human, strange, head missing
Leg, animal's, human's
Card V. D1.
F−.

Gate
Skeleton
Card V. D7. Middle part, between the wings.
F+.

Fox, with cap on
God
Head, with horns
Rabbit
Card V. D7.
F−.

Head of butterfly

CARD VI

DESCRIPTION: Black-and-white. Winged area on top. Spread bearskin-like area below. A lightly shaded rod-like area running through the center.
Card VI. Whole.
F+.

Animal
Animal skin, bird's, tiger's
Art, impressionistic
Bird
Human body structure
Insect
Monument surrounded with walls
Reflection
Something cut and halved
Statue on hill-top
Sparks of hot metal

Souvenir
Scenery
Shadow of water underneath hills
Skeleton, animal's
Tree
Tortoise
Card VI. Whole.
F−.

Camel
Crane
Fish
Lizard-like
Sea animal
Sea insect
Woman, standing
Card VI. D1. Spread bearskin-like area.
F+.

Animal skin, any
Animal, with skin off
Cape
Earth
Front part of body, with ribs
Garment made out of tiger's skin
Map
Moss
Tiger's skin
Tortoise
Water
Card VI. D1.
F−.

Chest
Fish
Locket
Volcano
Card VI. D2. Lightly shaded, middle, rod-like part in center.
F+.

Backbone
Like a peak
Light post
Monument
Post
River
Skeleton, man's
Snake
Spinal cord
Tube from throat
Veins on a person's back

Card VI. D2.
F−.

Animal
Flower plant
Insect
Inside of an insect
Instrument
Pen
Tree

Card VI. D3. Top flower-like part.
F+.

Animal
Cross
Flower
Grasshopper
Hide of tree
Insect

Card VI. D3.
F−.

Aquatic animal
Chest
Fish
Light rays
Statue, human
Tree

Card VI. D12. Middle part of the central, rod-like area.
F+.

Candle
Dagger
Gas post [lamp post]
Leg of bed
Nib with pen
Sharp-edged sword
Trunk of banana tree

Card VI. D12.
F−.

Animal
Insect, aquatic

CARD VII

DESCRIPTION: Black-and-white. Two figures on sides with large white space in the middle.
Card VII. Whole.
F+.

Two human or animal forms
Art
Animals, sitting on rocks

Cloud, bits of
Caricature
Earth, in two parts
Entrance of cave
Flames of incense
Flower plant
Garden
Gate
Humans, rulers of kingdom
Islands, many
Map
Mountain, broken
Necklace
Rock, bits of
Sand
Sky full of clouds
Smoke of cloud
Statue on rock, of gate, of stone
Tree, floating on water
Women, two

Card VII. Whole.
F−.

Anatomy
Butterfly
Chair
Flesh, bits of
Frog
Inside of human body
Moth-eaten skin
Satya-Rajas-Tamas ('Doing good deeds without expecting rewards' [*saatvik*];
     doing deeds for material comforts [*raajas*]; and doing deeds to harm and
     hurt others [*taamas*])
Tree, with nest of vultures

Card VII. D1. Top part of figures; often seen as face.
F+.

Animal, wild
Cloud
Head of, child, dog, dragon

Card VII. D6. Light shaded vertical opening in the middle of the lower, butterfly-like
part.
F+.

Canal
Door
Fall
Fountain
Hilly track
Man
Person

Rectum, animal's
Road
Screw
Screwed object
Card VII. D6.
F−.
Coconut tree
Instrument
Card VII. D7. Butterfly-like area at the bottom.
F+.
Bird
Butterfly
Cloud
Hill
Card VII. D7.
F−.
Aeroplane
Clash of clouds
Beast

CARD VIII

DESCRIPTION: Muticolored. Two pink, rodent-like figures on each side; a light aqua, mountain-like area on top; a dark aqua, flag-like figure just below the mountain-like area; one pink-orange colored butterfly-like figure just below the flag-like area.
Card VIII. Whole.
F+.
Art design, badge, jewelry
Animals on colored rocks with reflections
Anatomy
Flower vase, decorated
Heart
Human body, inside of
Human form, seated
Jumping wolf, with reflection
Meditation
Mountain
Pattern
Receptacle
Reflection
Shield (cup, trophy)
Scenery
Skeleton
Card VIII. Whole.
F−.
Animal structure

Card VIII. D1. Rodent-like figures on sides.
F+.
   Animal(s), hilly,
   Bear
   Cat
   Fox
   Guinea pig
   Mongoose
   Kangaroo
   Leopard
   Lion
   Panther
   Squirrel
   Tiger
   Wild cat
   Wolf
Card VIII. D1.
F−.
   Skeleton
   Yogin ('female saint')
Card VIII. D2. Lower pink-orange, butterfly-like area.
F+.
   Butterfly
   Frock
   Garment
   Heap of earth [dirt]
   Hill
   Petals of flower
   Rock
   Shirt
Card VIII. D2.
F−.
   Animal skin
   Breasts
   Heart
   Human anatomy
   Liver
   Lungs
   Tree
Card VIII. DS 3. Whitish area in the middle between the top mountain-like figure and the flag-like area below it.
F+.
   Backbone
   Bones
   Ribs
   Skeleton, animal's, human's

Card VIII. DS 3.
F−.
  Animal skin
  Dragon-like
Card VIII. D4. Top mountain-like area.
F+.
  Bat
  Branch of tree
  Hill
  Tree
  Taazia (From Arabic word *taaziah* meaning grieving. A triangular object,
    signifying *maqbaraa* ['funeral mound of a holy man'] used in *Muharram*
    ['grieving'] procession, mourning the death of Hazrat Imaam Hussain)
  Umbrella
Card VIII. D4.
F−.
  Animal skin
  Bone
  Gorilla
  Map [of India]
  Lizard-like
*Card VIII. D5. The dark, aqua, flag-like figure below the mountain-like figure on
top.*
F+.
  Blouse
  Butterfly
  Flag
  Leaf
  Rock
Card VIII. D5.
F−.
  Animal skin
  Body (human)
  Chest
  Lungs
  Shadow of a dead person and his reflection
Card VIII. D7. Lower half of the pink-orange area.
F+.
  Forest
  Mountain
  Tree
Card VIII. D7.
F−.
  Branch of a tree
  Crown
  Flesh
Card VIII. Dd 24. Uppermost stick-like part of the mountain-like area.
F+.
  Stick

Card VIII. Dd 24.
F−.

    Anus
    Root structure
    Leaf

CARD IX

DESCRIPTION: Multicolored. Two orange, human-like figures on top; two bison-like green figures in the middle; four pink roundish areas at the bottom; a vase-like, whitish figure in the center; a rod-like, white figure in the middle of this vase-like area.

Card IX. Whole.
F+.

    Anatomy
    Body, human
    Cloud, of different colors
    Garden
    Mountain
    Meditating recluse
    Picture, exquisite
    Sketch
    Scenery, of sea bottom
    Tree, with flowers
    Worldly matters

Card IX. Whole.
F−.

    America
    Animal form
    Body, animal's

Card IX. D1. Two bison-like green figures.
F+.

    Animal
    Cloud, of autumn
    Earth, heaps of [dirt]
    Hill
    Leaves, collection
    Lion
    Man, well-dressed
    Sky, blue
    Tree-top

Card IX. D1.
F−.

    Bird
    Body part
    Fossil, of monkey
    Insect
    Liver

Lump of flesh
Rat rib
Stomach
Card IX. D3. Two orange, humanoid figures on top.
F+.

Animal
Bird
Creeper
Flower
Hare with horns
Hill after sunset
Hilly track
Mountain
Person
Tree
Card IX. D3.
F−.

Beak, crane's
Bone, of hind legs
Lungs
Lizard
Smoke
Stomach
Card IX. D5.
F+.

Backbone
Bamboo pole
River
Stem of flower
Stream of water
Card IX. D5.
F−.

Bone
Butterfly
Inside of chest or stomach
Skeleton
Card IX. D9. Four, pink, roundish areas at the bottom.
F+.

Canopy
Cloud
Flower
Footprint
Four heads
Rock
Stones
Tree
Card IX. D9.
F−.

Brain

Breast fossil (bird's)
Liver
Medical literature [pictures in medical textbooks]

CARD X

DESCRIPTION: Multicolored. Two spider-like, blue figures on sides; two alien-like figures on both sides of a pole; a caterpillar-like green figure at the bottom; two lion-like yellow figures at the lower end; two bird-like, brown figures on sides; two large, pink, cloud-like, long figures in center; a brassiere-like blue area in the middle.

Card X. Whole.
F+.

Design
Bottom of sea
Birds-animals-insects
Collection
Collected insects
Colored insects
Decorations
Flower, inside of
Garden with *sadabahar* ['evergreen'] trees
Mosquitos
Pictures, many
Printed cloth
Path of sin
Place under sea
Scorpions
Scenery
Wall, decorated

Card X. Whole.
F−.

Animal
A type of bear
Bones, of animal
Body, animal's
Body, human's
Ferocious creature
Sea animal
X-ray impression

Card X. D1. Blue, crab-like figures on top, sides.
F+.

Animal
Aquatic creature
Branches of tree
Chinese cock [male chicken] flying with wings open
Crab
Dragon, many-legged
Flowers (*jaba*)

Insect
Lily, of deep water
Lobster
Octopus
Spider
Water hyacinth

Card X. D1.
F−.

Flea
Lungs
Moss
Oal (a vegetable with roots underground)

Card X. D9. Long, pink, cloud-like areas in the center.
F+.

Anatomy
Bone
Caterpillar
Divers
Flower cup
Hill
Lungs
Mosquitos, magnified
Mountain of sea foam
Path, hilly
Person
Stretch of land

Card X. D9.
F−.

Bit of flesh
Face
Gate
Inside of animal or human
Intestinal section
Tree

Card X. D10. Caterpillar-like, green figure, at the bottom.
F+.

Aquatic animal
Caterpillar
Earthworm
Horns of bison
Instrument for sacrificing (*hadeed* ['sharp instrument'])
Insect
Peacock
Snake(s)

Card X. D10.
F−.

Fish
Sensitive organ (sex)

REFERENCES AND SELECT BIBLIOGRAPHY

Acklin, M.W. (1995). 'Integrative Rorschach interpretation'. *Journal of Personality Assessment*, 64, 235–38.

Akhtar, S., Pershad, D., and Verma, S.K. (1975). 'A Rorschach study of obsessional neurosis'. *Indian Journal of Clinical Psychology*, 2, 139–43. Abstract from DIALOG(R) File: PsycINFO (R) Item: 56–09982.

Arnheim, R. (1947). 'Perceptual abstraction and art'. *Psychological Review*, 54, 66–82.

Aronow, E. (1972). 'Comment of Raychaudhuri's "Relation of creativity and sex to Rorschach M responses"'. *Journal of Personality Assessment*, 36, 303–6.

Aronow, E., Reznikoff, M. and Moreland, K. (1994). *The Rorschach technique: Perceptual basics, content interpretation, and applications*. Boston, Mass.: Allyn and Bacon.

———. (1995). 'The Rorschach: Projective technique or psychometric test?' *Journal of Personality Assessment*, 64, 213–28.

Arora, U. (1982). 'A Rorschach study of alcoholics'. *Indian Journal of Clinical Psychology*, 9, 141–45. Abstract from DIALOG (R) File: PsycINFO (R) Item: 71–01580.

Asthana, H.S. (1963). 'A Rorschach study of the Indians'. *Rorschachiana*, 8, 283–87.

———. (1976). 'Some experiments with the Rorschach: Lecture II'. University Grants Commission, National Lecture Series, Sagar University, Sagar (MP), India (mimeograph).

———. (1994). 'Rorschach publications in Indian journals in past five years' (Personal communication).

Banerjee, S. (1985). 'A resolution on the epileptic personality: A psychodiagnostic approach'. *Journal of the Indian Academy of Applied Psychology*, 11, 7–11. Abstract from DIALOG (R) File: PsycINFO (R) Item: 74–28521.

Beck, S.J. (1944). *Rorschach's test, Vol. I: Basic processes*. New York: Grunne and Stratton.

———. (1945). *Rorschach's test, Vol. II: A variety of personality pictures*. New York: Grune & Stratton.

———. (1952). *Rorschach's test, Vol. III: Advances in interpretation*. New York: Grune & Stratton.

———. (1961). *Rorschach test, Vol. I: Basic processes*. New York: Grunne and Stratton.

———. (1976). *The Rorschach's test: Exemplified in classics of drama and fiction*. New York: Stratton Intercontinental Medical Book Corp.

Bohm, E. (1958). *A textbook in Rorschach test diagnosis: For psychologists, physicians, and teachers.* (Trans. Anne G. Beck and Samuel J. Beck). New York: Grune & Stratton.

Boring, E.G. (1950). *A history of experimental psychology* (Second Edition). New York: Appelton-Century Crofts.

Boyer, L.B., Dithrich, C.W., Harned, H., Stone, J.S. and Walt, A. (1988). *A Rorschach handbook for the Affective Inferences Scoring System* (Revised first edition). Berkeley, CA: Boyer Research Institute.

Bruner, J. (1948). 'Perceptual theory and the Rorschach test'. *Journal of Personality*, 17, 156–68.

Bulfinch, T. (1981). *Myths of Greece and Rome* (With an introduction by J. Campbell). New York: Viking Penguin Books.

Campbell, J. (ed.). (1971). *The portrait of Jung.* New York: Penguin Books.

Chandra, Sarat (1990). 'Devdas'. In V.N. Mukerjee (ed.). *Sharat Samagra: Pratham Khand* ('Complete works of Sarat Chandra: Vol. 1'). Varanasi, India: Hindi Pracharak Sansthan.

Coomaraswamy, A. (1939). 'Ornament'. *Art Bulletin*, 21, 375–82.

Descharnes, R. (1985). *Salvador Dali.* New York: Harry N. Abrams, Inc. (Originally published in 1976).

Dostoevsky, F. (1992). *Notes from the underground* (Bantam Classic Edition Reissue) (Trans. by M. Ginsberg). New York: Bantam Books.

Dubey, B.L. (1977). 'Rorschach analysis of impotence cases and their response to psychotherapy'. *Indian Journal of Clinical Psychology*, 4, 145–49. Abstract from DIALOG (R) File: PsycINFO (R) Item: 61–04063.

————. (1979). 'Rorschach indices of psychiatric patients in the army'. *Indian Journal of Clinical Psychology*, 6, 175–79. Abstract from DIALOG (R) File: PsycINFO (R) Item: 65–08086.

Dubey, B.L. and Dosajh, N.L. (1979). 'Rorschach responses in normal army personnel'. *Indian Journal of Clinical Psychology*, 6, 169–73. Abstract from DIALOG (R) File: PsycINFO (R) Item: 65–07991.

Dubey, B.L., Pershad, D. and Verma, S.K. (1981). 'An evaluation of Rorschach as a clinical tool'. *Indian Journal of Clinical Psychology*, 8, 157–63. Abstract from DIALOG (R) File: PsycINFO (R) Item: 68–07073.

Dutta, K.S., Jha, B.K. and Shukla, T.R. (1976). 'A Rorschach study of peptic ulcer'. *Indian Journal of Clinical Psychology*, 3, 149–52. Abstract from DIALOG (R) File: PsycINFO (R) Item: 58–11949.

Ellenberger, H. (1954). 'The life and work of Hermann Rorschach (1884–1922)'. *Bulletin of the Menninger Clinic*, 18, 173–219.

Exner, J.E. (1974). *The Rorschach: A comprehensive system, Vol. 1.* New York: John Wiley.

————. (1989). 'Searching for projection in the Rorschach'. *Journal of Personality Assessment*, 53, 520–36.

————. (1991). *The Rorschach: A comprehensive system, Vol. 2* (Second edition). New York: John Wiley.

————. (1993). *The Rorschach: A comprehensive system, Vol. 1: Basic foundations* (Third edition). New York: John Wiley.

Fairbairn, R. (1992). *Psychoanalytic studies of the personality.* London: Routledge. (First published in 1952.)

Franck, K. (1958). 'Manual for Franck drawing completion test (FDCT)' (Mimeo.). Victoria, Australia: Australian Council for Educational Research.

Freud, S. (1900). 'The interpretation of dreams'. *Standard Edition*, 4 and 5. London: Hogarth Press (1957).

———. (1923). 'The ego and the id'. *Standard Edition*, 19, London: Hogarth Press (1961).

———. (1933). 'New introductory lectures on psycho-analysis'. *Standard Edition*, 22, 5–182. London: Hogarth Press (1964).

Gill, M. (ed.). (1968). *The collected papers of David Rapaport*. New York: Basic Books.

Gupta, P.K. (1977). 'Rorschach ranking conformity test: An evaluation'. *Indian Journal of Clinical Psychology*, 4, 51–53. Abstract from DIALOG (R) File: PsycINFO (R) Item: 60–10762.

Gupta, R.K., Verma, S.K. and Kulhara, P. (1989). 'Expression of hostility on Rorschach cards'. *Journal of Personality & Clinical Studies*, 5, 9–13. Abstract from DIALOG (R) File: PsycINFO (R) Item: 76–35130.

Hertz, M.R. (1970). *Frequency tables for scoring Rorschach responses* (Fifth edition, revised and enlarged). Los Angeles: Western Psychological Services.

Husserl, E. (1973). *Cartesian meditations: An introduction to phenomenology* (Trans. D. Cairns). The Hague: Martinus Nijhoff. (Original work published 1931.)

Jindal, C.R. and Panda, S.K. (1982). 'Anxiety and achievement: A Rorschach study of high- and-low achievers'. *Indian Educational Review*, 17, 118–24. Abstract from DIALOG (R) File: PsycINFO (R) Item: 71–18869.

Joseph, A. and Pillai, A. (1986). 'Projective indices of creativity'. *Indian Journal of Clinical Psychology*, 13, 9–13. Abstract from DIALOG (R) File: PsycINFO (R) Item: 75–28333.

Jung, C.G. (1990). *The archetypes and the collective unconscious* (Trans. R.F.C. Hull) (Second edition). Boolingen Series XX. Princeton, NJ: Princeton University Press. (Original work published 1934.)

Kafka, F. (1988). *The metamorphosis* (Trans. and ed. Stanley Corngold). Toronto: Bantam Books.

Kant, K. (1993). 'Eunuchs in the pages of history'. *The Times of India*, 29 July, p. 10.

Kaur, D. and Kapur, R. (1983). 'Rorschach study of hysteria'. *Indian Journal of Clinical Psychology*, 10, 97–102. Abstract from DIALOG (R) File: PsycINFO (R) Item: 71–09671.

Kernberg, O. (1970). 'A psychoanalytic classification of character pathology'. *Journal of American Psychoanalytic Association*, 18, 800–22.

———. (1984). *Object relations theory and clinical psychoanalysis*. Northvale, NJ: Jason Aronson.

Klein, M. (1952). 'Some theoretical conclusions regarding the emotional life of the infant'. In Klein, M. (ed.). *Envy and gratitude and other works, 1946–1963*. New York: Delacorte Press.

Klopfer, B. and Kelly, D. (1942). *The Rorschach technique*. Yonkers-on-Hudson, New York: World Book.

Klopfer, B., Ainsworth, M.D., Klopfer, W.G. and Holt, R.R. (1954). *Developments in the Rorschach technique, I: Technique and theory*. Yonkers-on-Hudson, New York: World Book.

Kohut, H. (1971). *The analysis of the self: A systematic approach to the psychoanalytic treatment of narcissistic personality disorders.* The psychoanalytic study of the child. Monograph No. 4. Madison, CT: International Universities Press.

————. (1977). *The restoration of the self.* Madison, CT: International Universities Press, Inc.

————. (1978). 'Introspection, empathy and psychoanalysis'. In P.H. Ornstein (ed.). *The search for the self: Selected writings of Heinz Kohut: 1950–1978 (Vol. 1).* Madison, CT: International Universities Press. (Originally published 1959.)

Kumar, P. and **Patel, S.** (1990). 'Rorschach study of women showing high and low adjustment in marriage'. *Journal of Personality & Clinical Studies,* 6, 73–76. Abstract from DIALOG (R) File: PsycINFO (R) Item: 78–27377.

Lambert, R. (1991). *The twentieth century: The Cambridge introduction to art.* Cambridge, UK: Cambridge University Press.

Lerner, P.M. (ed.). (1975). *Handbook of Rorschach scales.* New York: International Universities Press.

————. (1988). 'Rorschach measures of depression, the false self and projective identification in patients with narcissistic personality disorders'. In H. Lerner and P. Lerner (eds.). *Primitive mental states and the Rorschach.* New York: International University Press.

————. (1991). *Psychoanalytic theory and the Rorschach.* Hillsdale, NJ: The Analytic Press.

Lerner, H.D. and **Lerner, P.M.** (eds.). (1988). *Primitive mental states and the Rorschach.* Madison, CT: International Universities Press.

MacNeil, R. (1995). 'The glorious messiness of English'. *Reader's Digest,* October 151–54.

Mahler, M. (1952). 'On child psychosis and schizophrenia: Autistic and symbiotic infantile psychoses'. *Psychoanalytic Study of the Child,* 7, 206–305.

Mahler, M., **Pine, F.** and **Bergman, A.** (1975). *The psychoanalytic birth of the human infant.* New York: Basic Books.

Majumdar, P.K. and **Mukerji, K.** (1969). 'Examination of certain Rorschach ratios: A factorial study'. *Manas: A Journal of Scientific Psychology,* 15, 71–78. Abstract from DIALOG (R) File: PsycINFO (R) Item: 43–11359.

Malaviya, P. (1973). 'A replication of Rorschach signs with suicide attempted schizophrenics'. *Indian Journal of Psychology,* 48, 53–58.

Mayman, M. (1967). 'Object representation and object relations in Rorschach responses'. *Journal of Projective Techniques and Personality Assessment,* 31, 17–24.

————. (1977). 'A multidimensional view of the Rorschach movement response'. In M.A. Rickers-Ovsiankina (ed.). *Rorschach psychology* (Second edition). Huntington, NY: Robert E. Krieger Publishing Co.

McCully, R.S. (1971). *Rorschach theory and symbolism: A Jungian approach to clinical material.* Baltimore, MD: The Williams & Wilkins Co.

————. (1977). 'Jung's depth psychology and Rorschach patterning'. In M. Rickers-Ovsiankina (ed.). *Rorschach psychology* (Second edition). New York: Robert E. Krieger Publishing Co.

Miale, F.R. (1977). 'Symbolic imagery in Rorschach material'. In M. Rickers-Ovsiankina (ed.). *Rorschach psychology* (Second edition). New York: Robert E. Krieger Publishing Co.

Minhas, L.S. (1981). 'A factor analytic study of psychometric and projective indices of creativity and those of intelligence and personality'. *Personality Study & Group Behavior*, 1, 29–38. Abstract from DIALOG (R) File: PsycINFO (R) Item: 68–02522.

Misra, R.K. (1976). 'Drug addiction: Problems and prospects'. *Drug Forum*, 5, 283–88.

———. (1980). 'Achievement, anxiety, and addiction'. In D. Latteri (ed.). *Theories of Drug Abuse*. Baltimore, MD: National Institute of Drug Abuse.

Misra, R.K. and Kilroy, M.A. (1992). 'Immigrant mental health: An experiential approach'. *Psychology and Developing Societies*, 4, 149–63.

Mookerjee, R. (1982). 'A study of Rorschach's indices of intelligence'. *Asian Journal of Psychology & Education*, 9, 8–14.

Mujtaba, B. and Mujtaba, V. (1985). 'Homosexuality and paranoid schizophrenia: A Study through Rorschach ink blots'. *Journal of Personality & Clinical Studies*, 1, 27–29. Abstract from DIALOG (R) File: PsycINFO (R) Item: 75–14057.

Mukerji, K. and Majumdar, P.K. (1968). 'A comparison of direct and projective method of personality assessment'. *Manas: A Journal of Scientific Psychology*, 15, 19–24. Abstract from DIALOG (R) File: PsycINFO (R) Item: 43–11340.

Mukerji, K. and Raychaudhuri, M. (1970). 'Assessment equivalence of clinical ratings, structured and projective measures of personality'. *Manas: A Journal of Scientific Personality*, 17, 67–76. Abstract from DIALOG (R) File: PsycINFO (R) Item: 47–09277.

Mukerji, M. (1961). 'Normal Indian personality as projected in the Rorschach test'. *Research Bulletin*, Faculty of Arts, University of Lucknow, September, 62–64.

Murray, H.A. (1938). *Explorations in personality*. New York: Oxford University Press.

Murthy, K.S. and Ram, P.K. (1986). 'Impulse life, emotional reactivity, introversive and extratensive balance in criminals on Rorschach'. *NIMHANS Journal*, 4, 121–24. Abstract from DIALOG (R) File: PsycINFO (R) Item: 75–17242.

Nagar, A.L. (1984). *Yey Kothey-waaliaan*. ('These dancing girls'). Allahabad: Lok Bharti Prakashan.

Nanda, S. (1990). *'Neither man nor woman: The hijras of India'*. Belmont, CA: Wadsworth Publishing Co.

Narayan, R.K. (1992). *Swami and friends*. Mysore: Indian Thought Publications.

'Neeraj', G.D. (1961). *Praan-Geet* ('Songs of life') (Third edition). Delhi: Atma Ram & Sons.

Pal, A.K. and Chakravarty, C. (1968). 'An enquiry on the construct of the schizophrenic pattern of ideas'. *Manas: A Journal of Scientific Psychology*, 15, 79–85. Abstract from DIALOG (R) File: PsycINFO (R) Item: 43–11670.

Pandit, P. (ed.). (1987). *Urdu kay lokpriya shaair, Firaaq Gorakhpuri* ('Firaaq Gorakhpuri: The popular Urdu poet'). Delhi: Hind Pocket Books.

Pershad, D. and Dubey, B.L. (1977). 'A proposed statistical design for Rorschach indices'. *Indian Journal of Clinical Psychology*, 4, 191–92. Abstract from DIALOG (R) File: PsycINFO (R) Item: 61–02590.

Phillips, L. (1992). 'A letter from Leslie Phillips'. *SPA Exchange*, 2, 9.

Piotrowski, Z. (1957). *Perceptanalysis*. New York: Macmillan.

Poddar, H.P. and Goswami, C.L. (eds.). (1939). *Kalyaan: Geeta Tattvaank* ('Bhagvat Geeta: The divine song'). Gorakhpur, India: The Geeta Press.

Prabhu, G.G. (1967). 'The Rorschach technique with normal adult Indians'. *Indian Psychological Review*, 3, 97–106. Abstract from DIALOG (R) File: PsycINFO (R) Item: 41–08936.

———. (1970). 'Clinical utility of Piotrowski's alpha diagnostic formula'. *Indian Psychological Review*, 6, 110–12. Abstract from DIALOG (R) File: PsycINFO (R) Item: 46–09289.

———. (1984). 'Hermann Rorschach: A centenary tribute'. *NIMHANS Journal*, 2, 77–92.

Prasad, K. and **Asthana, H.S.** (1947). 'An experimental study of meaning by Rorschach method'. *Indian Journal of Psychology*, 22, 55–58.

———. (1949). *The psychology of meaning*. Lucknow, India: Maxwell Press.

Pratap, S. and **Filella, J.** (1966). 'Rorschach correlates of the Taylor's Manifest Anxiety Scale for a group of normal people'. *Journal of Psychological Researches*, 10, 103–9. Abstract from DIALOG (R) File: PsycINFO (R) Item: 41–07327.

Pratap, S. and **Kapur, M.** (1984). 'Rorschach study of literate manics'. *Indian Journal of Clinical Psychology*, 11, 29–34. Abstract from DIALOG (R) File: PsycINFO (R) Item: 75–35948.

Rao, G.P., Verma, S.K. and **Kulhara, P.** (1987). 'Rorschach responses of obsessive neurotic and schizophrenic patients'. *Journal of Personality & Clinical Studies*, 3, 43–47. Abstract from DIALOG (R) File: PsycINFO (R) Item: 75–20308.

Rapaport, D., Gill, M.M. and **Schafer, R.** (1945, 1946). *Diagnostic psychological testing, 2 vols*. Chicago: Year Book Publishers.

———. (1968). *Diagnostic psychological testing* (Revised edition) (Edited by R.R. Holt). Madison, CT: International Universities Press.

Raychaudhuri, M. (1971). 'Relation of creativity and sex to Rorschach M responses'. *Journal of Personality Assessment*, 35, 27–31.

———. (1972). 'Some thorny issues in cross-cultural research on creativity: A rejoinder to Aronow's comment'. *Journal of Personality Assessment*, 36, 305–6.

———. (1988). 'The Rorschach testing and the trend in teaching of the Rorschach in India: An overview'. *Manas: A Journal of Scientific Psychology*, 35, 3–17. Abstract from DIALOG (R) File: PsycINFO (R) Item: 76–36543.

Raychaudhuri, M. and **Mukerji, K.** (1971). 'Rorschach and Kataguchi–Rorschach (Ka–Ro) ink-blot series: A comparative study'. *Behaviorometric*, 1, 67–71. Abstract from DIALOG (R) File: PsycINFO (R) Item: 50–09268.

Rickers-Ovsiankina, M.A. (ed.). (1977). *Rorschach psychology*. Huntington, New York: Robert E. Krieger Publishing Co.

Ritzler, B. (1995). 'Putting your eggs in the content analysis basket: A response to Aronow, Reznikoff, and Moreland'. *Journal of Personality Assessment*, 64, 229–34.

Rorschach, H. (1975). *Psychodiagnostics: A diagnostic test based on perception*. New York: Grune & Stratton. (Originally published in German in 1921).

Sandhu, J. (1978). 'Rorschach responses in schizophrenia'. *Indian Journal of Clinical Psychology*, 5, 145–53. Abstract from DIALOG (R) File: PsycINFO (R) Item: 64–03461.

Schachtel, E. (1966). *Experiential foundations of Rorschach's test*. New York: Basic Books.

Schafer, R. (1954). *Psychodynamic interpretation in Rorschach testing: Theory and application*. Austin Riggs Foundation Monograph Series. New York: The Psychological Corporation Hartcourt Brace Jovanovich, Inc.

Schlesinger, H. (1973). 'Interaction of dynamic and reality factors in diagnostic testing interview'. *Bulletin of the Menninger Clinic*, 37, 495–518.

Shakespeare, W. (1944). 'Macbeth'. In Black's Readers Service *The works of William Shakespeare: Complete*. Roslyn, New York: Walter J. Black, Inc. Black's Readers Service.

Shanker, P. (1968). 'Education and Rorschach affective factors of the Harijans'. *Indian Psychological Review*, 4, 95–100. Abstract from DIALOG (R) File: PsycINFO (R) Item: 43–11367.

Shetty, K. (1990). *Hijras: Vivaah say vaidhavya tak* ('Hijras: From wedding to widowhood'). *India Today* (Hindi Edition), 30 June, pp. 78–84.

Shukla, V., Tripathi, R.R. and **Dhar, N.K.** (1987). 'Validation of Piotrowski's signs of "organicity" against Bender Visual Motor Gestalt test'. *Indian Journal of Clinical Psychology*, 14, 84–86. Abstract from DIALOG (R) File: PsycINFO (R) Item: 77–01959.

Singh, S. and **Kapur, R.** (1984). 'Psychometric and behavioral correlates of group Rorschach measure of hostility'. *Indian Journal of Clinical Psychology*, 11, 35–44. Abstract from DIALOG (R) File: PsycINFO (R) Item: 75–35449.

Sinha, B., Singh, A.K. and **Singh, S.K.** (1986). 'Delinquents: An observation of their Rorschach protocols'. *Indian Psychological Review*, 30, 4–8. Abstract from DIALOG (R) File: PsycINFO (R) Item: 75–26881.

Summers, F. (1994). *Object relations theories and psychopathology: A comprehensive text*. Hillsdale, NJ: The Analytic Press.

Sugarman, A. (1991). 'Where's the beef? Putting personality back into personality assessment'. *Journal of Personality Assessment*, 56, 130–44.

Thapa, S. (1983). 'Personality patterns of Nepalese people in two diverse social groups as portrayed by Rorschach ink-blot cards'. *Indian Journal of Clinical Psychology*, 10, 451–58.

Ulett, G. (1994). *Rorschach introductory guide*. Los Angeles, CA: Western Psychological Services.

Upadhyaya, S. and **Sinha, A.K.** (1974). 'Some findings on psychodiagnostic tests with young retarded adults'. *Indian Journal of Clinical Psychology*, 1, 73–79. Abstract from DIALOG (R) File: PsycINFO(R) Item: 54–0557.

Vagrecha, Y.S. and **Mazumdar, D.P.** (1974). 'Relevance of Piotrowski's signs in relation to intellectual deficit in organic (epileptic) and normal subjects'. *Indian Journal of Clinical Psychology*, 1, 64–66. Abstract from DIALOG (R) File: PsycINFO (R) Item: 54–05656.

Van Breda, H.L. (1989). 'Introduction' (Trans. by R.W. Jordan). In P. McCormick and F. Elliston (eds.). *Husserl: Shorter Works*. Notre Dame, Indiana: University of Notre Dame Press.

Verma, J. (1987). 'A case study of a withdrawn boy as measured through Rorschach'. *Indian Journal of Applied Psychology*, 24, 96–100. Abstract from DIALOG (R) File: PsycINFO (R) Item: 75–35464.

Viglione, D. and **Exner, J.E.** (1983). 'Current research in the comprehensive Rorschach systems'. In J. Butcher and C. Spielberger (eds.). *Advances in personality assessment (Vol. 1)*. Hillsdale, NJ: Lawrence Erlbaum.

Weiner, I.B. (1966). *Psychodiagnosis in schizophrenia*. New York: John Wiley.

————. (1994). 'The Rorschach inkblot method (RIM) is not a test: Implications for theory and practice'. *Journal of Personality Assessment*, 56, 453–65.

Welsh, G.S. (1959). 'The Welsh figure preference test' (Research edition). Palo Alto, CA: Consulting Psychologists Press.

Yadav, R.A. (1977a). 'Rorschach responses of the institutionalized offender'. *Social Defence*, 47, 34–38. Abstract from DIALOG (R) File: PsycINFO (R) Item: 60–09567.

————. (1977b). 'Rorschach responses of the institutionalized offender'. *Indian Journal of Clinical Psychology*, 4, 151–56. Abstract from DIALOG (R) File: PsycINFO (R) Item: 61–04379.

Zimmer, H. (1992). *Myths and symbols in Indian art and civilization* (Edited by J. Campbell). Bollingen Series VI. Mythos Edition. Princeton, NJ: Princeton University Press. (Original work published 1946.)

INDEX

ABOUT THE AUTHORS

Rajendra K. Misra is currently Psychologist at Extended Care Associates, Kent, Ohio, and Therapist at Boys' Village Foster Treatment Center, Maple Heights, Ohio. A practising psychologist and academic, he also teaches at the Cuyahoga Community College, Cleveland, Ohio. Dr. Misra has previously taught at the universities of Lucknow, Allahabad and Jodhpur. His previous positions include Director of Research, Community Action Against Addiction, Cleveland; Executive Director, Northeast Community Mental Health Center, Cleveland; and Chief Clinical Officer, Wood County Mental Health Center, Bowling Green, Ohio. Rajendra Misra has the distinction of conducting the first ever Rorschach workshops in India. Apart from being widely published in professional journals, he has also written two books: *Manovigyan Maapan* ('Psychological measurement') and *Baaten Man Kee* ('Reflections of an immigrant').

Meena K. Kharkwal holds a Ph.D in Psychology and has previously worked as Lecturer at the Post Graduate College, Pithoragarh, UP. She has received advanced training in clinical-cultural psychology as a Research Psychologist at the Northeast Community Mental Health Center, Cleveland. Dr. Kharkwal has published 10 research papers in various professional journals and is currently a practising psychotherapist in Pithoragarh.

Maurita A. Kilroy, Licensed Professional Counselor (L.P.C.) of the State of Ohio Social Worker and Counselor Board, is Program Manager, Jewish Family Services Association, Cleveland Heights Ohio. She has been working in the field of mental health, providing a wide range of clinical services including diagnostic assessment, crisis/emergency intervention and counseling for mental patients in various age groups, and has previously been Emergency Mental Health Counselor at the Ravenwood Mental Health Center, Chardon, Ohio. Her research interests include personality disorders, cross-cultural mental health and quality improvement.

Komilla Thapa is currently Senior Lecturer at the Center for Advanced Study in Psychology, Department of Psychology, Allahabad University. A trained clinical psychologist, she completed her post-doctoral training at the Maudsley and Bethlem Royal Hospitals, Institute of Psychiatry, London. Dr. Thapa has worked extensively with disabled children and their families, and currently provides counseling services to students and clinical services to psychiatric patients. Her research interests include dsyfunctional families and the mental health problems of the elderly.